THE CASSOWARY'S REVENGE

Title page illustration: *Casuarius unappendiculatus* (courtesy of the Zoological Society of San Diego)

The Cassowary's Revenge

THE LIFE AND DEATH OF MASCULINITY IN A NEW GUINEA SOCIETY

Donald Tuzin

The University of Chicago Press / Chicago & London

The University of Chicago Press, Chicago 60637
The University of Chicago Press, Ltd., London
© 1997 by The University of Chicago
All rights reserved. Published 1997
Printed in the United States of America
09 08 07   4 5 6 7
ISBN: 0-226-81950-7 (cloth)
ISBN: 0-226-81951-5 (paper)

Library of Congress Cataloging-in-Publication Data

Tuzin, Donald F.
    The Cassowary's revenge : the life and death of masculinity in a
New Guinea society / Donald Tuzin
        p.   cm.—(Worlds of desire)
    Includes bibliographical references and index.
    ISBN 0-226-81950-7.—ISBN 0-226-81951-5 (pbk.)
    1. Arapesh (Papua New Guinea people)—Rites and ceremonies.
2. Arapesh (Papua New Guinea people)—Religion.   3. Arapesh (Papua
New Guinea people)—Psychology.   4. Cults—Papua New Guinea—
Ilahita.   5. Parricide—Papua New Guinea—Ilahita.   6. Masculinity
(Psychology)—Papua New Guinea—Ilahita.   7. Ilahita (Papua New
Guinea)—Social life and customs.   I. Title.   II. Series.
DU740.42.T84   1997
306'.089'9912—dc21
                                                        96-40395
                                                        CIP

⊗ The paper used in this publication meets the minimum requirements of the
American National Standard for Information Sciences—Permanence of Paper
for Printed Library Materials, ANSI Z39.48-1992.

In memory of Gidion Kambapwi

Contents

Contents

Photographs follow page 67

Preface

This book is about something that happened in Ilahita, a village in the interior lowland of northeastern New Guinea. The year was 1984. The event was a murder; not a senseless or anonymous killing, but a conspiratorial act carried out by men with a purpose. The assailants had known their victim all their lives and for most of that time had regarded him with profound respect, possibly even love.

The shocking truth is the killing was a parricide. The old man had been a tyrant in his day; perhaps he deserved to die. And yet, it counts for something that his brutalities had all been intended for the good of his children. He may have used fear, even terror, on a regular basis, but he also trained the children to survive and prosper in a dangerous world. Even as they struck the final blow, the perpetrators realized they were destroying a part of themselves, which is why—as Freud knew and the Old Testament tries to deny—parricide by sons is the most primitive homicide of all, the primordial deed of blood and moral ultimacy. Rooted in such ambivalence, parricide is inherently dramatic and almost always calls forth a story.

The essence of parricide is not the fact of one human being killing another, but the enormity of the feelings, emotions, and experiences surrounding this supreme act of repudiation. Thus, it implies no great metaphoric leap to observe that the victim in this case was not a human being, but an institution: a vast, fatherly ritual system that for generations Ilahita men had operated for the good of society and the good of themselves; a cult predicated on male secrecy, supremacy, and sanctuary; a magnificent masculine pageant of ideas and practices. Just as there is a provocative moral element in parricide, so in its cultural counterpart we are drawn to ask why the men would choose to destroy a tradition that had sheltered them so well for as long as they could remember.

The story behind this deed is actually three stories in one, wrapped around one another like strands of a coaxial cable. The first story tells

ix

why, and with what consequences, the secret men's cult collapsed. Much has been written about such institutions in Melanesia and elsewhere but to my knowledge the ethnographic literature lacks an extended study of the demise of a men's cult. This omission is surprising: men's cults have been dying for as long as anthropologists have been studying them; often, postmortem analysis might have revealed important features that were not obvious in the living body. In the Ilahita case, my previous acquaintance with the cult late in its heyday affords an opportunity to reconsider certain findings made at that time. Examined in retrospect, facts previously gathered take on a different, more fully realized character. As in the deathbed openings favored by biographers, the story of the cult's collapse entails revisiting facts we knew, or thought we knew, about this old man's controversial career.

The second narrative strand pursues another kind of revisitation—this time, the culture's own return to its mythological origins. Under conditions they thought were apocalyptic, the people fell back upon the prophetic scenarios of their epic creation myth—the story of "Nambweapa'w," a primal Cassowary-Mother whose animal skin is secretly purloined by the First Man. He holds her in domestic bondage as his wife and the mother of his children until she recovers her skin and takes her revenge. The phantom of Women overturning the dominion of Men haunts other stories in the Ilahita canon but the men's particular recall of "Nambweapa'w" indicates a reanimation, a reversion to mythic origins in order to confer mythic significance and direction on the present.

The third narrative is awkward to tell, for it is about my return to Ilahita after an eventful absence of thirteen years and my disturbing, uncanny involvement with the recent collapse of the men's cult. Swept into the current of events and fantasies, this return encounter rewrote the significance of my original visit, merging it into a stream of prophecy to which the ethnographer was now a reluctant, hapless contributor. This account is about exorbitant expectations; dreams of a millenarian Event following upon the death of the cult; startling coincidences pounced upon as divinatory; returnings from death, through doors that separate and yet connect that space and our own.

The telling of what happened in Ilahita requires, then, three different arguments, three different voices, three different domains. Coordination occurs through a shared interest in the parricidal deed, but also through the recurrent, shared theme of return and remembrance. Rediscovering, restarting, revisiting, reconsidering, folding back—these are the convolutions of symbolic process, and therefore these must be the apparatus of understanding. Ethnographers return to the field and modify the meanings of previous facts in the light of intervening events; cultures return to their mythic charter and unwittingly edit it to accord with historical experience; individuals return to places of precious memory, thinking to recapture some fragment of the experience—never to succeed.

Always, one must go back, searching for what things of the past "really" meant as a clue to present realities. Going is never the same as going back. Going is mundane, going back is mythic, because it confronts the self in memory. Indeed, in a curious way that poets understand, it is through memory that past and present are finally reconciled, finally realized, and the future is made possible. Individuals relate to themselves in this way, and so do cultures.

Acknowledgments

It is a pleasure to acknowledge those institutions and individuals whose kind assistance has made this book possible. Fieldwork in Ilahita during the period 1969–72 was supported in major part by the Research School of Pacific Studies, Australian National University, with a supplementary grant-in-aid from the Wenner-Gren Foundation for Anthropological Research. The return trip to Ilahita in 1985–86, upon which this book is principally based, was funded by a research grant from the National Science Foundation (No. BNS-8406936). Support during periods of writing and scholarship was provided by a fellowship from the National Endowment for the Humanities (No. FA-28279-89) and a sabbatical leave granted by the University of California, San Diego. I thank these institutions for their generosity and forbearance.

The following friends and colleagues read all or substantial parts of the book while it was in draft. Their comments and criticisms were full of useful insights, but they must be held blameless for any deficiencies in the final work. I thank Thomas Gregor, Stephen Cox, Gilbert Herdt, Rena Lederman, David Gilmore, Axel Aubrun, Philip Young, and Jeffrey Rakoff.

Other friends and colleagues assisted me on specific points of fact, insight, or scholarly coverage. In addition to those cited in the text under the rubric "personal communications," I am grateful to Suzanne Brenner, Karen Brison, Lesa Burton, Robert Cancel, Kathleen Creely, Donald Gardner, Maurice Godelier, Stephen Leavitt, Tanya Luhrmann, Clive Moore, Gotfried Oosterwal, Nicholas Rugen, and Marc Swartz.

To the people of Ilahita I owe more than can be measured or repaid. From among the many who were unfailingly helpful and hospitable, and fearing inadvertent omissions, my family and I most warmly thank Councilor Kunai, Supalo, Wa'angowa, Ongota, Ribeka, Hengewen, Wa'akea, Kwambafum, Ta'ola, Mangas, Napaf, Maufena, Ulula, Akotan, Samuel, Malalia, Gatowen, Nawalop, Stanili, Timoti, Kalum, and Salalaman. In addition, we are grateful to Heather Campbell, Mavis Platt, Leonide Graumann, and other field staff of the South Sea Evangelical Church for their friendly cooperation and material assistance during our stay in Ilahita.

In Ilahita and afterwards, Beverly, Gregory, and Alexander have been my eyes, ears, collaborators, editors, audience, critics, and conscience. They have lived with the project, and this is their book, too.

Chapter One

GOING HOME

Ilahita is an Arapesh-speaking village located in the East Sepik Province of Papua New Guinea. With more than two thousand inhabitants, Ilahita is one of the largest traditional villages in the entire country; its six residential wards and scores of hamlets and outlying settlements sprawl across a series of ridge tops in the hilly hinterland of the coastal Torricelli mountains. The people are mighty yam growers whose magnificent, manicured gardens also bear taro, banana, sugarcane, papaya, and various other vegetables and leafy greens. These cultivated foods, together with coconut, breadfruit, sago, and the occasional wild pig, cassowary, or marsupial, comprise a subsistence regime of considerable variety. The people of Ilahita were proud of their hunting and gardening abilities; they were proud, also, of illustrious traditions that supported a rich social and ritual life and of a history of warfare and diplomacy that made them lords of much of the surrounding area. They were proud, that is, until things fell apart.

In September 1984, the people of Ilahita experienced an event of historic significance to themselves. During a Sunday church service, several men in their forties came forward to the platform, and by prearrangement each in turn confessed to the women in the congregation that the secret men's cult—known locally and throughout this region as the *Tambaran*—was a lie. To be exact, the secret was that there was no secret. Contrary to what the women and their foremothers had been told for generations, the spirits of the Tambaran did not materialize and sit with the men in their secret conclaves, did not eat the sacrificial feasts, did not sing in voices of another world. These were merely illusions, created by initiated men with the help of imaginative tricks, prodigious appetites, and clever man-made devices such as flutes, trumpets, whistles, gongs, and bullroarers.

The men's confession also carried a warning, which was that in a truer sense the Tambaran was not a hoax at all. The spirit venerated in the cult was and is real; its power was lethal in the past, and it could kill again.

1

With newfound Christian enlightenment, they realized that the names by which they had known this spirit—Nggwal, Holof, Waf, and, in Melanesian Pidgin, *tambaran* and *kastam*—referred in fact to only one being: Satan. By unmasking Satan and ridding themselves once and for all of his presence, the men were determined to cleanse the community spiritually and prepare it for Christ's Second Coming, which was and is thought to be imminent. This was to be done by exposing and reforming Satan's human agents and eradicating the institutions through which they have always operated.

Why did the men do it? What would have incited them to obliterate, in the space of a few moments, the soul of an ancestral tradition that encompassed a vast range of cognitions, values, and social relationships? On the face of it, the men threw over the Tambaran to embrace Christianity: Good triumphant over Evil, Jesus over Satan, Light over Darkness. This is a possible way to look at it; certainly, it is the perception of local European missionaries and most village Christians. But why then did they do that? And why did it take thirty-two years of exposure to Christian teachings before they made the final leap to faith? The most general answer is that it took a generation's worth of challenging circumstances, grudging adjustments, and spiritual decay before the Tambaran, hugely successful in its time but also fraught with moral contradictions, finally became unwelcome in its own home. In other words, it was not only that Christianity—its tenets and promises, as construed by the villagers— pulled Ilahita in that direction; something else, something old and internal to the culture, pushed it there. This antecedent cultural motive is not difficult to discern; for, in thinly veiled symbolic form, it is enshrined in the story of the Cassowary-Mother, "Nambweapa'w," which is both the Ilahita Creation epic and, as recent events have shown by way of fulfillment, a mythically constituted prophecy of things that were to come.

To fathom the enormity of the men's act, one must begin by appreciating that the Tambaran completely dominated traditional social life and ideology. Its cult was the organizational framework for most collective activity, the sponsor of great works of art and architecture, and the source of much cultural meaning. In a book on the subject, I once described the Tambaran cult and its imagined spirit beings as "the personified mystique of a total way of life" (Tuzin 1980, 325). The phrasing may have been a little dramatic, but it captured the people's own sense of the Tambaran— its ideas, objects, practices, and implications—as comprising much of the body and all of the essence of Ilahita tradition. And when I speak of "meaning," I refer to the irradiation of mundane acts and objects with an aura hinting at forces beyond the apparent, an attribution that effects the integration of personal and collective significances. Such is the mark of culture everywhere. What is to be remarked in the Ilahita case is the extent to which diverse phenomena formerly cohered around this central institution. The Tambaran conferred meaning on ideas and practices by creating a whole, so to speak, and assigning them places in it; hence the identification of the Tambaran with Ilahita tradition, as an indigenous self-objectification.

For example, when I first lived in Ilahita, men did not grow yams and hunt pigs simply for nourishment, but as provender for the Tambaran in the great secluded feasts the men hosted and in which they shared. For that matter, men did not catch or produce food only to consume it, but to present it to one of several hereditary exchange partners, according to a structure of reciprocity dictated by the Tambaran. And what did these ritual exchange feasts accomplish, other than full bellies? Nothing less than the satiated Tambaran's renewal of all species, and rebestowal of material prosperity, happiness, and spiritual vitality on the village. Men did not organize themselves into totemic clans, subclans, moieties, submoieties, partnerships, neighborhoods, wards, and villages merely by accident or for the sake of social convenience, but because each of these units had a designated role in the ritual work of the Tambaran. Boys did not naturally grow into men, nor did men into old men: masculinity was acquired, fulfilled, and retired through a series of five Tambaran initiations, carrying the male from his mother's arms to the gates of great old age.

The Tambaran also ruled over matters of blood and argument. Wars were fought for various mundane ends, but always under the aegis of the Tambaran. The magical power deployed by war sorcerers was that of the Tambaran, not of themselves; killings in battles and raids were credited to the Tambaran, not to the human victor, who remained anonymous; trophies of body parts were mounted on the Tambaran's house, not on a warrior's belt. It would not be going too far to say that the Tambaran was a cult of war. Equally, though, it was a cult of peace: only the Tambaran would proclaim truces between enemy villages, usually to allow hostiles to cooperate in initiations and other major ceremonial endeavors. Disputes within the village, when they set groups against one another, also drew the attention of the Tambaran. Resolution was attained by "summoning the Tambaran" (i.e., mounting a convocation of cult members) to preside over the speaking, singing, and feasting duels that would decide who wins and who pays a fine. When a death occurred in the village, sorcery was nearly always the presumed cause, but in many cases divination by cult elders revealed that the sorcerer had been acting as the Tambaran's executioner, administering punishment for some remembered violation of ritual values or cult protocol. Et cetera.

Two larger points of interest require introduction. First, the Tambaran's legitimacy across all its domains rested precariously on the women's not knowing what went on in the men's ritual seclusions. Such an arrangement is by no means unique to Ilahita: secret men's cults occur in many parts of Melanesia, aboriginal Australia, Amazonia, and elsewhere, and a sizable literature has grown up around them. But this frequency should not anesthetize our wonder and curiosity at a way of life predicated on extreme gender alienation. Adopting Freud's famous metaphor, just as the shattering of a crystal reveals its structure, so the eclipse of the Tambaran discloses certain unsuspected gender dynamics that had been obscured by the dazzle of its living presence.

Second, considering its embeddedness in Ilahita culture and society, the Tambaran's antiquity in the village was, surprisingly, not great. The evidence is that some time after the middle of the past century, the cult was adopted from the Abelam, a bellicose people who had jostled their way northward from the Middle Sepik area (Tuzin 1976) (see map 1). As will be seen in later chapters, one may question whether the Tambaran was ever fully naturalized to Ilahita culture. If not, then to that extent its destruction may be seen not as revolutionary but as resolutionary of moral strains and contradictions that had existed ever since the Tambaran arrived in Ilahita. Significantly, the aforementioned story of Nambweapa'w, despite its embeddedness, appears to have been adopted at approximately the same time but from a different direction. This coincidence will turn out to be a key element in our story about the life and death of masculinity in Ilahita.

In July 1985, ten months after the men's declaration, my wife, Beverly, and I arrived with our two sons, Gregory, age nine, and Alexander, age five, to begin a yearlong stay in Ilahita. We had been absent from the village for thirteen years. Beyond the specific research plan, which was to study the process of cultural acquisition in middle childhood, we yearned

to reunite with old friends and to introduce our boys to the place and
people that were a special kind of home for us. I was excited about returning to Ilahita, but ambivalent: eager to observe changes, but fearful
that these new images would scatter and usurp the place of precious memories from before; pleased to be going "home," but guilty that I had not
communicated for more than ten years. As departure time approached,
my dreams became gloomy and forbidding.

In all the recent attacks on ethnographic objectivity, no one as far as
I know has remarked on the difference between going to the field for the
first time and returning there after a lengthy absence.[1] Both situations
may involve observer bias, but returning to the field entails a larger, more
complex hazard because it means tampering with a relationship that already exists, laden with emotion, personal history, and moral ambiguity.
Warned by the saying "You can't go home again," I had braced myself for
distressing changes: the place would look different, I supposed, probably
less picturesque; friends would have died. So it was; so they had. In addition, during the thirteen years that I was advancing on middle age, raising
children, and burying parents, the villagers were doing likewise. On both
sides interests, attitudes, and values shifted in accord with accumulated
experience. Those sorts of changes could be accommodated to the psychology of the research situation; after all, those were the changes that I
was returning in order to observe. There was a different kind of change,
however, one for which I was not prepared. It concerned unsuspected
evolutions in myself and the effect of these on the ethnographic relationship. Let me try to explain.

When as a young man I first lived in Ilahita, everything about the
place was new and exotic to me. The customs were theirs, and my remoteness from them sustained a relative objectivity and emotional detachment in my observations. Upon returning, however, I was startled to discover that their customs had become my own. The intervening thirteen
years of writing, lecturing, and nostalgizing added up to an emotional
investment in all that the villagers were seeking to destroy. The wholesale
cultural self-loathing and repudiation were extremely painful to behold,
even as I admitted to myself that some of the reforms were worthwhile
and, in any case, inevitable. People's feelings seemed rawer, more insistent;
I found myself reacting to emotions with emotions, more than previously.
Would that my reactions had been the workings of greater empathy or
observational acuity; they were too undisciplined for that. Before long, I

realized that these feelings were expressions of the frustration, impotence, and moral entanglement I experienced before this scene of cultural immolation. Though strongly felt, my sense of "co-ownership" was unwarranted and could not be proclaimed without making me appear silly or presumptuous. Objectively, nothing had changed: the customs were still theirs to dispose of as they saw fit. And yet whatever detachment I could claim for my original fieldwork, it was considerably diminished on my return.

Such soul-searching might not require comment but for the fact that curious counterparts existed in the villagers' perceptions of us—memories and attitudes that affected not only the ethnographic relationship but also the flow of events in this highly fluid cultural situation. Indeed, their feelings may have been the more intense and coherent due to the triangulating effect of there being many villagers but only the two of us. Our nostalgia, though inclined to linger on certain individuals and neighborhoods, embraced the totality—people, place, and culture; in the reciprocal, there was only us. The Ilahita can be great flatterers, and it is hard not to feel warm and wanted when people recall minute incidents from earlier visits: where I stood, what I said, who else was present, how we laughed and ate together—what a jolly time it was! Beverly received the same kind of treatment from the women. To hear them talk, the villagers regarded our previous visit as an almost mythical event, one of momentous significance in the history of Ilahita. Children grew up hearing about us as characters from a kind of Golden Age. Those who had known us as adults would exaggerate our remembered nobility and generosity; for many, our return evoked fond memories of folks who had died during our absence.

It was tempting to see this outpouring as a sign of the villagers' esteem and affection for us as persons. This interpretation might even be partly accurate in the case of a few of our closest, most loyal friends. But the greater truth was that we were ciphers: lacking all context and almost all substance, yet seen as generally harmless, powerfully connected, and eager to please, we were ideal objects onto which the villagers could project their hopes and expectations—and suspicions. Performing as someone else's object is never easy, even when the other's pseudo-perceptions are intelligible and relatively compatible with one's own sense of self and purpose. When, as in the Ilahita case, the projections are unreal, cryptic, and sometimes fantastical, stresses arise that are particularly hard on the ethnographic relationship.

From the start, our homecoming took on strange, disturbing qualities, and many a sleepless moment was spent wondering whether our return had been a mistake. Like characters in some gothic romance, we returned to the ancestral Schloss to find the old patriarch recently expired, under suspicious circumstances, and obscure intrigues afoot among surviving relatives, friends, and retainers. Within a few days, once the initial round of greetings had been exchanged, it became apparent that something was wrong. People seemed tense, awkward, and expectant. This was particularly unsettling in that their behavior seemed to involve me—though not in any way people were willing to state openly. Instead, innuendos, gratuitous whisperings, and conspiratorial glances created a "You know, and we know you know" flirtation that was grounded in nothing I knew.

This was a new and hurtful experience. In previous fieldwork, though much was undoubtedly missed—bits of cultural lore that simply never came up in conversation, or important happenings that I did not find out about until it was too late—I never suspected that something of collective significance was being actively hidden from me. This time, even my old cronies squirmed and dissembled when I tried to get them to tell me what was going on in the village. There were divisions in the community, that much was clear; but it seemed they were expecting me to declare which "side" I was on before anyone would tell me what the issue was.

I never did learn all the details of what had been going on when we arrived. Information pieced together during the ensuing months revealed, however, that my family and I had arrived in the middle of a crisis—a crisis, strange to say, precipitated in substantial measure by the announcement of our return. Before explaining the circumstances of our unwitting complicity, I should say more about the situation as it gradually presented itself to us.

The crisis besetting the village had two interrelated aspects. Under the "Tradition versus Modernity" rubric, there was an open division going back many years, but newly agitated, concerning the place of traditional ideas and practices in Ilahita's future. At the same time, a covert struggle existed between adherents and critics of a millenarian movement that acted as underground auxiliary to a program of religious conversion known as the "Revival." These aspects were connected by a strong religious interest, in that both were involved in the search, rather desperate at times, for new footings amid the spiritual turbulence stirred up by the Tambaran's collapse ten months earlier.

The issue of whether to preserve tradition was usually argued in the context of economic and educational development, with Modernists sometimes tactically embracing Christianity as a doctrine compatible with, and obscurely facilitating, their personal and collective goals. This debate heated up as the time of our return approached, mainly because both parties expected to benefit from my endorsement: an educated American would surely be progressive in outlook, reasoned the progressives, whereas the conservatives pinned their hopes on my remembered sympathetic interest in customary practices. Although this issue touched virtually every dimension of village affairs, the liveliest debates, by far, occurred between competing religious constituencies. Religion was an available, almost inevitable, battleground, because for generations the Tambaran had presided over Ilahita's social life and cultural ideology and had trained the villagers into a deep dependence on ritual idioms when it came to formulating their disputes.

This was not an argument over the future status of the Tambaran, which both sides perceived to be dead. Reformers were glad to be rid of it; traditionalists bemoaned the loss, but felt that the revelations had both shamed them and irreparably spoiled the Tambaran. No one denied, either, that the revelation of cult secrets had destroyed the core of Tambaran ceremonialism. This awareness lay behind the traditionalists' avowal that they would never again stage a Tambaran event: now that the women knew of the trickery, for the men to persist in cult activities would be to make laughingstocks of themselves. And yet, in the same breath conservative cult elders predicted that without the Tambaran there could be no prosperity. Soon enough, they warned, the people will find that yams and pigs have become scarce, the peace of the village will dissolve in uncontrolled trespass between neighbors and kin, and Ilahita will lie weak and disunited before its enemies. "Never mind," said the traditionalists, darkly savoring the whiff of scorched earth, "let those who showed the secrets be responsible for the hard times ahead. When they and their children—and our own children, too—cry to us to bring back the Tambaran, we will not listen. And when we die, the knowledge of how to raise up the Tambaran will die with us." In other words, although the revelation of

secrets and the associated collapse of cult ceremonialism provoked recrim-
inations and dire predictions from certain disempowered segments of the
community, all parties agreed, in effect, that there was no going back:
what's done is done, what's broken cannot be put back together again.

By the time we arrived people were arguing about secondary reforms.
If the end of cult ceremonialism was the death of the Tambaran, as most
villagers believed it was, there were a great many postmortem issues still
to be decided. Simply put, what was to become of the Tambaran's vast
ideological estate? Traditionalists were trying to minimize the social impact of the secrecy revelation, both to salvage what power and mystique
they could and to hold open the possibility of a Tambaran revival, based
on a willful "forgetting" of the revelation. To prevent this from happening, reformers were trying to maximize the effect of the revelation on
society and the moral order. It was becoming clear to both sides that
eradicating Tambaran ceremonialism had not nullified Tambaran consciousness. True, without the nurturance of ceremonial performances
these mental habits would eventually wither away. Meanwhile, the Tambaran thinking that suffused everyday life was capable of sustained resistance to change; hence the reformers' targeting of many traditional practices for eradication.

Ritually authorized sorcery activities were the first to go. But they
were only the most obvious, most dreaded expression of Tambaran consciousness; masculine assertiveness in virtually all traditional areas was uni-
formly tainted with Tambaran values.[2] Relatively benign practices now
condemned included competitive hunting and gardening, featuring the
ostentatious production, display, and distribution of food surpluses; ceremonial feast exchanges in celebration of life-crisis events; formal speech
making in the stylized mode of harangue; beneficial, or at any rate non-
destructive, magic; various artistic enjoyments; and the cosmetic uses of
feathers, flowers, bones, shells, and paint. The reformers cast themselves in
the role of inspired revolutionaries: enlightened, unflinching progressives
who, after boldly destroying the ideological center, would prowl the society searching not only for pockets of overt resistance and reaction but for
all customs, attitudes, and ways of thinking held over from the ancien
régime. Having made their successful coup, the reformers were determined to obliterate anything that might be a reminder of the old customs,
an invitation to nostalgia, a counterrevolutionary rallying point. Not just
the Tambaran, but what the Tambaran stood for—all must be destroyed.

Social revolutions, almost by definition, move quickly. Taking advantage of the confused early stages, activists rush to gain and secure as much political ground as possible before the forces of reaction can regroup against them. This is what happened in Ilahita after the revelation of the cult secrets. With the Tambaran poleaxed, the society was suddenly disengaged with itself—shifted out of gear, so to speak, and open to the possibility of runaway change. To this generic situation was added a reformist urgency from a seemingly independent source. Many villagers believed that a Great Cosmic Event was at hand. Just what form this Event would take was unclear, except that Jesus, God, and the Holy Spirit were presumed to be involved, probably in person; most believers understood that the Event would be the Second Coming promised in the Gospels. Just what would happen was also obscure, except that the Event would surely deliver rewards to the faithful and punishments to the heathen. In that apocalyptic judgment, worthiness would be proved not simply by Christian conversion, or even by sincere belief, clean living, and a record of regular church attendance, but by having confessed one's sins and been spiritually "cleansed" during a Revival service. The agents of this cleansing were women, who were graced because they were untainted by past Tambaran involvement. These female prophets, known as *tok profet* (MP), policed the new religious order by receiving Holy Spirit messages during trance, which revealed misconduct or breaches of faith and charged the perpetrators, who were nearly always men, to confess their crimes, which nearly always involved offenses against women.[3]

Previous millenarian enthusiasms had also prophesied an Event at which rewards and punishments would be meted out according to one's standing in or out of the movement. Aside from simple peer pressure, the decision to join the movement had been a matter of one's greed or credulity balanced against one's skepticism concerning the millenarian threats and promises. The Event, at any rate, would happen willy-nilly, regardless of the presence of disbelievers in the community. This time, by contrast, it was thought that the Event could be prevented from happening unless and until everyone was spiritually cleansed and the community's offensive traditions were purged. Or worse, the Event would happen, but Ilahita would be shunted to some kind of cosmic sideline, the skeptics in the village thus ruining it for everyone. In a manner very reminiscent of the village spiritual unity formerly exalted in Tambaran ideology, fate would not allow a majority, or even a consensus, decision: unanimity—nothing less—was the necessary and possibly sufficient condition for bringing the Millennium to Ilahita. It was not enough to keep the Tambaran on the run, dismantle its institutional framework, and wait for its consciousness to wither away. The Tambaran stood in the way of the Event, and the Event might not wait for long. Believers were quite certain, in fact, that the Time was Now, and nearly every week rumors flew that the Event had arrived and was unfolding—someplace else. A state of emergency prevailed among the Revivalists, who were wildly impatient at the traditionalists, the "Tambaran men," with their Millennium-spoiling resistance to the movement. The prospect of our return, announced more than a year in advance, helped to precipitate the emergency because many of the Revivalists attached vital significance to the coincidence of that event with the cosmic Event for which they prayed.

When we arrived, those who had been against the revelation of cult secrets were struggling dispiritedly to prevent further unraveling of their lives. Since I was remembered as having had an appreciative interest in the Tambaran and other customs gone by, these village traditionalists, who were in the minority, hoped I would contribute to their cause, perhaps even assist in a civil suit that was vaguely planned against individuals who had destroyed cult paraphernalia. And yet, they could not be certain of my alliance. For one thing, historical momentum favored the reformers, who viewed the elimination of the Tambaran as the crucial launching event for the eradication of tradition on a grand scale. Would I be able and willing to take sides and make a difference, or would I resist political entanglement, as I had done before? Moreover, in the wake of recent shocking changes, who could be sure that Beverly's and my attitudes had not also changed? Worse, the traditionalists were demoralized by knowing that the reformers were confidently expecting us to embrace the Revivalist cause, interpreting our return in the positive light of their own millenarian program.

Claims and accusations concerning this program made up the other, more covert aspect of Ilahita's social crisis. Although I did not know it at the time, traditionalists hoped to discredit and destroy the reformist cause by proving that it was an illegal cargo cult.[4] The reformers clung fast to their denial, insisting that the repeal of ancestral traditions was necessary because most elements in that tradition—sorcery in particular, but many other beliefs and practices as well—were incompatible with a wholesome Christian life. Their goal was spiritual salvation, the reformers rejoined, not worldly goods. Traditionalists thought they knew better what the re-formers were up to, but could not risk being candid with me, not until they were sure that I was not part of the "cargo" conspiracy. Whence their doubts concerning my position? As I gradually came to realize, they originated in events and circumstances going all the way back to our first fieldwork and its aftermath.

Fieldwork during the year 1971 was dominated by ritual activities that happened to be centered on Elaf, the hamlet in which we lived. Elaf contained the main ritual plaza of Ililip, one of Ilahita's six residential wards (see map 2);[5] there, in that year, a magnificent spirit house was built in anticipation of a major Tambaran initiation the following year. The construction work extended over many months, consumed a conserva-tively estimated ten thousand man-days of labor, and was punctuated at each major stage by all-night feasting, dancing, and flute playing, some-times repeating itself for several nights in succession. All this was very exciting for me: what good fortune to have such sensational, ethnographi-cally throbbing activities literally on one's doorstep! It was also very, very tiring. Whereas the participants could handily retire to their sleeping mats in home hamlets for an hour or two during the endless night, or, if pride and stamina drove them until dawn, for a generous stretch of uninter-rupted sleep the next day, Beverly and I had nowhere to go. Not that we would have wanted to escape, anyway; too much of interest was occurring on the margins of the dance plaza. Around the many smoking and cook-ing fires dotting the fringe, men from different parts of Ilahita and from other villages mingled in conversation about ceremonial matters or about the Tambaran's relevance to various recent events. Sometimes voices would be raised (in jest or friendly raillery, for there was a strong taboo against belligerence in the presence of the Tambaran) or someone would be inspired to make a speech while the drummers and dancers were resting.

As occasions when gossip is exchanged and opinions are aired among men who normally interact infrequently, and when self-important cult elders dilate on ritual truths, those meetings were as welcome to me for my reasons as they were to the participants for theirs. That grand ritual season culminated eighteen months spent in familiarizing myself with the villagers: their personal characters; ties of kinship, descent, and marriage; friendships and animosities; political standings; and, in the case of males, ritual memberships. Large gatherings were no longer so bewildering, for I now understood the customs motivating them, the current social and political issues occupying the minds of the participants, and also some of the unspoken—if not hidden or downright secret—objectives being pursued through nuances of speech and action. My hard-earned competence as an observer of the Ilahita scene was certainly very far from perfect; but it was as advanced as it would ever be, and thus the great ritual extravaganza of 1971 could not have come at a better time. During that year my record of attendance at Tambaran ceremonies held in Ilahita and nearby villages was probably unequaled, even by senior cult members. This was noticed by the people.

In October 1971, Beverly and I returned to Canberra, where, except for a three-week return to the village in September 1972, I worked at writing my doctoral thesis. It was in January 1973, a few months before the thesis was to be completed, that I first noticed a lump in the nape of my neck. The lump persisted. Worried, but telling myself that it was probably some treatable ailment caught in the tropics, I kept the lump to myself and pressed on with the final chapters. The examination and biopsy finally occurred in April, resulting in a diagnosis of Hodgkin's disease, a malignancy of the lymphatic system. This began two years of traumatic, debilitating therapies, demoralizing prognostic uncertainties, and weary hours spent sitting around clinic waiting rooms decorated with that forced cheeriness oncology patients learn to associate with their nausea. The stress of those two years was compounded by the demands of removing to and establishing myself in a teaching position in the United States and by the death (by cancer) of my mother. With nothing but bleakness to feel and communicate, with no wish but to hide, I allowed all my personal correspondence to lapse—including the intermittent exchanges I had maintained with some of the people of Ilahita.[6]

Toward what proved to be the end of my medical ordeal, Beverly received a letter from Gidion Kambapwi. Five years my senior, Gidion was our closest neighbor and friend in Ilahita, a man of outstanding character, and one of the finest human beings I have ever known. Gidion asked Beverly if it was true what he had heard—that I had died. If so, he explained, as my "elder brother" in the Mano'um clan he would take charge of arranging a funeral feast in Ilahita. Touched by Gidion's thoughtfulness, we responded at once that I was alive and recovering; that I had been dangerously ill, but now appeared to be defeating the sickness.

Gidion's question was not accidental or unreasonable. In a previous letter, written during the dark, uncertain early days of the Hodgkin's experience, I had told him that I was ill with *sik kansa,* this being my best guess at what a Melanesian Pidgin equivalent might be for "cancer." In those days the people of Ilahita knew about malaria, tuberculosis, and leprosy but not about cancer, so Gidion would not have known what kind of sickness sik kansa was. Years later, I learned from a younger clan brother that Gidion—a prominent but decidedly unconfirmed Christian—had taken my letter to a European missionary, who told him that sik kansa is nearly always fatal—that being much truer then than it is now. What else was said cannot be known, but it would be consistent with the situation for there to have been references to the possibility of miraculous intervention and to the need for prayer. For many Sundays the village Christians, a tiny band in those days, offered up prayers for my survival. But the pessimism of European missionaries and administrators concerning cancer, along with my silence, led Gidion and the others to conclude that I had died; hence his letter to Beverly.

To my permanent shame and sorrow, after reassuring him that I was alive, I never again communicated with Gidion. When I finally did write to him, ten years later, informing him of my plans to return, the reply came from his daughter, Naipe'w, who in our absence had grown up and become a nurse's aide. Her father, she said, had died of liver cancer just three weeks before my letter arrived.[7] The people now knew about cancer.

I later learned that Gidion's disease was thought to have been an act of Tambaran retributive justice stemming from an incident that had occurred several years earlier. It began when Gidion was alerted that some men from Mamilimbi, an enemy group, had violated a court order by processing a sago palm on land that was being disputed between the two villages. Gidion's clan, the Mano'um, was the main litigant on the Ilahita side. As the chief spokesman for Mano'um interests in court, Gidion rushed off to summon the police. When the police and Gidion arrived in Mamilimbi to arrest the trespassers, they were told that the men had gone to Ilahita—to Gidion's own hamlet, in fact—to deliver a statue they had pledged to contribute to an upcoming initiation ceremony. The posse then rushed to Elaf, just as the Mamilimbi men and their Ilahita hosts were sitting down to a ceremonial repast in celebration of the ritual donation. Rather than let them finish their meal, Gidion demanded and obtained the immediate arrest of the culprits, who were carted off to jail, humiliated and with empty bellies. According to those who years later divined the cause of Gidion's terminal illness, his fate was sealed with that breach of Tambaran courtesy.

Gidion, I was to hear, had spoken of me often over the years. Everyone else believed that I would never come back, or that I was dead—perhaps had never actually recovered from the sik kansa. Gidion, almost alone among the villagers, never stopped believing I would return, and he restated this conviction as one of the last things he said before dying. In Ilahita, as elsewhere, deathbed utterances are taken to be especially significant. The choice of certain thoughts or memories out of a lifetime's accumulated possibilities cannot be random or accidental, but must spell oracular awareness that emerges as the dying person starts to acquire ghostly omniscience. That is why my letter, arriving so soon after Gidion's demise, excited speculation over the significance of my coming: were the two events connected? was it that Gidion, after dying, had found me in the Hereafter, and had sent me to Ilahita? If Gidion's lethal cancer was caused by the Tambaran, did my "lethal" cancer have the same source? This speculation reactivated the original opinion concerning my supposed cancer "death," namely, that it was caused by unusually close and prolonged exposure to the Tambaran's powerful magic. Had dead Gidion sent me to avenge the both of us against the Tambaran and its men? If such was the purpose of my return, its larger significance must have to do with furthering the impending millenarian Event—as harbinger, skirmisher, inquisitor, or as the very Event itself. By preemptively destroying the Tambaran before I arrived, the village would avert catastrophe and attain eligibility for a share in the apocalyptic rewards to come.

Little wonder that the people greeted me with a mixture of hope and apprehension. Little wonder, either, that a sizable, curious company came along, when, within hours of my arrival, I went to pay my respects to Gidion's grave, or that anxious glances were exchanged when I casually remarked that the grave was still mounded, its year-old backfill surprisingly fresh in appearance. In Ilahita, people do not visit cemeteries for purely sentimental reasons; in fact, they positively avoid them, except when something needs to be buried or dug up.

My impression is that most people eventually came to accept my visit as the mundane, nonmiraculous thing I claimed it to be. If there was disappointment, it was probably mixed with relief that the glorious but terrifying Apocalypse was not quite yet. The most militant Revivalists, however, among them our nearest neighbors, never stopped watching and waiting, hoping to catch Beverly or me with our guard down; wanting to be there when, for one stray, incriminating moment, my true mission would be revealed. Our words and actions were closely monitored, and the slightest oddity would set the Revivalists' network jangling with rumors. In this respect, at least, Ilahita's society of rumor had not changed a bit: it was still Shakespeare's "blunt monster with uncounted heads" that gobbles up, especially in states of enthusiasm, all coincidences and anomalies, however minor, and absorbs them into its organism.[8]

Despite what has been said, I do not for a moment imagine that the prospect of my return was sufficient to panic the men of Ilahita into publicly renouncing the Tambaran. An institution so entrenched as the Tambaran was in Ilahita society and culture cannot be undone by something so flimsy as the rumors and surmises surrounding my return; many other factors contributed, as well, to the men's act. Also, in this large village, many persons would have scarcely noticed that I had returned or made less than a passing connection between that event and the grand happenings that were afoot. But if the whole uncanny business of Gidion's death and my return was but a sideshow to the main events, it was nonetheless highly consequential for me and my work, for it remained a fugitive element in my dealings with people through virtually the entire period of fieldwork.

Being both inside and outside the community one studies is a liminal position familiar to ethnographers: their cozy methodological vantage point, their fly-on-the-wall perch. For the people, however, once the novelty is gone, the presence of this quasi-person can be puzzling, troubling, even irritating. It is a disturbing presence and, in its ambiguities, ghostlike. As it happens, the Arapesh word for "white man," *dowank,* is synonymous with *kgamba,* meaning "ghost."[9] One should perhaps not make too much of this semantic connection, since it dates to the time of first contact, when white men were scary, luminous, murderous creatures of doubtful humanity, who had the habit of casually putting off and taking on their "skins." No one any longer openly admits to such lurid fantasies, and the word *dowank* has become a mildly pejorative racial epithet. (Normally they use the nonpejorative Melanesian Pidgin word *waitman.*) And yet, as we shall see, current Revival thinking resurrects such notions in a modified form. There were times when I felt that the ghostish meta-phor, which had only lightly haunted my original stay in the village, was made serious and literal by the circumstances of my return. Going home to Ilahita was not the joyful, uncomplicated reunion I had hoped it would be.

Chapter Two

THE MISSION

During much of the year of our return, public life in Ilahita was ablaze with Christian fervor and expectancy. The main church overflowed every Sunday and holiday and from time to time was the scene of religious conclaves attracting hundreds of participants from all over the region. On other days—morning, evening, and night—the small churches in each of the wards carried forward the enthusiasm. Casual greetings and leave takings were tagged with Christian benedictions. Universal love and harmony were the goal, and the Melanesian Pidgin phrase *wan bel,* meaning "spiritual oneness and accord," was a slogan—more an incantation— heard many times during the day.

The answer to a missionary's prayer? On the contrary, it was in the very midst of this Christian excitement that decades of continuous white mission presence came to an abrupt, unhappy end. The last white person at the Ilahita station was a young, likable, slightly manic New Zealander nurse. Her coworker, also a nurse, had returned to New Zealand a couple of months earlier, pessimistic and burned out after seven years in Ilahita, and still shaken from having been assaulted the previous year by a young tough wielding an ax. Almost immediately after her partner left, the younger woman began to cave in under the strain of isolation and fear. Before long, she was sick, debilitated, and terrified of the local people and had overmedicated herself to the brink of psychosis. Field authorities, alarmed by reports of her condition and by the frenzied state of Revival activities in the village, decided that her life was in danger. The nurse was evacuated, and her superiors announced that they would never again assign a white person to Ilahita.

Thus ended a relationship that had begun thirty-four years earlier, when the South Sea Evangelical Mission arrived in Ilahita, just after that village had come under Australian administrative control. For decades the Tambaran successfully resisted Mission Christianity, but in the end it was Ilahita's own, indigenized Christianity that finally drove the missionaries away. This "Revival" Christianity did not merely succeed the Tambaran as the village's spiritual guide; in curious ways it was the Tambaran's natural, chosen, inevitable heir. Totalistic systems, such as the Tambaran (and the Soviet Union), change according to their kind: abruptly, uncompromisingly, often violently, always totalistically. They do not evolve gracefully. For Ilahita, the Revival's moral universalism, adherence to the foreign doctrine of Christianity, millenarian promise, and exaltation of women's spiritual superiority made it the precise opposite of the Tambaran and therefore the irresistible object of defection.

The nexus of relationships between Mission Christianity, Revival Christianity, and the Tambaran is important to understand; otherwise it would be too easy to assume that Ilahita's wholesale shift to Christianity and the revelation of cult secrets were engineered or forced on them by European missionaries. To be sure, Mission Christianity was part of the historical backdrop against which Revival Christianity arose. But during their final decade in the village, resident missionaries found themselves increasingly relegated to the sidelines of village Christianity: ambivalent, perplexed, mostly unwelcome spectators to Ilahita's elaborate countercultural show. Ironically (because now both sides claimed Christian authenticity and priority), the Mission's rather helpless position in relation to the Revival was nearly a replica of its previous position in relation the Tambaran. To the missionaries, Ilahita's notorious resistance to their teachings—resistance to Christ—had plainly been due to its being, in the words of one Mission publication, "the stronghold of Satan." Eventually, most villagers would reach the same dismal conclusion about their ancestral traditions. But the fact that the Christianity they finally embraced was politically assertive and flagrantly defiant of the Mission suggests that the Tambaran's intolerance of outside interference continued in spirit, measured by Ilahita's determination to retain control not only of its daily religious affairs but of its metaphysical self. That is why, for as long as it persists as a village, Ilahita will be an intensely religious place.

It is hardly sufficient, however, to say that the Tambaran earlier persisted in spite of the Mission purely by virtue of its peculiar strength and vitality. In the past two millennia, many institutions far mightier than the Ilahita Tambaran—the Roman Empire, for one—have yielded to the sticks and carrots of Christianity. Of equal importance in the Ilahita case was the restraint exercised by most of the individuals who actually worked there, an attitude that resulted from a combination of Mission policy and personal style. Although doctrinally Protestant-evangelical and deeply committed Christians, they were not the sorts of zealots who barged and bullied their way into some other parts of the Sepik region; none here resembled, for example, the Catholic priest whom people still tell about, who long ago rode a white charger through the nearby Wosera region, setting his torch to every spirit house he could find.[1] On the Sepik River, Mission-sponsored cultural vandalism sometimes took the form of publicly revealing secret Tambaran paraphernalia, in the hope that the men, once their all-powerful spirits were exposed as mere bits of wood and feather, would be so humiliated that they would abandon their cult.[2] Resident missionaries in Ilahita, on the other hand, never resorted to such tactics, nor were they implicated in the men's self-revelation. Considering the extreme vulnerability of cult secrets to exposure by outsiders, how tempted must the missionaries have been simply to explode the men's ritual pretenses; how available a shortcut, one would suppose, to all their salvational goals! Why didn't they take it?

One possibility is that the missionaries never got close enough to the Tambaran to discover just how important secrecy was to the whole institution. They knew, of course, that women and children were terrorized by the Tambaran and that a good deal of what the men did was sham and trickery. But they also knew in their religious hearts that Satan is the greatest, the original Deceiver. To these Christian trench warriors, his sponsorship of the Tambaran implied that the evil of all the men did was an exudation of that greater, personified Evil that was Satan himself. Curiously, although missionaries and cult elders disagreed over the moral value of the Tambaran spirits, they did not disagree over the reality of those spirits. This is the crucial point. By virtue of their own belief system, the missionaries were disposed to accept the men's claims of alliance with spirits of terrifying force and opinion. All other aspects of the Tambaran, including its ceremonial sham and secrecy, were eclipsed by the fact of Satan's evil immanence: when a lie represents The Lie, then it is no lie at all, but the plain truth. In form, this is not unlike how Arapesh cult elders rationalize their own deceit, when, as Tambaran men, they manipulate truth and illusion in the service of ritual goals (Tuzin 1980, 261–65; 1995b).

This view of missionary awareness is based on many clues and much circumstantial evidence. I could not have discussed these matters in such terms without exposing the Tambaran to risk. Moreover, the missionaries were wedded to a fundamentalist worldview requiring that the satanic meaning of the Tambaran be inherent, not attributed or negotiable. This is why, I suggest, whenever I discussed matters of "native superstition" with local missionaries, theirs was an attitude of credulity rather than skepticism.

For example, several months into my original fieldwork, a Mission schoolteacher a few years my senior and recently arrived from Germany asked what my researches had uncovered concerning the efficacy of sorcery. Taking him to mean the efficacy of a personal belief in sorcery— that is, as a psychosomatic phenomenon—I began to respond in terms of the power of suggestion, the crippling potential of fear, "voodoo death," and the like. But no. He quickly brought me back to his question, which concerned sorcery as a literally efficacious magical technique. When I gently protested that sorcery in this sense was a fantasy, he replied with a condescending chuckle, "Come now, we had sorcerers in Europe in the Middle Ages. We even have them today! Why could there not be sorcerers here in Ilahita?" The corresponding lesson given from the pulpit is not, "You need not fear sorcery, because it does not exist," but rather, "You need no longer fear sorcery, for Christ will protect you." Thus, the effect of the missionary's conviction of a world divided between Good and Evil is to bring the two belief systems into alignment, into a common universe of discourse and morality, and, in practical terms, to reinforce sorcery ideas and practices by crediting to them the prestige of white European knowledge.

Fifteen years later, I heard the same attitude expressed by a middle-aged American mission worker from a distant village. Perceiving what he took to be startling resemblances between the religious frenzies of the Revival and those of the European Reformation, this man allowed himself a friendly view of what was happening in Ilahita and was willing in principle to countenance claims of miraculous intervention by the Holy Spirit. "Why can't these miracles be as real as those of the Middle Ages?" he asked rhetorically. "You must understand, these are exactly the kinds of conditions that result from the actions of the Holy Spirit; this is when miracles happen." Unlike some of his colleagues, who charitably felt that the Revivalists were well intentioned but religiously confused, he did not regard the bizarreness of some of the expressions (e.g., pay telephones to the dead) as any cause for alarm or censure. He accepted them as the workings of the Holy Spirit—New Guinea style—just as sorcery is Satan's handiwork in this time and setting. Again, such credulity, coming from such a prestigious quarter, acts as an extremely powerful endorsement for the irrational, sometimes fraudulent, claims of the Revival leaders.

The belief-driven logic of the missionaries thus acted to strengthen the same customs they were there to combat. This ironic situation, along with the missionaries' fearful, principled incuriosity about the details of "Satan's cult," helps to explain why the Tambaran was able to flourish alongside the Mission presence. An equally important factor was the extraordinary character and personality of the woman who, for many years, was Christianity's chief representative in Ilahita.

Go back to an earlier time and picture Miss Liesbeth Schrader, a robust, jolly Pomeranian lady gone gray in the fields of the Lord. She usually wears a light cotton housedress, belted, with sensible shoes that can stand up to mud and white socks reaching just above the ankle. Her hair is in a braid loosely coiled on her head, a style I think of as "Nordic." Neither her age nor a slight lameness in one leg prevents her movements from being quick and determined. Miss Schrader is capable of managing the station on her own—preacher, teacher, and nurse, all in one—but this has rarely been necessary, and in any case Mission authorities dislike placing fieldworkers (especially women) on their own in the villages. She has been a missionary in the South Seas for thirty-five years.

It is mid-morning and Miss Schrader is teaching. Her pupils are boys and girls around ten or eleven years old, most of them boarders from other villages. Having gained precarious order in her classroom, Miss Schrader is into the day's lesson. Suddenly, from down the lane—the village's main artery, which passes through the Mission station—comes the sound of whistles, trumpets, and songs announcing the approach of the Tambaran. Pandemonium erupts. Desks are overturned, books and papers go flying, as the children dive for windows and doors in their escape to the safety of the jungle environs. Across the way, women are bolting from the Mission clinic—trailing bandages, clutching babies yanked from the examining table or the nurse's arms, making a mad dash of their own. In a moment the Mission compound is deserted—except for the teacher and the nurse, who stand in their doorways shaking their heads to each other in exasperation over this unholy disruption of their good works.

From previous experience the ladies know that the more seriously ailing clinic patients will drift back after the emergency but that the flown children are gone for the rest of the day, already dispersed and larking about on their surprise, Tambaran-given holiday. They know, too, that this is no isolated incident, for it implies that the year's ritual season has begun and that many similar interruptions can be expected in the weeks and months ahead. And if a lower-grade initiation is on this season's agenda, some of the boys in the class will be absent for many days or weeks at a time.

The cultists arrive shouldering a litter on which rides the spirit effigy that is the cause for all the commotion. Words are exchanged. Neither side is willing to be intimidated. As head of the station, Miss Schrader becomes schoolmarmish and scolds them for their heathenism, ingratitude, and selfish disregard for the welfare of the women and children, the sick and the helpless. A few of the men flare back at her for her intrusion (her intrusion! she sputters), some are insolently amused. But most of the men only shrug in mild apology, as if to say, this is how it must be—as if to say, don't take it personally. The fact is, they all like the German lady and would prefer not to upset her. Several of the men have known her as a presence in their lives since childhood, and all have received her kindnesses from time to time. And so the men do not tarry but continue on their way, leaving Miss Schrader to wonder—for the umpteenth time in her nearly twenty years in the village—whether there is any hope for this place after all.

It would be easy to say that the Mission had no right to be there in the first place; to side with the cultists in their legitimate desire to go about their business without interference; to view the Mission as outside "the culture" and therefore ineligible for a place in the ethnographic account. And yet, like it or not, the Mission (and increasingly the ethnographer, for that matter) is very much a part of this ethnographic scene, and the social relations linking it with the indigenous villagers are based on understandings that over the years have become integral to those constituting the culture as we now find it. Taking for the moment the ethnographic situation as it is, accepting the Mission's presence as fait accompli, it is possible not only to appreciate the pathos of the missionary's situation but to discover analytic interest in it as well. As a perhaps useful corrective to the not uncommon anthropological stereotype of missionaries as arrogant, fanatical, and spiritually rapacious, let me be the devil's advocate and suggest that, in the face of the frustrations that constantly beset them, these missionaries displayed remarkable restraint in not violating the men's secrecy or otherwise forcing Christianity on the people. Again, why did not the missionaries simply explode the men's cult?

The organization in question is the South Sea Evangelical Mission (SSEM). From its Australian headquarters, the SSEM established itself in the Solomon Islands early in the century and became the pioneering mission in this part of the Sepik region during the decade following World War II.[3] Unlike, for example, the Anglicans, Lutherans, and various Roman Catholic orders, which are missions nurtured by a mother church, the SSEM draws its field personnel and much of its funding from independent Protestant evangelical churches in Australia and New Zealand. Additionally, since around 1960 a significant number of fieldworkers have come from the affiliated Liebenzell Evangelical Mission, which is headquartered in Germany and has been the chief Protestant presence on the New Guinea island of Manus since 1914.[4] These differences in national origins and specific church backgrounds limit the generalizations one might safely make about the belief style and comportment of SSEM workers in their various locales. Although I have met many of its field (and also headquarters) staff over the years, my view of the Mission is largely shaped by those who served in Ilahita, whom I knew best and who, until the late 1970s, happened to be of German nationality.

More specifically, the formative period of Ilahita's mission experience was directed by Miss Schrader, who founded the station in 1952 and remained its head, almost without interruption, until her retirement in late 1969. Though she was from Germany, Liesbeth Schrader was not a Liebenzeller but a member of a small, allied religious order known as the Friedenshort Sisters.[5] She first worked as a missionary with the SSEM on Malaita, one of the Solomon Islands, was evacuated to Australia at the outbreak of World War II in the Pacific, and afterward joined the newly opened SSEM field in New Guinea.

Miss Schrader's final three months in Ilahita, prior to retirement, coincided with the start of my fieldwork there. Even at the time, I realized how fortunate I was to know her, but in particular to know her at the end of her career as a practicing missionary, just at the time she was perhaps most inclined to philosophize about what it all meant.

Looking back after many years, I am slightly amazed that Miss Schrader was the first missionary I ever met and that until then I had imagined such people to be almost as alien, personally and culturally, as those I was going to New Guinea to study. My doctoral advisor at the

Australian National University, Derek Freeman, had counseled me to consider missionaries and administrators as part of the ethnographic scene, to put aside preconceptions and respect them as persons who, certainly at the outset of my fieldwork, would know much more than I would about the local people. Excellent advice, and yet as regards missionaries, who were more preconceived, I could not rid myself of vague notions gotten from unflattering literary or historical treatments, alternating between images of milquetoast piety and bombastic, burn-'em-at-the-stake fanaticism. Although not so naive as to believe that such images would be met in the flesh, I was worryingly sure that missionaries, for their part, placed anthropologists just one rung above Satan on the great ladder of moral worth. If they asked whether I was a Christian—surely the first thing such people always want to know—I would have to disclose the distance I had slid from my church upbringing, and the relationship would be downhill from there on. Polite avoidance was clearly in order.

Miss Schrader proved not to be so avoidable. She was disarmingly hospitable and even acted glad to see me—anything to break the routine and sense of isolation, I suppose. It was early September 1969. The early rains that year had forced me to spend an unscheduled five days stranded at the Maprik subdistrict administrative station. There, I busied myself with census and court records, waiting for the rain to stop and a government vehicle and driver to carry me and my supplies to Ilahita, some twenty-five kilometers away (see map 3).

Our slow, muddy journey followed the gently broken terrain of this hinterland region, across numerous streams and one fordable river, through stretches of grassland, jungle, and majestic old rain forest, past new and old gardens and picturesque little Abelam-speaking hamlets and villages. At length, we mounted a ridge where our pony track entered and dissolved into a cluster of houses arranged around a clearing. That cluster led us immediately to another cluster, which led us to another, and another, and another. Off to the side of the ridge were spurs studded with smaller clusters; and across the way another ridge could be seen, with clusters and spurs of its own. We had entered into the midst of a complex of hamlets that was simply vast in comparison with any of the previous settlements we had passed. "This is where the road ends," announced the laconic driver. "This is Ilahita."

The village appeared deserted when we arrived—it was early afternoon and people were still in their gardens. In those days, each village was required to maintain a simple "rest house" for use by official visitors. Ilahita's stilted *haus kiap* (MP), which was to be my home for a month, overlooked a large ceremonial plaza at about the geographical center of the village. Forty meters obliquely across the clearing was a nuclear-family dwelling—Akotan's, I would learn—while directly across the way was a shelter for use by police and carriers on patrol. The only other occupants of the plaza were a gigantic fig tree and a large frangipani tree, whose constant flowering scented the place with one of the sweetest of all tropical fragrances.

The government driver deposited me and my gear in front of the house, shook my hand, and drove away. As I sat on the stoop of the rickety, thatch-roofed structure, listening to the engine die away, feeling farther from home than I had ever felt and wondering what to do next, I heard a semidistant "Hullooooo!" and observed a woman beckoning excitedly from the door of the semidistant Mission residence—which until then had also seemed deserted. Since it was only the two of us, with no Arapesh present to witness me associating with a missionary,[6] there was nothing to do but answer the summons.

Minutes later, contentedly working on a second helping of apple pandowdy, I was describing to Miss Schrader my intended study of the local customs. "Well, you've come to the right place, young man," was her slightly glum response, "for there are many in Ilahita who remain in Darkness." The heartening effect of this news must have shown, for Miss Schrader added, warily, "And if you do not obstruct God's Work, you will be welcome here, as far as I am concerned." When I replied, truthfully, that there was nothing about my work that should obstruct God's, she gave a satisfied nod, as if to say we now understood each other.

Thenceforward, although religious subjects came up many times in conversation—both because Christian faith was the idiom through which she expressed herself, and because traditional religious practices were of great interest to each of us for very different reasons—Miss Schrader never once steered the topic toward my personal beliefs or my observer's opinion of the Mission. Whatever hints she may have picked up, I am reasonably sure they did not enter as a factor into our relationship. If anything, the reflective mood of her final months in Ilahita tilted the communication the other way, and it is not impossible that my position as someone apart from her social routine and studiously nonjudgmental helped her to objectify herself in a way that she might not have done otherwise. At any rate, to this green and terribly earnest outsider, who at age twenty-four could have been her grandson, she generously confided many of her ideas and experiences concerning the people and customs of Ilahita. Not only was all of this valuable as data and as part of my general orientation to the place; more important, the opportunity of seeing her at work was crucial, I now realize, to an understanding of the entire career of Christianity in Ilahita.[7]

As mentioned, Miss Schrader introduced Christianity to Ilahita and for nearly a generation was the source of the villagers' understandings of this new body of ethical and religious ideas. As a missionary, she was there to teach the people stories and lessons from the Bible and, above all, to convey to them a sense of the meaning of Christianity. In the early days there were very few speakers of Melanesian Pidgin; even in the 1980s there were enough (elderly) nonspeakers of that language that preachers relied on phrase-by-phrase vernacular renderings. Problems of translation have always been monumental, going well beyond obvious challenges, such as how to express "The Lord is my Shepherd . . ." in idiomatic Melanesian Pidgin, let alone Arapesh.[8] The greater difficulty lay in the fact that many of Christianity's key concepts—universal brotherly love, spiritual salvation, etc.—were alien to local thinking, and any discussion of such matters in locally known languages could hardly avoid being ludicrously inadequate.

Never mind, though, that progress in theological development was slow and halting, Miss Schrader was all the while defining Christianity in her own person. Missionaries put a lot of stock in setting a good "Christian example," and well they should; for in the early days of contact, villagers, because they are unversed in the Christian ideals against which to compare the behavior of these missionaries, have no alternative but to assume that Christianity is what the practitioner does. "Don't judge Socialism by the people who practice it," advised George Orwell, which is all very well if one already knows the tenets of socialism. In the absence of such knowledge socialism (or Christianity) must be judged by its examplars. Thus, even as Miss Schrader strove to behave in what she consciously understood to be a good Christian manner, the people were all the time learning what Christianity was by what she said and did.

For present purposes, the most important aspect of Miss Schrader's personal style was her doctrinaire abhorrence of the Tambaran, which she viewed as Satan's handiwork, combined with a good-hearted acceptance of people who continued to adhere to it. Of course, most of the villagers whom she knew best belonged to the small church congregation, and toward them she showed an especial friendliness befitting their membership in the community of Christ. But with a few exceptions[9] the many who remained outside this group were treated with tolerance, respect, and sometimes overt affection.

Kwamwi, for example, was not only of the highest ritual rank, he performed as a master artist and one of the village's leading shamans. In the opinion of neighboring enemy villages, Kwamwi was a dangerous sorcerer, a cold-blooded killer who fueled his mystical power by eating human corpses. Taking pains to look like a man of parts, he was always decked out in shell jewelry and a jaunty comb-and-feather arrangement in his hair. Around his neck hung an unadorned little bundle, containing, he said, the magically efficacious finger of a bush demon he had once killed in the jungle. Although Kwamwi could be scary when it suited him and could more than hold his own as a magician, artist, and orator, off-stage he was remarkably sweet tempered and playful. Little children adored him; he was a gentle husband; and, to my knowledge, he was the only man in the village at the time who treated his dog with kindness, and who gave it a name—Kailal.

Much of what Kwamwi stood for publicly, Miss Schrader was bound to despise, and yet this did not diminish her enormous affection for him. They were about the same age—she a little older, perhaps—which may have facilitated the convivial, teasing banter that usually marked their interactions. Kwamwi, she liked to recall, had been one of her earliest friends in the village, in fact, her first clinic assistant; and she fondly recalled how, whenever she was doctoring a wound, Kwamwi, bending forward to get a better look, would block her own view while tickling her face with his feathery headdress.[10]

Kwamwi's case is extreme but instructive, for time and again I saw evidence that Miss Schrader hated the sin and loved the sinner. This attitude might not seem exceptional in a missionary: after all, it is both central to the ethic of Christian charity and to the core methodology of Christian proselytization, in that it envisages the soul as rescuable from the acts and beliefs that weigh it down. My experience suggests, however, that most missionaries, like most people, are inclined to react to others according to the latter's exhibited characteristics, without immediate regard to their (sometimes subtle) redemptive qualities. This is surely a natural tendency, and the effort needed to resist it must be proportionately greater when one's own values are absolutistic and strongly contrary to those of the other. The value differences do not have to involve religion— scientific and political ideologues are also likely to hate the "sinner" because of the "sin"—but how more extreme can a situation be, than that of a German missionary of profound Protestant evangelical convictions sent to darkest New Guinea to combat the greatest evil the world has ever known? To be sure, charity requires that the people be viewed as innocents in satanic bondage; but what force of faith or discipline must it take to uphold the innocence of "heathens" who, like Kwamwi, year after year remained loyal to Satan? In the face of such chronic frustration, Miss Schrader's charity was remarkably sincere and consistent. Some of her colleagues even hinted (if I interpreted their sighs and shrugs correctly) that she was a bit too mellow in her attitude toward what needed to be done.

Miss Schrader's tolerance at the interpersonal level meant that during her tenure, Christ and the Tambaran coexisted in reasonable accord in Ilahita. There were moments, such as the school incident described earlier, when the two collided—but with little consequence to the relationship. Ilahita's Christians never numbered more than about 10 percent of the village population—too few to be a threat to the Tambaran, whose custodians did not object to the Mission's presence. If there was any discontent among the villagers, it was among the Christians, who quietly grumbled that Miss Schrader was too generous toward the heathens. Disillusionment with Mission Christianity would eventually erupt as the widely popular Revival movement, but the process of alienation between village and Mission began soon after Miss Schrader's departure in December 1969 and her replacement by a succession of persons unlike her in temperament and personal style. As an example, the one time I witnessed bullying tactics, they were employed by the person who, with his young family, was Miss Schrader's immediate successor in Ilahita.

Mr. M. had an executive air. His manner seemed to say that Ilahita had been the "Stronghold of Satan" long enough and that he would soon put the Devil to flight. This might have been all right, except that his nature seemed also to include an element of religious pride and a ready impatience with those who did not meet his expectations. Hearing that the men were gathering for an all-night ritual song festival within earshot of the Mission compound, the missionary angrily protested and imperiously ordered them to cancel their plans or at least to shift their heathenish revelry to a location where he could not hear them. Being new to the area, Mr. M. perhaps did not know that the sound of these affairs carries for miles, that their venue is ritually determined and not susceptible to last-minute changes, and that the cult leaders would not for a moment allow this bumptious intruder to tell them what to do. The singing went ahead as scheduled, whereupon Mr. M. punished the village (women and children included) by closing the clinic for three days. It was a cruel, foolish act, for which the community never forgave him. And often during the disapproving commentaries it was said, nostalgically, "Miss Schrader would not have done such a thing."

The villagers' reaction confirms the gentler tone of Mission conduct during the preceding period. The commentators were correct: such a thing would not have happened when Miss Schrader was in charge. Her approach was to set an example of good Christian living, teach the Scriptures to those who wanted to learn, and, perhaps above all, encourage each person to find Christ in his or her own way and own time. As much as this policy endeared Miss Schrader to the people, it did not produce many converts—a fact its author brushed aside, saying, with a gemütlich twinkle, "Let the Catholics measure success by the number of converts. I am interested in the quality of our converts."

This quality was supposedly guaranteed by the transformative effect of the Christian message on those who open their hearts to it. And yet the rudimentary conceptual grasp of this message by regular churchgoers, combined with the chronic problem of backsliding, left room for doubt precisely as to the authenticity of faith in the congregation. During a conversation shortly before her departure I carelessly remarked to Miss Schrader that the loyalty of the (few) Christians in the village was doubtless due to her generous, compassionate nature. This was the fact of the matter, as best I could judge from having gotten to know some of the village Christians; but the comment was also meant as a compliment, and as such it stumbled badly on a nerve that was obviously raw on the surface. "I should be very sorry if that were true," the lady said gravely, suddenly looking her age, "because if the people's attachment is to me and not to the Word of God, it would mean that my mission here has utterly failed."

Miss Schrader's tendency to hate the sin and love the sinner created what might be called the missionary's dilemma. Christian charity is universal or it is nothing. But if charity is granted indiscriminately, to heathens and converts alike, then where is the practical advantage in converting? Of course, Miss Schrader and her colleagues did not see this as a dilemma, for to them the advantage was self-evident, though perhaps not practical in the usual sense. Christianity, in their view, should not be adopted for mercenary reasons. Indeed, that one might become a Christian in order to "get something" was an idea Miss Schrader seemed unable to grasp; the question of advantage simply should not arise. She and her colleagues wanted not to entice people but to guide them to an evangelical Awakening all their own, leading to fulfillment in the inherent rewards of Christian living.

This is all well and good, but what would such a promise have meant to folks hearing of it for the first time? From their point of view, would it have been worth the costs entailed in becoming a Christian? Whereas the benefits were ethereal and distant, the prohibitions were stark and immediate. Not only Tambaran ceremonialism, but oratory, polygyny, magic, long-yam production and competition, the use of tobacco and betel nut—such traditional practices were incompatible with SSEM Christianity. The only ones seriously attracted to this regime were those with more to gain than to lose: men lacking ambition or structural position to participate successfully in Tambaran politics and, significantly, women of an enterprising sort. It is not impossible that some of the early converts sought, found, and were content with the kind of spiritual reward Miss Schrader herself enjoyed. If there were such converts, I never knew of them.

My clear impression, based on knowing several such original converts very well, is that their motives were predominantly, if not exclusively, materialistic; this despite teachings by missionaries (with their cars, airplanes, radios, bounteous food, and clothing—all effortlessly acquired) that Christianity allows one to be rich in spirit and still be poor in worldly goods. Obstacles of language and cultural understanding may have helped to obscure the fine distinction between spiritual and material largesse. To the early Ilahita Christians—not unreasonably—the correlation was clear, direct, and compelling, and any difference between the two was a difference that made no difference. Of course, the missionaries were alert to this hazard, and most of them tried to avoid suggesting that salvation meant material rewards in the here and now. Nevertheless, the apocalyptic provision of Christianity, especially as emphasized in evangelical Protes-

tantism, makes it extremely easy to imagine the there-and-then trans-
ferred into the here-and-now. Yet again, missionary argument was de-
feated by its own doctrinal postulates, concerning, in this instance,
salvation and reward: saying nothing about material rewards, they would
arouse suspicion; saying something, they would sow confusion; saying
more, they would "protest too much." Whatever was said, the small
group of Christian stalwarts, always enriching what they heard with what
they hoped for, fancied themselves in a kind of collusion with the missionaries. They saw the preacher's elision of "cargo" as a tactical ploy for
their benefit, a maneuver designed to obfuscate the "true message" for all
but the handful of committed converts who knew better—themselves.

These persistent churchgoers, resentful that heathenism was evidently
cost-free, looked forward to some terrible punishment being delivered
upon their godless neighbors. And yet, as the decades passed, the galling
injustice persisted: punishment never came to the heathen, neither did
any tangible rewards come to the blessed. As believers took to keeping
their hopes and admonitions to themselves, fearing derision from the others, frustration and disillusionment with Mission Christianity mounted. A
new paradigm was needed, one that brought the "true" truth of Christianity—the secret truth that white people would never divulge—to bear
on the material aspirations of the Ilahita people. When it finally came, the
Revival, as the new paradigm was called, was a devastating prelude to the
Refiner's Fire: a mass movement trampling all of tradition, chasing the
Tambaran from the village, righting all the old wrongs, and turning this
"Stronghold of Satan" into something far worse. The Revival was meant
to herald and to trigger the Apocalypse—and, in a way, that's just what
it did.

Chapter Three

THE REPEAL OF CUSTOM

The Arapesh liken the death of an important man to the falling of a great tree in the forest: the myriad vines connecting the giant with the surrounding canopy cause its tumble to tear at and shake the entire forest community. When we arrived in Ilahita, reverberations of the Tambaran's collapse were still pronounced. The hole left gaping in the social canopy distressed the traditionalists, while the modernists saw it as allowing a glorious sunlight to stream in, scattering the gloom of spiritual darkness, and creating the conditions for new growth.

The reformist movement did not stop at the destruction of the Tambaran—a loss over which, by itself, the traditionalists remained inconsolable; it went on zealously to repudiate all ceremonial life construable as related to the Tambaran, which included just about everything. The traditional grounds of male solidarity and association were obliterated. Without formal oratory, banned because its techniques were taught during one of the Tambaran's initiatory seclusions, speeches became merely ad hoc and informational. No more did famous orators, with great rhetorical and gestural flair, meet in colorful speaking duels over the proper application of custom to current events. Meanwhile, the Christian taboo against the use of tobacco and betel nut—a seemingly trivial injunction—did incalculable damage to casual male sociality. Their prohibition is indicative of the general calamity visited upon the men: without the Tambaran, without all of the ancillary topics and projects it gave men to talk about, without the stimulating need to coordinate competitions and displays, without even the companionable sharing of betel nut and tobacco, male society quickly declined. Without the cover of secrecy, without the protection of the Tambaran's canopy, masculinity as the Ilahita had known it for a hundred years could not continue. The Tambaran was *what men do* (Tuzin 1980, 212–13); so when it died, masculine identity, purpose, and agency died with it.

*   *   *

One important casualty was the male prestige complex centered on the production, display, competition, and exchange of long and short yams (Tuzin 1972). Apart from the loss of periodic excitement and pageantry, the change removed the cultural incentive for the production of food surpluses, which were an important subsistence cushion in rare, but potentially catastrophic, times of garden failure. People now plant only according to estimated subsistence needs, having recently decided that European missionaries were correct all along in insisting that the surpluses were wasteful and their purposes evil. The men now accept that the competitions fueled by the surpluses were socially disruptive, which is much less than half true, and that the magic used to grow the yams was heathenish, which is true only in a name-calling sense. One interesting consequence of this change is that garden work was converted from meaningful endeavor into unredeemed drudgery. In the past people at work would sometimes remark on how hot it was, but never would they complain about the work itself. Today, complaints about gardening are frequent. People resent the labor, even though today's gardens are smaller and shabbier than before, and the time spent in them is clearly much less.

Surplus yam production sustained the Tambaran in more ways than one. Yams, along with wild pigs, were the principal feast foods during the great cult ceremonials, and they were also needed in large quantities to feed ritual workers and celebrants during long periods when they were not engaged in subsistence activities. Under the aegis of the men's cult, yams were the principal currency in various forms of competitive exchange, nearly all of which occurred between partners whose relationship was defined by the Tambaran; that is to say, the partners were members, usually by inheritance, of ritually constituted classes. Indeed, it would not be inaccurate to describe the Tambaran as lord of an extraordinarily large and complex gift economy, directing the circulation of ritual goods and services within the village, and to other villages, friend and enemy, within Ilahita's ceremonial orbit. And because it was a finely geared system of *gift* exchange (Mauss 1925), with each of its many connections wrapped in moral obligation and privilege, the Tambaran's economy powerfully integrated village society.

In human terms the annihilation of this vast exchange apparatus subverted hundreds of close, affective male relationships. The Ilahita system was a dual organization of unprecedented complexity, comprising eight cross-cutting dual oppositions. These oppositions were layered on a gradient of social inclusiveness, from the ritually formalized opposition between actual brothers to the great totemic moieties arraying one half of the men of the village against the other half. Each opposition had its distinctive criteria, symbols, and activity domain (Tuzin 1976, chap. 8). Men inherited different exchange partners along each axis of the system: ritually designated "friends," "allies," "neutrals," and "enemies," as the case may be.

The importance men assigned to these relationships, regardless of ritual "content," is difficult to convey in words. Partners exalted, praised, and boasted of each other at every opportunity. Brothers and affines may bicker and be envious, though they are not supposed to; exchange partners (including ritual "enemies") never try to diminish each other—at least not in any ad hominem sense, outside the terms of the immediate competition. On the contrary, the motive is always to boost the other's fame and importance, for it reflects well on one's own standing to have an exchange partner of high quality: the greater he is, the greater you are. That principle extends even to defining the contingent nature of one's social existence. A man's personal male identity is constituted by his exchange relationships; through them he is fulfilled and made whole, in the abstract, shimmering, metaphysical way that is the mystery of livingness (cf. Strathern 1988, 159–60).[1]

The idea that living unity exists in the mediation of dualistic contrarieties is one that informs the entire Ilahita exchange system but is perhaps most clearly represented in the language of Tambaran symbolism. Thus, for example, initiation partners are understood to share a named Tambaran spirit. This spirit exists at all times in the Otherworld of such forms and is summoned to human company mainly in the context of Tambaran ceremonialism. Most crucial, it performs as the magical agent in the renewal and re-creation that occurs during initiation rites. Incarnated in paintings, sculptures, flutes, songs, and other cult paraphernalia, the spirit is given by the initiating partner to the novice partner. At the next initiation, it passes back again, to the son of the first partner—and so on, back and forth between interdigitated partnership generations. The logic is that there is no point of inertia: the exchange neither begins nor ends, but is in a state of perpetual, alternating disequilibrium; the spirit exists on neither one side nor the other, but in the relationship between them, in the never-finalized summation of the alternating half-exchanges. And because these puissant spirits are projections of the partners' own personhood and spiritual potency, each man's identity is renewed, re-created—fully realized—in the ritual transaction. Hence the thrilling sense of masculine vitality, and of masculine solidarity and common cause, which permeates Tambaran ceremonialism and its ancillary exchange operations (Tuzin 1980).

Try to imagine, then, the bleak prospects following on the collapse of the ritual exchange system. In this devastating combination of losses, virtually the entire foundation of Ilahita masculinity was removed. For men momentarily intoxicated with other spirits, viz., the promises and practices of the Revival, the depression was deferred. Not until this millenarianism has run its disillusioning course will they perceive the real damage done when they exposed the cult secrets, burned the statues, paintings, and shell treasures, and launched a campaign to repudiate and destroy all that belonged to their Tambaran past.

It is important to note, however, that considerable sociocultural erosion had occurred prior to the revelation of the cult secrets, as secular developments such as schools, village courts, and business enterprises increasingly drew time, interest, and resources away from the Tambaran and allied collective endeavors. Revivalist Christians may view the revelation as the ultimate triumph of God over Satan, but the secular truth is that this event culminated a trend that had been in place for at least a decade. Indeed, without the prior withering of Tambaran values and activities, a withering that was predictable in 1972 (Tuzin 1980, 325), the revelation would have been politically impossible. Still, the climactic event, which I did not at all foresee, was significant in that it strategically struck at the core of Tambaran ideology: the secret mandate authorizing the suppression of women. Knowing full well the implications of their act, the men who staged this event took history into their own hands and precipitated a crisis that they and their forefathers had always dreaded: the women's discovery that they had been duped by the Tambaran, that tricks and illusions had kept them in surreptitious ritual bondage, and that, all along, their husbands had been their jailers. In the late 1970s, a previous Revival attempt had faltered, and the people quickly reverted to the Tambaran. Said one Revivalist leader, this time, the secrets are exposed; there will be no going back.

Another casualty of the reforms was the elaborate, beautifully expressive observances surrounding death. One now hears that it is a "sin" to mourn a passing, to weep, for women to intone their lyrical wails, to make death payments to kin and ritual partners, to gather the community together in solemn observance, or to make any other "unnecessary" ado about it. Those who cannot help themselves and cry anyway are first shushed, then removed to a house where the emotional display will not embarrass the person or distract the others. A Christian death should occasion quiet rejoicing, Revivalists say, for the soul has gone to Heaven; a heathen death needs no attention at all, for that soul has gone to Hell. In either case, the body is a husk, and the sooner and less ceremoniously it is gotten into the ground, the better.

One can appreciate that beliefs involving the soul's ascent to Heaven and the Good News that one can expect to reunite with departed loved ones in Paradise, which are part of mainstream Christian traditions, can be consoling to the bereaved. One can also accept that some individuals and some cultures go to unhealthy extremes in their response to death: consigning oneself to widow's weeds for the rest of one's life, leaping onto a funeral pyre, or dutifully lopping off some little girl's finger are not customs one would necessarily wish to recommend. Both extremes, however, the one by denying the social and emotional trauma of the loss, the other by rejecting the possibility of social and emotional reconciliation to the loss, impede the mourning process. My view is that traditional mortuary practices in Ilahita, although involving some rather gruesome elements,[2] functioned extremely well to facilitate the mourning process. Now that is gone, replaced by alien understandings that, if I am not mistaken, are devoid of social or psychological relevance. The following incident struck me with particular force because, knowing the characters well, the element of denial was painfully clear to me.

I went to offer condolences to an unusually talented and educated forty-year-old man who, one hour before, had found his ancient mother expired in her bed. The death was unexpected. The old lady seemed to have been in excellent health and had been her usual jovial self when I had exchanged greetings with her the preceding evening. To my surprise, my friend was pleased and exhilarated over his mother's death; indeed, his behavior had a manic quality, indicating that he was possibly in a state of shock. Not only was she in Heaven, he declared excitedly, her death would spare him the continued bother of caring for her. After he had calmed down, I asked him to tell me things he remembered about his mother. He told of a woman who had been ever loving and caring toward him—a description consistent with my perceptions of her. When he recalled how, every week during the years he attended Bible school in Brugam, fifteen kilometers away, his mother would carry a heavy load of yams to him, his eyes welled with tears. But only for an instant: quickly recovering his chilling ebullience, he again reminded me (and himself) that her death was a good thing for both of them.

Traditionalists were greatly distressed over what they saw as a bloodlessness in the Christian construction of death. They also perceived that the attitude was profoundly subversive of broader cultural understandings because traditional mortuary procedures importantly affirmed a variety of descent and ritual relationships and also validated ideas concerning the nature of corporeality and social personhood. Indeed, because the Tambaran supervised most rites of passage through its five-tiered initiation structure, death was the only life crisis to receive elaborate ritual treatment in its own right.[3] With this in mind, the following incident illustrates the traditionalist criticism of Revivalist mortuary notions, capturing the bleakness of cultural loss and the despair of those who discover they cannot practice and preserve culture all by themselves.

One quiet afternoon a passerby told me that Mangumbwili was dead—had died, in fact, two or three days earlier. I was dubious. Mangumbwili was a prestigious cult elder, one of a group of four powerful brothers who had long dominated political and ritual affairs in the ward of Nangup. If he had died I could not have missed learning of it at the time, nor could I have failed to hear the slitgongs.[4] Customarily, when a person dies the event is broadcast by the nearest slitgong, with a signal composed of the distinctive tattoo of the deceased's own patriclan, followed by that of his mother's patriclan. In the case of a female decedent, the signals identify her husband's clan, followed by that of her father. After this signature, a funereal knell is sounded—rather the way the clock in the church tower announces the final quarter and then tolls the hour, except that the slow-paced knell may last for many minutes. On a scale that depends upon the renown of the deceased, other slitgongs within earshot join in: after repeating the signature pattern, each begins its knell in syntony with those preceding. And so the news radiates by leaps from the death place, until the entire countryside for miles in every direction is reverberating as if from the dolorous tread of some sad giant. For everyone who beats a gong, there is a special gift of food at the memorial feast that formally ends the mourning period.

Only the deaths of great men evoke the full majesty of this response. While Mangumbwili may not have been the greatest of men, he was certainly important enough for his death to be sounded throughout the village. But I had heard no gongs, and so distrusted the news that he had died. When I inquired of my neighbor Supalo, whom I knew to be Mangumbwili's ritual exchange partner, he confirmed that the death had occurred. Years of leprosy had left Supalo's face with a symptomatic leonine puffiness about the cheeks and eyebrows, fixing there a brutish scowl that hides the tender, intelligent, and playful sides of his nature. Rage and anguish are at home in such a face, and it was these that came to the window when I asked about the gongs. "They are silent because his children are Christian," he said bitterly.

> It is because they dishonor him so—their own father, who fed them—that I did not go to the funeral. And when I die, what will happen? Will they just throw me in a hole? It will not make death easy to know that the gongs will not sound for me, that my greatness will be forgotten, that my life will have been nothing.

The matter must have been weighing on Supalo, for he immediately launched into a heartrending soliloquy, by the end of which his lion cheeks were wet with tears.

> Why do the Christians do this to us? I am a heathen [MP: *haiden*], but when I see the yam sprout, I wonder, "Why is this?" and I think, "Maybe God did it." And when I see the sun rise, I wonder, "Where does this come from?" and I think "Maybe God sent it." And when I see a newborn baby, I wonder, "Why did this happen?" and again I think, "Yes, maybe God made it happen." *I will allow them their God! Why will they not allow me my custom!*

Supalo's indignation was genuine. Adding to it was mortification over the fact that under the circumstances he could not perform the exchange partner's traditional role at Mangumbwili's funeral. Formerly, Supalo would have summoned a group of men from his moiety to stage a mock attack on the funeral party. While the body is lying in state, the attackers, decked in feathers and paint, suddenly storm the proceedings, hurling harmless missiles into the crowd. Then, led by the bereaved exchange partner, the group files past the corpse, paying last respects before sitting to one side to be served their share of the funeral feast. The mock attack expresses the desolation felt by the exchange partner and his group; their rage against the deceased's kinsmen for letting him die; their own innocence of the death; and their determination that he be given a proper funeral.

All of this Supalo should have done. But it would have been humiliating, as well as futile, for him to have attempted to mount such an expedition: there were too few to join him, and too few to be attacked. Without others to assist him in carrying out his cultural role, Supalo was pathetic, and he knew it. "I can't do this alone," he said. That realization, perhaps more than any other aspect of the case, was the reason for his angry tears. The death of Mangumbwili removed a defined part of Supalo's identity as a man; the death of the Tambaran ensured that there was nothing he could do to valorize and thus redeem the loss.

Unlike most of the elder traditionalists, who were passively despondent or were cowed by events, Supalo jeered openly at the Revivalists and plotted against them. He accused them of deviating from genuine Christianity, thus seeking an ironic alliance between himself, who had always scorned the Mission, and whom Miss Schrader pitied as one truly lost in Darkness, and those few Christians loyal to the Mission-sponsored church and openly critical of the Revival movement.

Pursuing a different tack Supalo once put it to me—rather ingeniously, I thought—that the destruction of the Tambaran and its paraphernalia was illegal and that its executioners should be hauled into court and punished for crimes against cultural property. One zealot had chopped up the beautifully carved lintel from the collectively owned spirit house; other Revivalists, though, had burned priceless shell rings inherited from their fathers. When Supalo cited these cases as equally illicit, I mildly protested, wondering how he might respond. "Did these objects [the shell rings] not belong to them?" I asked, knowing that they did. "Were the rings not theirs to save or destroy, as they chose?"

Supalo replied,

It is true that the rings came to them from their fathers. But the rings are not theirs to destroy, only to hold and polish and protect, before passing them to their sons. The rings are the custom that belongs to all of us. To attack the rings is to attack our custom, *my* custom; to destroy the rings is to destroy me. Ownership does not give the Christians the right to do this.

Again, Supalo's sentiments are genuine. But this argument, like the one concerning Mangumbwili's funeral, is also self-serving, in that the culture he nostalgizes was ruled over by an oligarchy of ritual elders that prominently would have included himself. For him, the death of the Tambaran meant the loss of the ritual mandate he and his peers would have used to control and intimidate others. Nevertheless, in the present instance Supalo does make an interesting point, one that would surely appeal to the many millions of traditionalists around the world who see themselves as martyred by cultural vandalism, erosion, and neglect. Advocating custodianship rather than ownership as the tenurial mode appropriate to cultural property, Supalo implicitly affirms the rights of the collective over those of the individual.

The collective versus the individual, as alternative referents of social justice, is a choice familiar to us since the dialogues of Plato; but to the Ilahita the jural concept of the individual is a recent, not yet formulated challenge to the collectivist understandings that were culturally formulated, but transparent, to men of Supalo's generation. Custodianship, then, was Supalo's way of objectifying something he had always taken for granted: the collective, cultural foundation of belief and morality. It was a recognition brought about under conditions of culture contact, that is, by the discovery that there are other kinds of action, other beliefs, and that these represent alternative choices about which individuals and groups, according to their perceived interests, may differ.

Supalo's application of the idea of custodianship to the nature of rights concerning ritual paraphernalia was a skirmish in the battle being fought between collectivism and individualism all along the broad front of Ilahita society. The problem for Supalo and other rearguard defenders of collectivist traditions was that for generations the Tambaran had been the champion and master icon of that ideology. With the Tambaran dead, never to be revived, they had no way to think about collectivism, let alone defend it as a workable social philosophy under a different name. In Russia and the other post-Soviet republics, the discrediting of totalitarian collectivism has given collectivism itself a bad name, impeding the development of enlightened institutions that can effectively balance the interests of the individual and the state. In Ilahita, similarly, appeals for solidarity, proper conduct, and the public good used to be made in the name of the Tambaran. Now that name is anathema to the majority of villagers, none other has quite taken its place, and it is too early to predict whether village Christianity, Revivalist or otherwise, has the institutional potential to do so.

One change particularly indicative of the rise of individualism and the breakdown of community, and the attendant loss of control by Tambaran elders such as Supalo, was the advent of the village court system. Today, this highly effective institution manages many of the conflicts formerly contained under Tambaran jurisdiction. Village courts were instituted in 1975 as part of Papua New Guinea's move to national independence. The Ilahita court thus predated by nearly a decade the final demise of the Tambaran. Its effectiveness grew in step with the general deterioration of Tambaran hegemony, specifically its declining ability to enforce conventional behavior and to manage disputes, through the agencies of male society, as defined, organized, and united by the cult—a reminder that when the Revivalists administered the coup de grâce by revealing the Tambaran secrets to the women, they were killing something that was already functionally dead. This peculiarity will become important in following chapters when we address the mythic significance of the revelation. For now, let us consider the village court.[5]

The national system under which the Ilahita court operates is an ingenious blend of Anglo-Australian legal principles, abstracted indigenous understandings concerning rights, wrongs, and compensations, and guidelines for the judicial handling of the torts, misdemeanors, and lesser crimes that sometime disturb village life in Papua New Guinea. The latter calls for a village-based system of jurisdictions, each presided over by a panel of locally elected magistrates (usually five in number), one or more bailiffs, and a clerk. Village courts are empowered to impose moderately severe fines and jail sentences. Appeals are heard by the local court in Maprik, which is also the starting venue for legal matters of a seriousness that exceeds the village court's competence.

The Ilahita village court area includes Ilahita itself, its southern neighbor Ingamblis village, and a nearby Kwanga-speaking village, Kamanakor. In its fortnightly sessions and in the "mediation" hearings held by individual magistrates and bailiffs to attempt out-of-court settlements, the court disposes of nearly all legal problems that arise in the village. In Ilahita, at least, the system is a stunning success, both in the quality of its judgments and in the support it enjoys among the people.

During the colonial period, grievances had to be taken either to the Australian authorities in Maprik, whose remoteness from events, customs, and personalities often produced faulty judgments, or to the village's elected representatives (there were two) to the local government council, who lacked the training, organization, and police powers needed to dispense justice effectively. In the majority of cases, disputes continued unsettled, grievances unanswered. Conflicts escalated in scale or seriousness to the point where colonial administrators had to intervene, or they went underground, festering there until some new incident prompted their reexpression. Restorative measures authorized by the Tambaran continued to operate, but, ironically, their effectiveness was reduced in many instances by the villagers' belief that Australian law was more immanent, enlightened, and powerful than it actually was.[6] The limits of the Tambaran's jurisdiction receded before an Australian legal presence that never fully materialized except on paper. Increasingly, a good many cases of middling importance—those too serious for the village councilor but not serious enough for the Australian administration—did not receive satisfactory treatment. And it was thanks to the charismatic authority of the Tambaran, and its associated system of yam exchange, competition, and display, that these cases did not have a greater detrimental effect on village society.

The success of the village court system is understandable against the background of mounting frustration over the inadequacy of the prevailing legal alternatives. For the first time Ilahita had a resident, highly accessible court, presided over by magistrates with intimate local knowledge, and guided by principles and procedures that reflected the people's own legal understandings.

Another reason for the court's success is undoubtedly the charismatic person of its chief magistrate, Kunai. A man immensely magnetic to women—with six contented wives, he is by a measure of three the most polygynous man in the village—Kunai is also very popular among the men. He is sagacious and an extremely astute politician. In addition to his position on the village court, Kunai is chief magistrate of the local village court area, comprising twelve village courts. This means that in difficult cases that a village court is unable to handle, such as one in which a magistrate is a plaintiff or defendant, Kunai is called in to preside. Kunai is also one of Ilahita's two representatives to the Maprik Council. He is the longest-serving member of the Maprik Council, having been a councilor almost since the council was first proclaimed in the mid-1960s, has been returned to office in every election, and was elected president of the council during the period of our second fieldwork. Kunai, in sum, has risen to be one of the most important men in the entire Maprik District, and yet his success has done nothing to reduce either his boyish charm or his deep involvement with the present and future of Ilahita.

Every fortnight, officials, principals, witnesses, and spectators assemble in large numbers at the courthouse to enjoy—I think that is the right word for it—the airing of complaints, scandals, and diverse instances of their neighbors' folly and venery. In Ilahita, at least, thanks to Kunai's leadership, the dedicated panel of magistrates performs with remarkable effectiveness, and their decisions are rarely appealed.

One might suppose from this that the operations of the village court have reduced the amount of conflict in the village. Well, yes and no. On the one hand, the severity and social scale of disputes have been lessened by the ability of the court to intervene early in their development, the importance of which the court is very aware. On the other hand, just as Philip V of Spain forbade lawyers to land in the New World colonies, lest their presence foment strife among the Indians, so the advent of the village court has produced an enormously heightened appetite for litigation and a marked increase in the number of cases brought to public attention. Economic development has contributed to this increase by introducing new categories of litigation, for example, unpaid cash loans and contract disputes. Also, the recent advent of bride-price in place of sister exchange in marriage transactions has produced a regular stream of cases involving default. For matters great and small, villagers are now committed to the idea of having their day in court. Moreover, they participate in the legal process *as individuals.*

The effect of the village court system—descended, as it is, from Western principles of jurisprudence—has been to locate legal identity and accountability in the *person,* thereby undercutting group ties. Traditionally, and through the period of my first fieldwork, the individual could guarantee that his rights would be defended only by maintaining relationships based on family, clan, neighborhood, and ritual reckonings. Rather than acting directly, an individual who had been wronged would frequently adopt a morose passivity, expecting kinsmen or ritual allies to act on his behalf. Nowadays, if asked, the simple advice to one's brother is, "Take him to court!" The grievance is now the victim's own, and the institution that created this new situation stands ready to service it. The lesson, namely, that the individual is legally self-sufficient and responsible, is repeated several times every fortnight before a large and attentive audience in the village courthouse. It marks a change of great sociological moment, for it liberates the individual from legal dependency on the group. Projecting this to all individuals in all groups, the change repeals a prime constitutional element of corporate identification, to wit, its basis on ritual, descent, and residence criteria.

The preceding comments apply to the populace at large, but noteworthy in the scores of observed cases was the extent to which the village court functioned to articulate and protect the interests of the traditionally disenfranchised: women and young men. Most of these court cases have to do with breach of contract, such as delinquent cash loans, trespass and poaching, conflicts concerning women, such as adultery, wife beating, and delinquent marriage payments, and petty crimes, such as minor theft. In the past, these conflicts would have been handled by customary redressive procedures under the direction of clan and cult leaders. Occasionally, a competitive yam exchange would decide the matter. If the case was of sufficient scale, or if it involved the violation of ritual privilege, such as using a net-bag design that was the prerogative of a cult grade to which the offender did not belong, the Tambaran was summoned, and a substantial payment of yams and pigs would be demanded to "feed" it. In short, through its ritually mandated system of rights, wrongs, compensations, punishments, and competition conventions the Tambaran exercised reasonably effective control of Ilahita society, as evidenced by the village's extraordinarily large size and quality of integration over a period of many decades. Nowadays, that control is exercised by the village court or not at all.

One interesting pattern concerns the rise of individualism in the context of the loss of social control over the sexuality of young men—the latter being, as Gelber (1986, 39) correctly notes, an important function of male initiation systems in Papua New Guinea. In Ilahita, young men's sexuality was formerly constrained in several ways. First, considerations of masculine growth and purity, as well as practical exigencies of warfare and ritual seclusion, meant that adolescents and young men were separated from women for long periods and under the control of older males. Second, there was a specific taboo, strong and apparently effective, against premarital sexual contact.[7] This injunction was much stronger for males than for females, and in all my inquiries, censuses, and genealogies, no violations by males were uncovered; the few remembered premarital pregnancies were all the work of young married men. Third, prescribed sister-exchange marriage, usually arranged by fathers when the principals were still infants or young children, reduced the need and opportunity for adolescent flirtation and hanky-panky. Arranged marriages also obviated the challenge young men would otherwise face in winning brides through their own courtship efforts. Now, with sister-exchange marriage rapidly disappearing, young men are entering unpracticed into the dating game, and, as Stephen Leavitt (pers. comm.) has also observed among the nearby Bumbita Arapesh, they are anxious and pessimistic about their ability to attract a wife.

Young people are now floundering in a transition period. The "old-fashioned" sister-exchange system is being phased out, and, with unprecedented amounts of cash coming from external work opportunities, bride-price is being phased in. Young men are finding that getting a wife means raising enough money—something they are increasingly able to do on their own—and, importantly, the *number* of one's wives is a function of finances, not social connections. Accordingly, callow young men are experimenting with polygyny, with results that often end up in the village court. In a moment I will describe Ta'af's travail; first, let us examine how polygyny is supposed to work.

Ta'ola is a successful polygynist with three wives, and his advice on the matter is plainly worth listening to.

> Show each wife that you care for her. Provide each wife with a house of her own, and be sure to rotate among them as regards meals and sex. But always remember that the first wife is special; she may be older and less pretty than the others, but she is the most important, and if you treat her thus, the others will understand and respect you. Sleep with the wives in turn, but live with—keep your belongings in the house of—the senior wife.

Ta'ola goes on to advise that before you take a second wife, you would do well to get the first wife's agreement. If you are sensitive to her feelings, she might even help in the negotiations, for the second wife should be her companion and coworker. And before you take a third wife, be sure that the first two do not object.

Ta'ola's pointers suggest that for polygyny to succeed, the expansion must occur incrementally, with the consent of preceding wives and with the household explicitly organized as a cooperative social and economic venture in which all interests are protected.[8] It takes considerable maturity on the part of the husband to manage such an establishment, and this is probably why young men generally make poor polygynists. Take Ta'af, for example, a man in his early twenties who bungled things rather badly.

Ta'af appeared in village court to ask that they order his first wife, Teresia, to return home to him from her father's house, where she had been living for four months. Teresia told the magistrates that she had received wretched treatment from Ta'af, who insulted her in the ways he gave preference to his newer wife, Kwailas. Also, Teresia told the court, Ta'af had not provided each wife with a house of her own, and she was "afraid" of the house in which they all lived. She suspected that Kwailas, with or without Ta'af's collusion, had placed magic traps for her, devices such as "broom magic," which rivalrous women use to sweep their co-wives out of the house, or concoctions that would weaken or kill her or render her infertile. Kwailas had a two-year-old baby boy, but Teresia was childless; could the reason be that Kwailas had slipped something into her food or under her sleeping mat? Because of the lack of physical evidence, this possibility was scarcely mentioned during the court session; but discreet questioning afterward indicated that it was prominent in the minds of those present.

As examples of Ta'af's favoritism toward Kwailas, Teresia described how, when the family left for the gardens, Ta'af would always go off early with Kwailas, leaving Teresia to walk by herself with little or no instruction or guidance. And when they came home from the gardens, both wives would cook food, but Ta'af would always accept the bowl offered by Kwailas, putting the one from Teresia to one side. Later, if someone came to visit their hearth (as would commonly happen), it was the food from Teresia they would be given. Teresia delivered this testimony with cold, contemptuous glances at Kwailas, who occasionally snarled and sputtered in anger at something that was said. It was not hard to believe that the two women had trouble living together under the same roof.

Teresia claimed that as Ta'af's senior wife and the one acquired through a sister-exchange transaction, she was entitled to more respect and consideration. Nomba, her father, tactfully avoided taking sides for or against his daughter. Hoping to strike a chord of reconciliation, he testified that Teresia had, indeed, been treated shabbily, but that Ta'af, too, was entitled to more than an absentee wife. Nomba wanted Teresia to return to her husband. He did not like having her as his responsibility, for it was only a matter of time before she would start taking lovers, with the result that he would probably be blamed for permitting or, indeed, encouraging it. "Let everyone hear that I do not favor this separation, and let them remember this if worse things happen."

The court agreed that Teresia should return forthwith to Ta'af. They tended to dismiss as unfounded—because there was no evidence—Teresia's fear that the house held sorcery traps. On the other hand, the court strongly upheld Teresia's rights to be treated with all the respect due to a senior wife. They especially emphasized that the Ta'af-Teresia bond was doubly important because it involved a sister-exchange transaction with another couple. Trouble within one would likely cause trouble in the other, for the other couple would be divided in their loyalties to spouses and siblings. "Teresia is your exchange wife," the court told Ta'af, "and you must treat her well. You simply paid money for Kwailas, and so she matters less." So, in returning Teresia to him, they instructed Ta'af to improve his behavior toward her. They also advised, especially under the circumstances, that he provide separate houses for his wives.

Sometime after Teresia had gone to live with her parents, Ta'af had obtained money (110 kina) from them to be held as security in case she did not return to him.[9] The Court ordered that this money be returned to Nomba. Ta'af had only K100 with him, which he turned over, and this satisfied the court.

Probably it has always been the case that many more young men attempt polygyny than succeed in it; the preceding case gives clues as to why this happens. One problem seems to be that the successive wife(s) is added too soon, that is, before existing unions are solidified. New marriages may have many rocky intervals, especially now that young women are more assertive than were their foremothers. Rather than working through and resolving the problems, the inexperienced husband may seek the solution of courting and taking an additional wife. This is especially tempting when the first marriage was part of a sister-exchange transaction, possibly arranged while the principals were still children.

During the turbulent early period, after the first baby is born and the husband faces a period of sexual abstinence and relative inattention from his maternally absorbed wife, he begins to feel sorry for himself. Gambling and drinking beer with his friends, some of whom are in a similar situation, provide a diversion; but this only makes matters worse at home, where his young wife complains about his wasteful frolicking, in contrast with her labors in the gardens and groves, baby on hip. Arguments and bickering become common, almost daily occurrences. Eventually, the husband seeks to escape, either to a job in a distant town or into the arms of another woman. Sometimes these routes coincide, and one day the man returns with a woman he met in another part of the country. For the man who stays in the village, acquiring a second wife no longer entails the socio-structural impediments it once did, for, as previously noted, bride-price is rapidly replacing sister-exchange as the normative procedure, and a young man with cash and other attractions is an independent agent in the marriage market. Even if the woman in question is already married, a cash compensation under the aegis of the village court is a nonviolent, face-saving way for shifting a woman between husbands; it simply means buying a woman from her husband, rather than her father. Under certain circumstances (such as premarital pregnancy) the girl's family might settle for a deferred payment, though it is known that such obligations are sometimes never honored. In the past, women were objects of exchange; now, they are chattel.

These circumstances practically guarantee that the junior wife will enjoy preference from her husband; indeed, as will be seen again in the case of Rosa (chapter 7), she and the husband are likely to team up against the senior wife. Furthermore, the trouble that is sure to ensue will add disproportionately to the public's growing impression that domestic life in Ilahita is in disarray. This is because the young men in question are typically among the most visible, enterprising, and economically successful members of their generation. In the past, these men would have been groomed to be artists, magicians, or ritual leaders—closely managed by Tambaran elders. With today's newfound freedoms, they answer only to themselves, with expectably chaotic results. The village court functions to pick up the pieces; but, in truth, there is little left to be put back together.

If, for the young men, the village court is a welcome change from the Tambaran in defining and protecting their individual rights, the same is even truer for the women. The trend Richard Scaglion identifies (1990) in the nearby Abelam village of Neligum is occurring in Ilahita also, with possibly even greater force. "Clearly," Scaglion writes,

> Abelam women are now making good use of the Village Court in pursuing their grievances. In 1977, they were the plaintiffs in only about 22 per cent of disputes resulting in Court Orders. It was clear from the context of many of these disputes that males were bringing cases on behalf of their female relatives. By 1987, however, it appears that women have taken matters into their own hands: they were the complainants in 53 per cent of all Orders. It thus seems that Abelam women are now able to remove their grievances from the male-dominated forum of village politics and still have them heard by a body that recognizes local custom. (1990, 29)

In Ilahita, the women's newfound legal assertiveness is compounded of two trends: first, the increasing readiness by women to seek satisfaction in the court for wrongs associated with their traditional subordination to male authority figures—wrongs that have always been there; second, the emergence of new kinds of conflict between men and women, resulting from disrupted domestic culture, particularly in the area of women's self-determination. Even with the marked increase in its domestic cases, however, one must suppose that most gender-related disputes never reach the hearing of the court. Still, in its position the court is a window looking out upon the distressed scene of male-female relations in the aftermath of the death of the Tambaran.

In the village court, for example, the man Galan is charged by his wife, Ao'ola, with having savagely beaten her about the head and body with a heavy stick. She alleges that he also beat her sister and coplaintiff, Mangia'w. According to Ao'ola, Galan took the stick to her after wrongly accusing her of having an adulterous liaison merely because she returned somewhat late one afternoon from washing coffee beans.

Galan's defense began as follows. It is true that he may have overreacted to his wife's late return from the coffee work, but he was distraught at having learned that the wife of his younger brother had been seduced during his (the brother's) extended absence at the plantation. The news put him in mind of the faithlessness of women. The magistrates reply that this has no possible relevance to Galan's wife, and they press him to declare the true, hidden reason behind the beating. After much foot-shuffling agitation, Galan finally admits that he was sick and tired of his wife's constant attempts "to make me the wife and herself the husband." Fighting back tears of mortification, Galan says,

> She always insists on having the upper hand in every decision and in every disagreement. She is always putting me down because she is a Christian and I am not. When she arrived late from the coffee work I went to strike her with my hand, but her mother seized one of my hands, her sister the other, and Ao'ola herself grabbed my scrotum and gave it a terrible yank. [Some court spectators titter.] It hurt very much. [More titters.] I lost my temper and beat Ao'ola and her sister with a stick.

With head and back bowed and hands wringing, Galan was a study of abused, abject, ganged-up-on masculinity. After reprimanding him for using a stick, the court leniently charged him a K10 court fine and a K5 compensation payment to Mangia'w, but denied compensation to Ao'ola, who, they ruled, had sufficiently provoked the assault. Ao'ola did not protest the ruling, but she was visibly dissatisfied. As the group filed out of the courtroom, she glared at Galan with a wait-'til-I-get-you-home kind of look.

Galan's domestic plight became fully public only when it had led to the assault and ensuing court action, by which time his male ego was livid from repeated bruisings. Galan was not a strong man, physically or politically, but he was proud enough to be ashamed that his wife dominated him. Whereas she enjoyed plenty of support from the Revivalist community, especially the women members, Galan had nowhere to turn: not to the Tambaran, for it was dead; not to the male community, which was either Christian and therefore gratified by his discomfiture, or traditionalist and therefore contemptuous of his inability to control his wife. So Galan suffered in silence until the festering rage and resentment violently burst against his wife. Galan's dilemma was not unique.

Mangas, a man of about sixty who was a leading hunting and gardening magician, admits privately that he has been having murderous impulses toward his wife, Kotawa. His complaints, echoing those I heard from many men during the year, have to do with Kotawa's constant surliness, her gratuitous defiance of his authority, and her insolent neglect of her domestic chores. She no longer tends the garden with Mangas, neither does she cook his food. Instead, with the other women, she attends church services every evening, sometimes until three o'clock in the wee hours, only to reassemble a short while later for the daily morning worship. "When I try to tell her, gently, that she is behaving badly, she either screams at me or begins to tok profet. Kotawa used to be a good woman, but now she had changed. Our gardens are dying—I am dying—and if things continue this way much longer, I must run away to [the provincial capital of] Wewak, or else I must kill her."

Mangas is not a violent man. On the contrary, he is humane, temperate, and socially responsible, the kind of man who is always there to break up a fight, not start one. Now he is also a deeply unhappy man, who views his wife's behavior as a sign that there is nothing right with the world any longer. Like many other men of his generation and situation, including Supalo, he does not tolerate well his sudden powerlessness and the appalling sense of deprivation that comes from seeing life's noble virtues shattered.

The kind of marital defiance attributed to Kotawa is frequently evinced by younger wives, with the result that violent discord has increased markedly in this sector of the community. The situation is exacerbated by the fact that married women under thirty generally are Christian, while their husbands generally are not. For example, when the young man Tunde awoke hungry in the middle of the night and stirred his sleeping wife to get up and cook food for him, she sullenly refused. He beat her, but to no avail: she had refused before and would refuse again. She cried loud, long, and plaintively over her wounds, but in the end Tunde went hungry. Other young men complain that their wives constantly nag them about the time and money they spend drinking beer and playing cards. This, too, leads to arguments, beatings, and increased unhappiness. Still other men find their wives refusing to have sex with them, ostensibly because the Holy Spirit will not possess or come close to them if they detect the scent of sexual intercourse (Macdonald 1995, 187). This reverses a traditional situation in which men would frequently refuse to have sex with their wives, because of their need (real or pretended) to maintain ritual purity in preparation for war or some magical or ritual project. In those days women who were frustrated might sometimes grumble, but in general there was little they could do but resign themselves to the way things were and supposedly had to be. Today, however, men in this situation react angrily, and a good many beatings from this cause were recorded during the year's fieldwork.

Among the areas of domestic bondage from which Revivalist women felt newly liberated, child care was especially prominent and problematic. The loss of exclusive male society meant that husbands were no longer absent from the house much of the time on social and ritual excursions. Wives quickly came to expect that, with all that free time, and in keeping with their (the wives') superior responsibilities within the Revival movement, husbands should be doing more around the house. Conflicts occurred. The worst episodes happened every few weeks when hundreds of Revival women would convene (usually in Ilahita, which was the center of the Revival) for a religious retreat. Husbands were left at home for several days to look after themselves and the children. Women seemed to take particular glee in imposing this duty on the men, who were relatively powerless to resist it, short of letting their children go hungry. Whereas Revival men usually accepted this arrangement stoically, as a kind of religious obligation, male nonbelievers such as Galan or Mangas (above) were invariably enraged, because, short of violence, there was nothing they could do to prevent this insubordination by their wives.

Even without the Revival, child care and other domestic issues might well be problematic because of recent startling changes in Ilahita's settlement and demographic features. Returning in July 1985, I perceived that the village had grown both larger and more dispersed. Census figures confirmed both changes. The village population had risen from 1490 to 2085, an increase of 40 percent in fifteen years, and the proportion of residents living in external settlements had increased from 28 to 38 percent.[10] More graphically, while the population of the main village had increased by 20 percent during the sixteen-year period, that of the external settlements had appreciated by 87 percent. Correspondingly, as the number of households in the main village rose by only 3 percent, those in the external settlements increased by a whopping 101 percent.

Several factors contributed to this dispersion. Overarching them all was the decline and eventual death of the Tambaran, whose activities had formerly nucleated the village by drawing men together in frequent social and ceremonial events; the center was where the action was, and men wanted to live near it. In its absence, Ilahita is coming apart, as the Tambaran men said it would, scattering itself toward the boundaries of its hinterland. This in turn is causing domestic strain by distancing people from their traditional support groups: married women have to travel farther to visit their parents and siblings, while men find themselves having less and less in common with anybody, other than a shared chronic feeling of malaise.

Ilahita's stunning population growth is the result of several factors. Standards of sanitation, hygiene, and diet have improved considerably, and there is an increased acceptance of Western medical knowledge and technology, especially in the pre- and postnatal care of mothers and infants. At the same time, medical authorities have encouraged earlier weaning, thus shortening the period of sexual taboo following the birth of an infant. (Formerly, the average age of weaning was thirty-six months, ranging up to fifty-two months.) This combination of decreased birth intervals and an increased rate of child and infant survival has already had an explosive effect on the bottom levels of the age pyramid. During my first fieldwork, nuclear families typically had three or four children, at evenly spaced, four-year intervals. Now, families of eight to ten children are not unusual; neither is the sight of a mother leading a toddler by the hand while nursing an infant at the breast and carrying a third child in her womb. A few villagers—mostly young, unmarried, educated women— see where the situation is heading and publicly advocate birth-control and family-planning measures.[11] The vast majority, however, are either oblivious to or fatalistic about the local population curve, or they regard this as a distant problem that they will not be alive to face. Barring any intervening factors, at its present rate the village population will exceed 3400 in the year 2001, and, with shortages already evident in productive resources, conditions will be grim.

All these trends create enormous stress on traditional domestic practices. Women are dead tired of having babies and caring for battalions of children. They resent the little ones, and they resent their husbands even more. Men are generally sympathetic with their wives on this issue, but they are reluctant to endorse contraception and family planning for fear that if given the choice, women would stop having babies altogether. And, worry the men, if the women stop having babies, or choose never to start, they might soon discover that marriage itself is not necessary or in their interests. As discussed earlier, these are men who lack confidence of their worth in female eyes. Insecure, emotionally dependent, without

gender protectives such as arranged marriage and Tambaran male exclu-
sivity, they worry about abandonment. People in that state are difficult to
live with.

Many more examples of gender-based conflict could be given, but the
preceding are perhaps sufficient to indicate the discrepancy between the
gender reforms optimistically proclaimed by Christian enthusiasts and the
distressed condition of men and women in their dealings with one another. Although the reordering of gender relations in Ilahita has occurred
at the highest level of social ideology and institutional practice, the place
where it is being most severely felt is in the everyday lives of men and
women. The death of the Tambaran, and the corresponding loss of the
masculine legitimacy, has driven men more into the domestic sphere,
where their authority is resented and resisted. Confused and enraged by
the women's Revival-authorized insolence, the men react with fists and
sticks. Physical violence by men against wives and mothers is now far
more frequent and severe than ever was the case under the Tambaran. A
similar situation is described by Macdonald (1995, 336) for Malahum, a
nearby Balif Arapesh village, which is within Ilahita's ritual (both Tambaran and Revival) sphere of influence. "Physical violence has become
domesticated in practice and privatized in ideology. By 'domesticated,' I
mean that violence when it occurs is almost always between spouses or
other close kin; by 'ideologically privatized' I mean that an ideology
which sustains a belief in familial harmony disguises domestic violence by
ignoring it."

One might hope that, eventually, after much pain, a system of culturally embedded expectations will form within these intimate relations; one
that will reliably influence actions and restore the people's sense of meaning and stability in the world. On the other hand, with increasing population and environmental depletion, it is perhaps more likely that things
will get worse. For the time being, at any rate, neither men nor women
know what to expect or even what they have a right to expect. In gender
terms they are seeking themselves, and until they find them, the distress
will continue.

The loss of privilege can be tragic, comic, or merely gratifying, depending
on where one sits. It is tempting to regard the Tambaran as having gotten
its just deserts and men like Galan, Mangas, and Tunde as having gotten

a taste of the abuse their wives and foremothers have endured for genera-tions. The case for retributive justice is muddied, however, by the fact that the relentless misogynism of the Tambaran belied the generally benign, protective behavior of men toward their wives. The Tambaran required the men to act toward women and children in a manner that was often troubling to the men themselves. This contradiction is important as a source of male guiltiness discernible within the dynamics of ritual violence in the past (Tuzin 1982); its resolution was a motive in the recent reve-lation of cult secrets, and it even accounts for some of the ambivalence that is emerging as postmortem memories of the Tambaran begin to take shape.

Furthermore, that this contradiction between ritual ideology and per-sonal behavior is genuine and not an artifact of method is confirmed by its reported presence in other Arapesh groups. Thus, Mead reports (1935, 67–68) that the Mountain Arapesh tempered the secrecy, sexual hostility, and hazing of the Tambaran, which are featured in the cults of other Sepik groups. "In a community where there is no hostility between men and women, and where the old men, far from resenting the waxing strength of the young men, find in it their greatest source of happiness, a cult that stresses hate and punishment is out of place." Similarly, Macdonald's observations (1995, 199–200) among the nearby Balif Arapesh could equally apply to Ilahita. In the past, despite the ideological excesses of the Tambaran, "relations between men and women were not necessarily antagonistic . . . Sufficient older women recall their husbands and fathers (ritual 'bigmen' they say) as men who were considerate husbands and kind tolerant fathers to make such an assumption questionable."

In summary, the domestic travail the men now suffer is not simply a just requital for their having been brutes in the past, but for the institution they had inherited and had formerly espoused. The Tambaran—the apo-theosis of "what men do"—was the real culprit, but it is ordinary men who are being punished in its place, just as they once enjoyed the unmeri-ted privileges of its tyranny.

Perhaps, then, it is a manifestation of cultural reassertion that, even within the midst of the spiritual cleansing, there are hints of recognition that the punishing has gone too far. Privately, some women who are active in the Revival movement are beginning to doubt the wisdom and fairness of demonizing Ilahita's Tambaran past, because to do this they can hardly avoid demonizing the men themselves. As part of the dramatic power reversal, these women are discovering what their male predecessors knew for themselves: that gender dominance entails moments of guilt and moral vulnerability, regardless, one might add, of which gender is on top. Such a woman is Akwaliwa, the widow of Asao and a tok profet in the Revival. Her story is worth telling in full for its insight into the discrepancy in male behavior—public and private.

During my first fieldwork, Asao was the scariest man in the village— a *sangguma,* and proud of it. People would have openly despised him, only it was too dangerous to do so. It was safer to fear him, and that they certainly did. As a young man Asao had been sent by his father to Salata to be trained in the assault sorcery for which that Bumbita Arapesh village is infamous in the region. Sangguma are said to acquire ghostly powers by mastering magical skills, submitting to harsh bodily disciplines, and drinking the fluids of a rotting corpse. Asao did not simply admit to all of this, he boasted of it. Animal familiars (mostly night birds) spied for him and brought him news of distant places. Asao claimed the ability to fly and to make himself invisible. With ostentatious glee, he told of participating in attacks (sangguma usually work in teams of two or three) on selected victims. The usual method was for the target to be waylaid at a lonely spot, done to death with dagger or club, and then be sent home— disguised as his living self—to pretend to take sick, decline, and die a seemingly natural death over the next few days. Asao was known to receive unsavory visitors at odd hours; people would gossip that he had been seen talking to strangers. Occasionally, he would be mysteriously absent for days or weeks at a time, presumably in retreat to purify his magical powers or on commission to stalk and attack someone in another, possibly distant, place.

Despite the fantastical nature of these pseudo-accomplishments, I did not think that Asao was demented or that he took himself literally. It was apparent that Asao liked being feared, liked being outrageous, liked being thought of as a scoundrel and a ghoul. My rapt, note-taking acceptance of his fly-by-night claims was a new sort of affirmation for him. My company stimulated invention more than memory, however, for there were moments when Asao flashed the this-guy-will-believe-anything kind of contempt one gets from a carney barker.

When I knew Asao, he was about forty-eight years old, slightly below medium height, and with a wiry build. Constant betel chewing gave his mouth a bleeding-gash look across his usually scowling face. In public, he tended to strut rather than walk or saunter. A broad-brimmed, slouchy hat contributed an incongruously rakish effect. It was said, cattily, that Asao wore the hat to hide a developing bald spot. With his brothers— but only with his brothers—Asao sometimes became relaxed, quipping and laughing with the others. Most of the time, however, he exuded menace and self-importance.

Asao's baleful reputation carried social costs. With his three wives and two children, he lived in a bleak, unshaded camp thirty minutes' walk from the village. There were reasons, he explained, why he preferred living in isolation away from the village. A populous, noisy, congested, sexually polluted settlement is no place for delicate magical procedures; and, lack of tranquillity aside, one cannot enjoy simple privacy or avoid being drawn into neighborhood squabbles. These were plausible reasons for Asao's household to live apart. What he did not mention, though others did, was that no community in the village would have him. Asao was a pariah. Even his own kinsmen did not like to have this golem around, living and lurking nearby. Twice during the preceding couple of years, he and his wives had settled in a village hamlet, only to have some real or imagined trouble arise and lead to their being shown the road. Asao was not the only nefarious character in the village, but he was the most notorious; his complicity as a sorcerer was suspected in nearly every adult death, of which there were some thirty recorded during my first fieldwork.

These particular suspicions did not attach to Asao because he was a sangguma—those ghouls generally do not prey upon fellow villagers— but because he was also adept at more commonplace forms of sorcery, which feature the theft and manipulation of a victim's personal leavings. When directed against fellow villagers such sorcery is criminal, in theory; but in Asao's case, because he was a cult elder, his alleged acts were in large part ritually legitimate. Notwithstanding his career of rejection, op-probrium, and alleged dark deeds, Asao was not perceived to be a crimi-nal, but an agent of the Tambaran, which was known through divination often to decree that the deaths should occur as punishment for past ritual offenses. As to how, precisely, Asao and other wizards received the Tam-baran's commission in these matters—that was another one of the myster-ies enshrouding the men and workings of the cult's highest grade. At any rate, reviled and respected at the same time, Asao was viewed as a kind of public executioner.

This office was nobler in the past than in postpacification times, because it was bound up with the tradition of village war sorcery. Echoes of that past sounded in 1972, when a sorcery bundle was found hidden near one of Ililip's hamlets. Suspecting that someone from Mamilimbi, a group that is part of the enemy village of Lehinga, had planted it there, the Ililip men called upon Asao to assess the bundle's character and strength and the damage it may have done and to initiate appropriate mystic countermeasures. Like a doctor summoned to a sickbed, Asao took charge of the situation with a cool, professional air, plainly gratified by the community's urgent, if temporary, reliance on him.

In the setting of his encampment Asao was friendly and hospitable toward me. This contrasted with his mocking, faintly insolent manner when we were in the main village. With other men present as his audience, his manner seemed to say, "You may be white, but you are young and weak and without knowledge. Let others toady to you. I do not demean myself by treating you as important." Toward the end of fieldwork, as I became openly sympathetic with Gidion in his feud against Asao and his brothers—especially his youngest brother, Akotan—Asao's manner toward me changed from mocking to hostile and distinctly threatening. One can truly appreciate a glare only if one is its victim. Asao was a most practiced glarer.

By the end of fieldwork, little affection remained between us. In the years following my departure, I would recall Asao as one who exemplified what might be called the cynical, "dark side" of the Tambaran: that aspect of deception, intimidation, and terror which masqueraded as ritual necessity. And because women were so much the victims of that aspect, I naturally assumed that Asao incarnated, as well, all the misogynistic impulses of the Tambaran.

When I returned in 1985, Asao had been dead for about four years. I duly logged the fact into my census record and thought little more about it. Then, a few days before the conclusion of that fieldwork, I was unexpectedly visited by Akwaliwa, Asao's senior wife, who was living as a widow among her relatives, a few hamlets away from my own. I had noticed her loitering in the shadows, some distance from where I was sitting with a group of men, but did not realize that she was waiting for a moment when I would be alone. When that moment came, she strode forward in a deliberate manner and, in surprisingly fluent Pidgin for a woman nearing fifty, announced that she had something very important to tell me, in private.

This was an unusual overture. I scarcely knew Akwaliwa; she was certainly not one of the dozen or so women, mostly close neighbors, who were comfortable being alone with me at my place. What could this be about? Was she going to ask for some item of our household gear, as others were doing in anticipation of our imminent departure? Knowing I was about to return whither I had mysteriously come, was Akwaliwa going to propose a secret, millenarian arrangement for herself? These were the thoughts that passed through my mind as she seated herself, rather primly, and cleared her throat. What followed was completely unexpected. Desiring nothing but a few minutes of my attention, Akwaliwa announced that she had come to tell me about herself and Asao. "You must not leave," she said, "without knowing."

To paraphrase what became a lengthy, uninterrupted declaration: Akwaliwa recalled that her first marriage had been to Kunai, who was now charitably, but discreetly (so as not to arouse gossip), helping to support her in widowhood. Because Falipa'w (Kunai's senior wife) and one or two of the other cowives did not like her, the original union soon dissolved, and Akwaliwa took up with Asao as his second wife. Not long afterward, the first wife died. The two lived monogamously for three or four years before Asao casually asked what she would think of his taking another wife. Akwaliwa, angry and jealous at the question, and still bruised by the troubles she had had as a cowife, refused to hear of it. Asao quickly dropped the subject. Afterward, however, touched that Asao so clearly respected her feelings, Akwaliwa inwardly relented. Accordingly, when Asao next raised the question—saying gently that she would have someone to help her in the gardens and groves, someone to keep her company during his frequent, prolonged absences—Akwaliwa gave her consent. A second wife joined the household soon afterward. After some initial difficulty, which Asao skillfully resolved, the two women got along very well together, and in due course a third wife was smoothly added to the household. "We all lived very happily together," said Akwaliwa.

This last was murmured with a sigh, and it was from then that Akwaliwa's voice would occasionally break and tears would appear. "Asao was a *good* man," she said, "a good husband and father." Without prompting, she described how Asao always honored her as the senior wife but was careful to eat, work, and sleep with each of the wives in turn, so that none would feel neglected or envious. An expert, kindly manager, Asao would never let trouble develop or fester. He consulted his wives on matters affecting the household and conscientiously assigned tasks each morning.[12] Asao had only two children, both daughters: one died young; the other he doted upon—dandling her, giving her things, at length helping her to marry the man of her choice, and, when that did not work out, using all his influence to arrange for her an attractive match with one of Kunai's sons. The daughter, for her part, was desperately saddened when Asao died.

And die he did, as he had lived, the presumed victim of a sangguma from the nearby Kwanga village of Kamanakor. The alleged motive was revenge for a Kamanakor death that diviners there had blamed on Asao. In his line of work, Asao knew that his days were numbered by inevitable acts of revenge or countersorcery that would finally catch up with him. Many times he tearfully confided to Akwaliwa his worries for her welfare if and when he died and would not be there to protect her. By this time Asao was estranged from his brothers, especially the violent, volatile Akotan, and he warned Akwaliwa that they would probably move to exclude her from clan property once he was out of the picture—which is exactly what happened. Indeed, it was out of concern for his wives' welfare that Asao, in the few years before his death, undertook to teach them Melanesian Pidgin to such a level of fluency that if necessary they could seek lives for themselves in one of the towns. "You know, it was hard sometimes, always having to speak Pidgin [*tok pisin*] rather than our own language around the house. But Asao was strong for our sakes, and now you see how well I speak. When I married Asao, I did not speak Pidgin at all; now, it is like my own language to me." For a long moment Akwaliwa gazed in reverie at her hands resting on her lap. Then, softly, "Asao has been dead these four years, but every day I think of him, and every night I cry for him."

Akwaliwa's visit left me with much to think about for the rest of the evening—and for many evenings thereafter. Had I misjudged Asao? Only to the extent that, having never given much thought to Asao's home life, I would have guessed (if asked) that he was difficult to live with, just as more than one set of neighbors had evidently discovered for themselves. Was I surprised that Asao was more complex than I had imagined? Not really: most people are, I daresay, and even some of history's worst villains have been loving family men. Nor did the visit alter my conception of public and private moralities among Ilahita men. I already knew and had written about the interesting tension between these spheres (Tuzin 1980, 1983), though it did interest me to learn that Asao's extreme belligerence in public was matched, apparently, by an equally extreme tenderness in private.

More remarkable, however, was that Akwaliwa took it upon herself—at some emotional cost and with no material gain—to tell me her story about dead Asao. For all she knew, I had no opinion whatever concerning her late husband; I may not even have remembered him from my first fieldwork.[13] If she assumed that I was aware of his reputation for sorcery, her proud loyalty to Asao, in life and in death, implied that she did not see this as a stain on his character or as a libel about which the ethnographic record needed to be set straight. The eloquent, devotional tone of Akwaliwa's testimonial confirmed that the public world of the Tambaran—the harangues, threats, punishments, masculine megalomania, and real and figurative violence against innocents—was, for this woman, only half the measure of her husband's moral being.

How much of her perception is discountable as the maudlin effusions of a bereaved, emotionally frustrated widow? To be sure, Akwaliwa was emotionally driven; but the ideological battles under way in the village, my well-known interest in them, and my imminent (perhaps final) departure conferred a particular anthropological significance on Akwaliwa's visit: namely, that she—a woman—perceived the moral dualism inherent in her man's position and beheld with compassion his corresponding predicament. "Asao was a *good* man," she had said. As much as any man in Ilahita, and far more than most, Asao played his public role to the maximum: a truculent, unbending, cold-blooded champion of the Tambaran. But at the end of the day Asao went home to dandle his little daughter and to make his wives glad he was there. In her own way, speaking from her own experience, Akwaliwa was exonerating the Tambaran past to which her husband belonged, a most unpopular opinion in Revival-ridden Ilahita. Hence the furtiveness of her approach to me, especially since she herself was a tok profet in the Revival movement.

Mention of the Revival leads me to ask whether Akwaliwa's benevolent insights existed when Asao and the Tambaran were still alive. Probably not, at least not explicitly. Akwaliwa's nostalgia doubtless amplified Asao's nobler qualities; her travail as a widow would have made former comforts rosier than they actually were. Her mission cannot be explained away, however, as merely the workings of faulty memory or of a desire to elicit my sympathy, though it may have had minor elements of both. Akwaliwa did not come to obtain pity for herself. She was enough her husband's wife to exude pride and toughness, even in her tears. Rather, she was one whose personal loss—stereotypic and commonplace in itself—gave her an awareness of the higher injury that the society was busily inflicting on itself. Hers was a personalized version of a sentiment that had been building, secretly and in snatches, among many men and (fewer) women who occupied the middle of the ideological spectrum separating traditionalist and reformist extremes. These were people who observed the social and moral devastation wrought by the collapse of the Tambaran and began to imagine that life with the Tambaran had not been so bad after all. For in those days, beyond the color and pageantry, the feasts and dances and speeches, the mighty works and sense of village unity and greatness—people knew what the Tambaran expected of them.

Hence the larger poignancy of Akwaliwa's visit. Asao had been a Tambaran man par excellence; thus, for Akwaliwa, the literal death of her husband mingled in significance with the figurative death of the Tambaran.[14] Thoughts about Asao spilled over and became thoughts about the Tambaran. To defend or rationalize the one was to defend or rationalize the other. The political risk suggested by her clandestine manner attached not to her status as a widow—no one would impugn loyalty to a dead husband—but as a *Tambaran* widow. In the long afterthought since Asao's death, Akwaliwa, perhaps as part of the mourning process, reconciled herself to the relationship she had had with Asao and to the gendered ritual order of which it was a miniature. After months of indecision during which my fieldwork proceeded, she finally decided not to miss the opportunity to convey her thoughts and feelings to the one person interested, reasonably informed, and yet detached enough to understand what she needed to say. Again, Akwaliwa did not seek sympathy for herself—her plight as a childless, unwanted widow she seemed to accept as a matter of fact—but for Asao and his world. In the old days it took a brave or foolish woman to speak out against the Tambaran; nowadays it takes a brave or foolish woman to speak out *for* the Tambaran. Polarities have reversed, values are inverted; but the old tyrant of consensus survives, hale and reborn, into the new village order. Thus does culture avenge itself upon history.

* * *

One should not underestimate the Tambaran's baleful misogyny: its duplicity, exclusiveness, exploitation, and rhetorical violence. Nevertheless, the discovery that Asao had harbored a secret life of domestic felicity warns us that the ritually constituted ideology of sexual antagonism, in Ilahita and perhaps elsewhere in Papua New Guinea, may not faithfully reflect the tenor of male-female relations in ordinary, everyday life (Tuzin 1982). The sometimes violent rhetoric of the cult was directed against women, collectively, as a local political threat, not against innocent, Tambaran-abiding women or Universal Womanhood. A man would not speak disparagingly about his wife or kinswoman, or permit others to do so, simply to curry Tambaran favor. But, emphatically, this does not mean that ritual ideology was irrelevant to domestic life. On the contrary, by giving men an exclusive place, purpose, and identity—a masculine sanctuary—the Tambaran provided a public outlet for their angers, fears, and frustrations, thus in large part shielding the household from their effects. With the loss of the Tambaran, that outlet is closed, and the violence has nowhere else to go but home. The troubles that now beset the hearth are a measure of how the Tambaran's gender tyranny actually helped to maintain good relations between the sexes. That is what Akwaliwa and some of the other women are beginning to discover.

What has happened in Ilahita is worthy of a Greek tragedy, in which the gods at play tease mortals with the illusion that their deeds and intentions are entirely their own. In Ilahita, actors behave according to perceived circumstances. But that social stage rides atop cultural imperatives of which, except at the rare moments that we call "historic," the actors are only dimly aware. The Tambaran had to die, it is said, because its evil prevented the Holy Spirit from delivering salvation and riches to the believers of Ilahita. Yet the Tambaran had been withering steadily for more than a decade and was virtually dead already. Why not simply ignore it and let its grave be unmarked?

For one thing, time was of the essence, for no one knew how long the Holy Spirit would wait before taking its rewards elsewhere. In addition, the coincidence of my return to the field, heralded by the dying Gidion, and the millenarian events seemingly rushing to fulfillment, convinced people that the Tambaran must be gone before I arrived. But perhaps most significant, because it brings motive into alignment with culture and makes the moment "historic": the Revivalists did not simply want the Tambaran to die; they wanted to *kill* it. The break with the past had to be decisive, a clear demonstration of Christian faith and resolve.

In the same gesture something else happened, something more historic though less explicit. The men rid themselves of the contradiction that had bedeviled them since the inception of the ritual system in the last century: the reliance on secrecy and deceit, which undermined the legitimacy of male authority and produced a sense of moral unease and vulnerability among the men themselves. Cult elders were aware of this dilemma, which, they claimed, was inherent in received tradition and was therefore beyond their power to change (Tuzin 1980, 264; 1982). Concealed behind all the talk about the Revival, this old contradiction pressed for its own resolution, guiding events mysteriously, predeterminately, as the Fates did in the mythic imagination of Sophocles. Appropriately, this motive was constituted in Ilahita's Creation myth about the Cassowary-Mother. The story of "Nambweapa'w" correctly foretells the death of male hegemony as an act of revenge, one to which, also prophetically, the men fatally, avoidably, expose themselves.

Intertwined, then, with the circumstances of the Revival movement, the fatal unmasking of the Tambaran, murder of masculinity, and rocketing of women into a position of ritual superiority enacted a revenge that had been prefigured in Ilahita's epic Creation myth. In the story, the Primal Mother's natural prepotencies had been deceitfully withheld from her by her husband. With the help of her oedipally inclined little son, she discovers the deception, recovers her true powers, and avenges herself by killing the husband-deceiver. The act of revenge engenders a period of blissful, magical fulfillment for the children. At some level of mythic awareness, amidst the frenzied expectations of the Revival, and knowing their "little brother" was about to return from America, the assassins killed the Tambaran in hope of producing the same beatific result. To explain why their plan was not as crazy as it sounds—in truth, was not crazy at all—I must tell the story of Nambweapa'w, the whole story, from their point of view and ours.

The full telling of this story must go far beyond the narrative text to include its place in Ilahita history, imagination, and culture and its prophetic relationship to the death of the Tambaran. This enterprise will occupy the next three chapters, which are the centerpiece of the study.

To orient the reader to what must at times be a complex, convoluted, and multivocal argument, let me outline its major features in advance.

The first chapter in the series, "The Cassowary and the Swan Maiden," identifies "Nambweapa'w" as belonging to a very large family of stories embodying the "swan maiden" motif. Members of this family are found as far away as Ireland, but there is an Oceanic subfamily of versions that is immediately traceable to the Malay Archipelago. It is argued that Ilahita acquired the motif indirectly from Malay sources no earlier than the mid–nineteenth century, that the Ilahita "swan maiden" story deviates from all other known versions in specifiable ways, that these deviations pinpoint moral and existential dilemmas distinct to Ilahita, and, finally, that these problems arose because of the contemporaneous adoption of the Tambaran, a foreign cult the main tenets of which were inconsistent with primordial Arapesh values. Hence the importance of knowing the source(s) and timing of the story. These are challenging claims, requiring extensive support in the scholarly literature and in comparisons of the Ilahita version with others in the vicinity and region.

The next chapter, "The Web of True Prophecy," turns from the external to the internal contexts of the story. The many strands connecting details of "Nambweapa'w" with details of Ilahita culture verify the story's deeply embedded, resonant character. When the story speaks to Ilahita listeners, it does so with a fine insight into their existential concerns. When the story posits certain structural and logical relationships, it closely mirrors Ilahita understandings about such matters. When the story predicts the future, its divinatory authority comes from introspection into Ilahita motives and desires. Nambweapa'w's intimate knowledge of her people—a knowledge at once enshrined and alive—requires extensive demonstration, because it supports an unlikely analytic claim—that her story genuinely prophesied the death of the Tambaran and was later invoked to preside over the mythic construction of the event and its circumstances and aftermath.

The final chapter of the set, "Millennium," brings myth, fantasy, and personal narrative into joint focus upon the event of my return to the field and its place in the millenarian hopes of the Revivalists. An act of name bestowal identifies me with (or *as*) one of the characters in the story of Nambweapa'w. Dreams and visions cast me as an envoy, companion, or literal transformation of dead Gidion. These fantasies have it that I am returned from the Otherworld, bearing material and spiritual rewards, which, with the Cassowary's Revenge, the killing of the Tambaran, now achieved, are available for the people. Exorbitant or not, such notions are possible when culture, history, and psyche unite to create a "mythic" moment in which the barriers separating metaphysical domains are lifted.

Councilor Kunai (1970)

Gidion (1970)

Supalo (1986)

Ta'ola (1970)

Mangas returns from a successful cuscus hunt (1970)

Kwamwi (left) and his junior exchange partner, Dongwande (1970)

Asao (1971)

Samuel (1986)

Wa'akea and Salalaman (1971)

Casual male sociality is largely a thing of the past. Two of the men are shown sitting on a slitgong (1971).

The Nggwal Bunafunei spirit house, Elaf hamlet (1972) (courtesy of Malcolm Kirk)

Nggwal Bunafunei statue, showing a piglet drinking from the penis of a cult spirit while the mother pig looks on from above (1971)

The door to inner sanctum of the Nggwal Bunafunei spirit house stands open, due to the temporary removal of the sacred pipes and drums (1971)

Christian Revivalists gather at the church in Ililip ward to hear Salalaman preach

A carved house post is all that remains of the Nggwal
Bunafunei spirit house in Elaf hamlet (1985)

Chapter Four

THE CASSOWARY AND THE
SWAN MAIDEN

Within a few hours of my first arrival in Ilahita, after the get-acquainted chat with Miss Schrader, a small throng of villagers had assembled at the rest house that was to be my temporary home. Word had spread in the nearby hamlets that a lone white man had appeared with lots of gear and was staying at the *haus kiap* (MP). This was a most unusual happening for the villagers: a missionary would not be staying in the rest house, and a patrolling official would have carriers and a police escort. No other kinds of white people ever came to Ilahita. Who was I? they wondered politely. What did I want?

I explained in halting Pidgin that I wished to live in Ilahita for a long time, to learn its language, stories, and customs, and to put these things in a book that would be all about Ilahita. This seemed to strike the people as a fine idea. The mood turned more relaxed and friendly. I told them I was from America. This produced a gratifying buzz of cross-conversational enthusiasm lasting several moments. The clamor, of which I understood not a word, eventually settled on the idea that I should be taken forthwith to see the Water of Nambweapa'w—whatever that meant. Leading the way was Ribeka, a vivacious, attractive woman in her early thirties, who was to become my closest female confidante and principal linguistic informant. New friends, a festive excursion. I was starting to feel at home already.

The Water of Nambweapa'w turned out to be a circular pool located some twenty minutes' walk from the haus kiap, in the ward known as Balanga. Cool and spring fed, it lay nestled in a jungle grove just a short distance down the ridge from Eil, the ceremonial plaza of Balanga ward. The pool was a stone's throw across. Its mood was hushed, intimate, and tranquil. At that late afternoon hour frogs were starting to clear their throats for what promised to be a noisy nocturne, but this only seemed to accentuate the deeper stillness of the place. A picturesque spot, but otherwise nothing special, I thought, until my guides told me what had happened there, a long time ago.

After hearing the story, I did not doubt that the place *was* special. But it would take many years and the collapse of the Tambaran and its troubled aftermath to reveal Nambweapa'w's cultural and prophetic importance and its significance for Ribeka, the others, and myself.

As told to me, the story is long and detailed (Tuzin 1980, 1–8). In brief, it goes as follows:

> The First Man was walking along when he heard the unusual sound of laughter coming from nearby. He went to investigate and, from hiding, espied a group of cassowaries bathing in a pond. Having removed their skins, they had become beautiful (human) women. The man secretly stole the skin of the one he most fancied, so that later, when the cassowary-women emerged to resume their skins, the one he had chosen could not find hers. This led to the man's taking her home with him, where he tricked her into piercing herself to create her external genitalia. They began their married lives together. Her name was Nambweapa'w.

> Man and wife advanced to old age, producing a long line of alternately sexed children, who later intermarried and became the ancestors of all the world's peoples. The first born, a son, was the ancestor of the Ilahita Arapesh. The father would take the older children to the garden, while the mother stayed home to care for the youngest; then, the next day, the parents would reverse roles.

> This youngest child, a son, was about six years old when he discovered that his father kept a cassowary skin in hiding; this after the father had donned the skin a few times to frighten the youngster into ceasing his crying and whining. The next day, in exchange for some coconut tidbits that the boy cried for during meal preparation, he revealed this secret to his mother, who reacted by putting on the cassowary skin and running back to her natural home in the forest. Before finally leaving, however, she instructed her children on how they were later to join her.

> Accordingly, after some months they followed her, taking their old father with them. They hid him under a taro leaf at the

prearranged meeting place. The boys and girls climbed separate trees, with the oldest near the bottom, continuing upward in birth order, until the youngest was at the top. Starting with the oldest, each boy in turn blew a conch shell in the direction of the grass fields and then threw a grass spear. Each projectile went a little farther than the last, until that of the youngest flew far away, landing in a ground-crab hole right next to where Nambwea-pa'w was sitting, making vegetal salt.

Nambweapa'w went to them. After ordering the children down from the trees and telling her sons to take up their spears so that they (and their sisters) could come with her, she noticed that there was one unclaimed spear remaining. She identified this as her husband's and, finding him crouched under the leaf, crushed his head with it.

From there the story follows a course that recounts the creation of certain cultural and institutional forms: menstrual houses and Tambaran houses, and marriage—in this instance, between adjacent brothers and sisters, with Nambweapa'w taking the youngest, sisterless son for herself.

After a time, Nambweapa'w decided that it would not be good for the descendants of her children all to speak the same language. Accordingly, she sent the boys up a betel palm, in birth order, with the oldest at the bottom. She then called them down, and as each descended, he was bitten by a certain kind of insect, causing him to speak a different language. The oldest spoke the language of Ilahita, while the remaining sons spoke languages progressively farther afield. When the youngest alighted, he spoke a language utterly different from the others, a language now known to have been English.

Nambweapa'w's magic provided effortless abundance, a life in which death and pain and sorcery were unknown. This Edenic existence was lost, however, when her children—all but the youngest—fecklessly violated the one dietary taboo she had imposed. She punished them by turning herself into a wallaby[1] and tricking the innocent youngest son into killing her with a spear. Before she died, she revoked her sustaining magic and ordained that life thereafter would have pain and drudgery and death. The youngest son scolded his siblings. In a blaze of moral indignation, he was swept away by a sudden flood—to America, "as we now know," where he fathered the white race, and from whence he will someday return.

"Nambweapa'w" is by far the most popular tale in the Ilahita repertoire. I was to hear it often over the next two years. Tellers and audience, old and young, males and females—none seemed to tire of it. Even children could recite large parts of the story, indicating that "Nambweapa'w" is a living tradition, not something dusted off and displayed merely to satisfy the anthropologist. "Nambweapa'w" is *their* story. The people take pride in the belief—largely justified—that other villages acknowledge Ilahita's ownership of the story and of the events it describes. Telling the story was their way of introducing or, better, revealing themselves to me. "Nambweapa'w" holds a unique place in the Ilahita mythic imagination: all in one, it exhibits their sense of themselves as human beings, moral actors, residents of an illustrious village, and custodians of a shrine of universal importance; all in one, it projects their fondest wishes and fondest dreads.

I knew from their manner, that first day, that the story was terribly important to them. I could detect their intense interest in my reaction—which was, of course, eager praise for what a good story it is and tactical respect for their superstitious claim that it is a *true* story. A decade later, when I came to write a book on the Tambaran, it was obvious to me that "Nambweapa'w" should be the prologue (Tuzin 1980, 1–8) on the vague grounds that the tale was somehow crucial to an understanding of Ilahita religious imagination. The truth was that I did not know what to say that would do justice to the story's intuitive importance. Additional years and events have clarified and, in curious ways that this book tries to explain, *realized and fulfilled* those intuitions, revealing that the eventual truth of the story was far greater than even the villagers imagined.

It is hardly surprising that the people of Ilahita should be entranced by this tale of a wild creature turning into a lovely maiden, for many of the world's peoples have fallen under the same spell. Folklorists would instantly recognize Nambweapa'w as the "swan maiden," the enchanted heroine of what may be the oldest, most widely told love story on earth (Lessa 1961, 163). From its earliest known version as the story of Urvasi and Pururavas, in the Rig-Veda (ca. 3000 B.C.), the "swan maiden" appears to have spread to numerous European folk traditions. The motif is prominent in northern Europe and the British Isles, appearing in Celtic texts from ancient Ireland, in the Icelandic and other Norse sagas, and in various old Germanic and Slavic versions.[2] Tchaikovsky's haunting ballet, *Swan Lake,* steals the story, feathers and all, while in the courtly love imagery of medieval France, *Les belles dames sans merci* and the fairy mistresses sung of in the lays of *Lanval* and *Graelent* are transparent adaptations of old Celtic swan maiden tales (Cross 1915). The "Lady of the Lake" from Arthurian legend, "Orpheus and Eurydice" of the Greeks, and the saucy mermaid from off "The Eddystone Light"—they, too, draw their magic from that same ancient well of the imagination. La Llorona, the tormented, ghostly mother figure who haunts the pools and fountains of Mexico, may be a darker adaptation of the same tradition.[3] And in a recent study of swan maidens, demon lovers, and related motifs, Barbara Fass Leavy (1994) identifies Nora, the main character in Ibsen's play *A Doll's House,* as yet another avatar of this age-old mythic idea.

The basic swan maiden story goes as follows.[4] A young man espies a beautiful maiden bathing. He perceives that she is actually a swan who has removed her feathers or wings. The man steals the feathers, thus trapping the maiden in human form and bringing her under his power. They live happily as husband and wife, until the swan maiden recovers her feathers, often with the help of her (human) child, and flies to her freedom. In some versions, the bereft husband embarks on a quest to recover the swan maiden, and sometimes he succeeds in winning her back, if only by joining her in *her* world.

There are many variants. The swan maiden may or may not be aware that the man is in possession of her lost feathers. In some versions the maiden comes along voluntarily—may even contrive or initiate the original encounter—and stays with the man so long as he does not violate some injunction she lays upon him, such as not divulging to anyone the truth about her animal origins. It is because he thoughtlessly breaks the taboo or otherwise offends that the swan maiden departs. Instead of feathers or wings, as in the "classic" version, it may be her skin, tail, fur, jewelry, apron, skirt, or some other garment that the man purloins. Nor does the swan maiden have to be a *swan* for her story to qualify according to type: she has been a bear, seal, goose, grouse, crane, jackdaw, parakeet, cat, dog, pig, fox, horse, cow, buffalo, deer, fish, whale, porpoise, turtle, crab, clam, and bee. She has been a tree and a leaf. She has been a gorgeous celestial being, such as a "star maiden" or "sky maiden," or a water nymph.[5] It is also clear that the animal image is itself subject to metamorphosis as the story is borrowed, refined, or elaborated.[6] As one can see from its geographical range and the myriad variations on its theme, the basic story of the swan maiden is highly adaptable to local environments, cultural modalities, and existential issues.[7]

In addition to European exemplars we know from our own folk heritage, swan maiden tales are extremely common in the island societies of present-day Malaysia and Indonesia. Scholars (Dixon [1916] 1964; Lessa 1961) identify India as the source of this tradition, as well as that of Europe. Thematic similarities and known historical contacts suggest that from the Malay Archipelago the motif fanned out in a broad easterly direction. Swan maidens are found in cultures of the Philippines and Micronesia; along the north coast of New Guinea; in Vanuatu, New Caledonia, southern and eastern Australia; and in New Zealand, Samoa, and elsewhere in central Polynesia. Strengthening Dixon's original diffusion argument with many additional folktales, Lessa (1961, 160) concludes that

> there can be no doubt that the swan maiden theme was introduced into Oceania and is not an indigenous creation. It is found in many other parts of the world, where it has been long established. We know it to be present in Europe, Iceland, Turkey, Arabia, Iran, India, Ceylon, Assam, Burma, Siam, Annam, Tibet, Mongolia, China, Japan, Siberia, native North America, Greenland, Tunis, Algeria, Morocco, Zanzibar, and West Africa. There are written evidences of the motif in Indian literature dating back to a time before the settlement of much of Oceania.

Of course, none of this proves that the swan maiden theme is *not* indigenous to Melanesia and other Pacific regions; the known antiquity of the Indian version has nothing to do with the possibility that swan maiden stories arose independently in the Pacific and elsewhere. And yet, spontaneous generation on such a vast scale seems highly improbable.[8] At least as far as the southwest Pacific is concerned, the pattern of geographical distribution and thematic fidelity across diverse societies strongly favors a history of diffusion, with local modification, from immediate Malay sources.

This history of diffusion enables us to define what is distinctive in the "Nambweapa'w" variant. Contrary to the grandiose claims of early diffusionists,[9] to say that some cultural item is a product of diffusion rather than independent invention is not to say very much, unless one's interests are strictly antiquarian. This is because the *process of naturalization* through which an imported item enters the host culture is itself a (re)invention— a process involving selection, rejection, trial and error, and adaptation, almost as if the idea were endogenous. But if viewed in methodological rather than antiquarian terms, then the regional diffusion indicated for the Pacific "swan maiden" is heuristically quite useful, for it establishes a kind of standard against which to compare particular variants. Although in principle all details in the variant are significant, those deviating from the standard are doubly so; for in addition to their symbolic features, per se, they are the modifications wrought upon the story as part of the naturalization process. The deviations represent positive cultural "statements": themes of special concern or singularity that are created, elicited, or given a new "voice" by the imported story.

Diffusion is interesting, then, not because stories cross cultural boundaries, but because importing a story is an act of cultural opportunism, self-discovery, and self-creation on the part of the host tradition. In the same vein, Ilahita is entitled to regard Nambweapa'w as intuitively, uniquely *its own,* because for generations its storytellers have been perfecting the fit between the story's basic form and the pressing moral, aesthetic, and psychological issues that constitute the symbolic dimension of Ilahita culture.[10] Similarly, after demonstrating Celtic swan maiden elements in French love poetry of a later era, Cross notes (1915, 644) that his observations

> in no way contradict the fact that the [French] lays are in spirit
> courtly and chivalric. Their mystery and charm, such as they are,
> differ essentially from the mystery and charm of Celtic romance.
> The bones are Celtic; the flesh is French.

Ilahita's mythmakers did not adopt the swan maiden only to make her over into something genteel and fully human, nor did they accept her as she was. Instead, they took the image and intensified it: made the reds redder, the blacks blacker, the claws sharper, the attachments deeper, and the psychocultural stakes higher. As with the career of that other major import, the Tambaran cult, Nambweapa'w's conquest of the Ilahita mythic scene was accomplished through a process of involution. Instead of passively joining the repertoire of myths and legends, Nambweapa'w remained aloof, gathering themes to herself, growing and differentiating from within, until she controlled much of the emotional traffic in the mythic realm. Like the Tambaran—and the similarity is neither accidental nor inconsequential—Nambweapa'w has totalitarian tendencies.

What must be done, then, is to examine the details through which "Nambweapa'w" differs from other known swan maiden stories. This is an important exercise, for it is these distinctive features that reveal precisely what Ilahita is saying about itself through this narrative. Once this aspect of the story is presented, it will be appropriate to ask how and when Ilahita acquired the "swan maiden" motif in the first place.

In comparing "Nambweapa'w" with other swan maiden stories from the Pacific region, we note several features that emerge as distinctive. First, as swan maiden stories go, the Ilahita tale is uncommonly long and complicated—recall that the story presented earlier is condensed from the version originally collected (Tuzin 1980, 1–8). This is a somewhat wobbly distinction, since it could be a result of technical factors: the windedness of particular storytellers, their varying fondness for ornamental details, and the patience and purposes of different compilers. On the other hand, "Nambweapa'w" is long and complicated by Ilahita standards as well. The attention required to create and sustain such a story under conditions of oral transmission is a measure of Nambweapa'w's cultural importance, qualifying it as an epic. To be sure, other societies have epics; but, to judge from the published accounts, rarely if ever are they elaborations of a swan maiden story.

Second, "Nambweapa'w" is the only swan maiden story I have found (cf. Lessa 1961, 154) in which the man and his unusual bride are explicitly represented as the first humans—or, perhaps more accurately, the parents of the first humans. In other Oceanic versions, it is not rare for the swan maiden to be the source of certain foodstuffs (e.g., yams, pigs) or natural phenomena (e.g., thunder); in eastern Indonesia, the royal lines of Ternate and Tidore claim descent from a swan maiden, as do certain clans in Micronesia. But as the ancestress not just of a descent group, nor even of an entire society, but of all known races and languages—that boast is possibly unique to Nambweapa'w. This "origins" feature precludes certain characters who occur in most other examples of the story: the community of men to whom the male protagonist fatefully divulges the swan maiden's true nature; and, prominently, the man's aged mother, who typically assists the swan maiden in settling into human life and later in the story advises her son on how to recapture or "win back" his runaway wife (Lessa 1961, 145f.).

The fact that "Nambweapa'w" recounts the origin of all peoples and all languages predisposes the primordial couple to bear many children, rather than the one, two, or three appearing in nearly all other versions (Lessa 1961, 148f.). The Ilahita tale does not specify the number: it is sufficient that there be many;[11] that, for the convenience of (incestuous) marital coupling, they be born in alternating sex order; that the eldest be the Ilahita Arapesh ancestor; and that the youngest be a male, thus to justify his special, suggestively incestuous relationship with Nambweapa'w.

This arrangement aligns the story with a cultural pattern—evident in myth, ritual, descent ideology, inheritance, and respect behavior—which highlights the youngest and oldest of a line of siblings to the relative neglect of those born in middle position.[12] As the more developed and nobler character, it is Nambweapa'w's youngest child who attracts the listener's sympathy, while the oldest is stereotypically portrayed as the slow-witted heir of the unappealing father. The fact of there being many children actually facilitates the narrowing of the action on to the emotionally dense, composite triangle: Cassowary Woman—Wife—Mother // Husband—Father—Eldest Brother // Son—Youngest Brother—Husband. The story conflates father and eldest brother, personifying mundane, limited reality, and sets it against the mother and youngest brother dyad, which stands for the uncanny Other of unlimited, magical prepotency. In making the eldest son the *Arapesh* ancestor, the myth consigns the (Arapesh) beholder to the disenchanted state that is everyday existence; at the same time it mobilizes a counteridentity, expressed as a longing to reunite with those others who went away and to reattain the world as it existed when they were here.

An entailment of the "many children" feature is that by the time Nambweapa'w makes her escape, she and her unworthy consort have become old—another departure from the Oceanic "standard." (The absence of the mother/mother-in-law avoids the otherwise logical problem that would come from having the main characters advance to old age while the mother/mother-in-law is still there.) Men and swan maidens elsewhere rarely have more than three children—usually sons—implying that both main characters leave the story only a little older than when they enter it—at any rate, still in their prime. In the Ilahita story, the man's old age is explicit; crouched under the leaf, his decrepitude makes him pathetic and helpless before his wife's revenge, a kind of insect to be squashed without ado. Conversely, Nambweapa'w's (implied) old age is a source not of frailty, but of magical power and a fiercely commanding manner. Far from returning to the demure, blushing damsel she was when the man first spied her bathing, Nambweapa'w, after recovering her skin, becomes a phallically aggressive, husband-killing, no-nonsense mother, whom her children (all but the youngest, it would seem) fear. Consistent with Arapesh understandings about life stages, Nambweapa'w's old age makes her power credible and, in a psychodynamic sense, tolerable. For a woman of childbearing years to possess such power would be too disturbing to depict openly, for it would too openly recognize the deep ambivalence males feel toward their mothers, starting at an early age (chapter 7). Hence the need for the storyteller to make her old: old in her magical prime; old at the time her youngest son, having first displaced his father as the Ego of the story, marries her.

The age factor implies that Nambweapa'w's powers do not rest entirely on her condition as a recovered cassowary, formidable as those birds are. Her actions during the second half of the story (e.g., making salt, spearing her husband) are not those of someone running around in a cassowary suit, but of a woman—albeit a tough *old* woman, a woman whose powers disclose her as a daughter of the wild and of supernature. On the other hand, as we will see, the identity of cassowary does not oppose that of "woman," for in Arapesh reckoning the two are essentially the same, thus enabling the heroine to be both at once. What matters is that Nambweapa'w starts young and ends old; the many children make it so.

The fact—not unusual among swan maiden tales—that Nambweapa'w spends most of the story as a *mother* has serious entailments; for, as Leavy observes, it means that "the symbolic struggle with the otherworld to which she may at any moment return is intensified" (1994, 254). That "Nambweapa'w" is also (and unusually) an origin myth both ennobles the tale and, so to speak, raises its psychological stakes even higher. Nambweapa'w is more than a lover, more than a wife, more than a mother; she is The Lover, The Wife, The Mother. Although any woman of myth is potentially a target of these feminine projections, especially if the story casts her in the corresponding role, Nambweapa'w's wifely and maternal attributes are not only explicit, they are apotheosized: Nambweapa'w is the only wife/mother in the story, the first wife/mother, and the wife/mother of all humanity. And yet, from the moment the last-born child enters the story and the alternating baby-sitting routine is announced, the story casts Nambweapa'w as a domineering *mother,* in which role she slaughters her old husband. Thereafter, the action assumes the perspective of Nambweapa'w's children, increasingly that of the youngest son, who, in effect, delivers his father into his mother's clutches. Because her children are the parents of us all, we the listeners are induced to regard Nambweapa'w with their eyes; in other words, not simply as the grandmother to us and to all humanity, but as the *supermother.* All the good and bad emotions aroused by the maternal image are elevated here to cosmic proportions.[13] Nambweapa'w's story is not about some bizarre, trivial incident, as distant in mind as it is in time and space. It is a tale, the mythmaker insists, that involves us all.

The theme of universal origins prepares the way for yet another detail peculiar to the Ilahita version: the dramatic departure of the youngest brother for *America* ("as we now know"), from whence he will return. This ending is surely a relatively recent innovation. Although prior forms cannot be known, other stories in the Ilahita repertoire suggest that the young man would have departed in earlier versions, also, either to join his mother or, transformed into a bird, to fly to a distant mountaintop and become a spirit being. In either event, the connotations are of death: a condition, however, that is not necessarily final and from which one can conceivably return. More about death and Nambweapa'w in the next chapter; for now, it is enough to observe that the revised ending is a good example of how "Nambweapa'w" adapts itself to changing expressive needs and opportunities. Like politicians who slyly follow popular opinion while pretending to lead it, "Nambweapa'w's" prophecies, because they articulate real but unformulated tensions in the sociocultural order, have a way of coming to pass.

The revenge motif is another feature setting "Nambweapa'w" apart from its sister stories. In the others, the swan maiden recovers her free, wild self and escapes from domestic bondage; the only punishment she delivers on her husband is to desert him. The closest any of these versions comes to casting the swan maiden as a violent avenger is, in a few cases, having the husband die in his quest to win her back.[14] In the Ilahita version, there is nothing inadvertent or regrettable about the husband's death: ancient, creaky, bereft, no longer posing any threat to the swan maiden's freedom, he suffers his brains to be scattered for no purpose other than Nambweapa'w's pure revenge. Why else kill one who is, in effect, already dead? Perhaps in addition to the revenge motive, there is a wish to assert finality—to declare that there is no going back, and to commit the story to an entirely new direction.

Yet another detail of comparative interest concerns the personality of the swan maiden and, in particular, her sexual condition at the time of capture. Lessa (1961, 1420), drawing on many sources, summarizes the nature of the maiden as follows:

> She is hyperfeminine, being shy and submissive, delicate and sensitive, loyal and affectionate, patient and dutiful. But she maintains a steadfast quality of otherworldliness and never truly accepts the ordinary life of mortals. She seems to remain ever virginal, even though she bears children and rears them. Although she is a good wife she never seems to give herself entirely to her husband. She is often ready to abandon both her children and her spouse without too much remorse as soon as she finds a way to escape from her forced detention. One might describe her as . . . torn between the mundane and the superphysical. Her radiance and loveliness are out of place in a world of aggressive and misunderstanding human beings. She tries hard to be a real woman but finds she cannot cope with its practical implications.

Although these traits are not inconsistent with the *younger* Nambweapa'w, there remains the question of her sexual parts. Most other versions do not attend to anatomical details, except to imply that the unclothed swan maiden is a complete woman, though virginal. With the exception of the closely cognate Mountain Arapesh version (see below), only the Ilahita take the swan maiden's virginity to signify, rather drastically, the absence of a vagina. This detail, along with the man's corrective action, is enormously important, not just to the forward course of the narrative, but because it hooks the story into the web of cultural ideas concerning sexuality, gender, and cassowaries.

I commented earlier that one does not have to be a swan to qualify as a "swan maiden." In Ilahita, we see that the "swan" is a cassowary—a large, flightless bird at home in the rain forests of New Guinea, some of the off-lying islands, and northern Australia. Casting the swan maiden as a cassowary would have made simple sense to the Arapesh audience; but in being a cassowary, the swan maiden also elicited and formulated some of the culture's most primitive fantasies, causing her to act in ways that her sisters in other societies would find shocking—but also, perhaps, intriguing. In view of the cassowary's relatively restricted range, it might seem unfair or only trivially true to count it among the distinctive features of Ilahita's swan maiden tale. The claim is justified, however, by the significant fact that societies that *do* have cassowaries in their forest environs do not choose them as "swan maidens." Before examining this surprising omission in the light of local Sepik comparisons, it is worthwhile to consider how well suited the cassowary is to the role of the "swan maiden"—especially as the story is told in Ilahita.

My first encounter with a cassowary took place shortly after I had settled into the village. One day Moses, a knowledgeable, middle-aged man who lived in an adjacent hamlet, invited me over to see his cassowary. He kept it in a small pen behind his house. The bird stood about to my waist—a half-grown youngster Moses had captured as a chick in the forest.[15] Foraging nearby during the day, it returned home in the evening to be hand fed papaya before sleeping. Its adult coloration was coming in, and before long it would fetch a high price as the main course at someone's feast. As we watched it walk gingerly around the enclosure—unless aroused, cassowaries walk with an exaggerated elegance, as though expecting to step on a nail—I declared what a fine cassowary it was and then asked, in complete innocence, whether it was a male or a female. "What do you mean?" asked Moses with a puzzled (and puzzling) look. I elaborated. Eventually, after a few clarifying exchanges, he caught my drift and informed me that, of course, cassowaries are *only* female. "Everybody knows that," he added with a sniff.

Trying to conceal my excitement in this crystalline moment of ethnographic serendipity, I asked Moses to tell me more about cassowaries, beginning with how they reproduce. "Rocks," he said, "by eating rocks." Cassowaries are fiercely protective of their young, who flee to protection under their mother's vestigial wings, where, said Moses, they nurse from the ends of the tubular quills.[16] Cassowaries are proverbially aggressive and bad tempered, chronically dyspeptic because they do not menstruate. They do not menstruate, according to Moses, because they have no vaginas. Without the periodic discharge of built-up, blood-borne contaminants, cassowaries are in a bad mood all the time: permanent premenstrual syndrome, so it would seem. Abelam witches are mean and dangerous for the same reason: they, too, are females who do not have vaginas. For a long time I understood this attribution to mean that cassowaries and Abelam witches simply lacked the organ, showing smooth, unparted flesh where the vagina should be. (This is the impression one gets from the vagina-cutting episode in "Nambweapa'w.") Years later, I discovered that either the belief had changed or, perhaps more likely, I had all along misunderstood what was being described. Cassowaries and Abelam witches, I now learned, "lack" vaginas not because the vaginas are absent, but because they are *plugged*. "Plugged?" I asked. "With what?" The men I was with shrugged and let the question hang, unanswered.

In the presence of the men's silence, I would tentatively suggest that the vagina is plugged with a penis. Although to my knowledge the Arapesh stop short of having an explicit *vagina dentata* concept, the adjacent idea of *anus dentatus* occurs in myth and obscenity, and there are stories about women chopping off or stabbing men's penises, as well as ribald penis-as-maverick tales about ambulatory penises prowling around, up to no good (Tuzin 1972).[17] Traditionally, penises and vulvas were exhibited as war trophies on the facade of the spirit house. It is no great leap of imagination to move from these fantasies and practices to the idea that vaginas can be plugged with disconnected penises. Such an interpretation would account for the androgynous, awesome powers of Nambweapa'w and Abelam witches and their ability to inspire fear in men.[18] For, having incorporated the male member, they personify the ritually important Arapesh idea that coitus is a supremely creative act; it is a mythic, magical moment in which all opposites are fleetingly merged, the cosmic mechanism is temporarily disengaged, and impossible events become possible.[19]

The Ilahita are not unusual in treating cassowaries with special ritual and symbolic attention. Since the publication of Ralph Bulmer's classic article, "Why Is the Cassowary Not a Bird?" (1967), numerous ethnographers[20] have reported on the symbolic significance of cassowaries, especially their part in mythic and ritual constructions of sex and gender. Secondary cultural elaborations of the "cassowary" image certainly occur, but it is clear from all accounts that no adequate interpretation of the phenomenon can ignore certain natural oddities in this bird—anomalies that seemingly invite symbolic contemplation and usage.

First, let it be said that the Arapesh are quite aware that bird species generally include individuals of both sexes, that the sexes are usually distinguishable by form and behavior, that something like sexual intercourse is necessary for avian reproduction, and that cassowaries are birds. To be sure, they are strange birds: large, flightless birds who are powerful runners, leapers, and swimmers. Cassowaries have been described as "probably the most dangerous birds in the world" (Amadon and Gilliard 1954, 892). Aggressive when cornered or protecting their young, a cassowary can kill or maim with powerful kicks and raking motions with its rapier talons.[21] Such features are remarkable, but they hardly call for the exorbitant fantasies that typify cassowary lore among the Arapesh and other New Guinea peoples.

The confusion begins with the fact that cassowary sexual dimorphism is either minimal or the reverse of what one might expect from noticing other bird species. In size, coloration, and genital appearance, males and females are difficult to distinguish, although females are somewhat larger and more brightly colored about the head and neck, and their casque (a bony "helmet" on top of their head) is higher than the male's. Male cassowaries, somewhat unusually among birds, have erectile penises (Gardner 1984, 140), which, however, are so tiny (in the detumescent state, at any rate) as to be difficult to detect, even under dissection by an ornithologist. A prominent cloaca—the common outlet for intestinal, urinary, and genital products—yields such vast quantities of feces that it would be easy to perceive the orifice as an anus *only,* making it seem that the animal is without a genital system opening to the outside. From the cassowary's outward appearance, then, especially in comparison with humans and other mammals, it would not be outrageous to assume that the form is that of a female (because no visible penis) without a vagina (because no visible external genitalia). Nor would butchering a cassowary do much to reveal differences in sexual morphology.

Behaviorally, too, males and females are hard to tell apart. Cassowaries are solitary by habit, forming pairs only in the breeding season. Naturally, such pairs would be seen rarely or not at all, especially considering that cassowaries are extremely reclusive and largely nocturnal: trapping them is not too difficult, but, as weary field ornithologists have found, observing their natural behavior for an extended period is practically impossible.[22] After courting the male and laying as many as eight eggs (Coates 1982), the female leaves it to him to incubate and brood the nest and then defend the young for more than a year (Perrins and Middleton 1985, 26). True to the relevant images in "Nambweapa'w," cassowary sightings would be of solitary adults, single adults leading young offspring, or small groups of subadult siblings—not nuptial pairs. As with sexual anatomy, inferences from snatches of observed behavior might lead one to conclude that cassowaries come in one sex and one gender—and those are female and feminine.

As a final note, cassowary habits are markedly seasonal. There are times of the year when some hankering seems to draw them away—a simple result of the fact that they peregrinate across large foraging ranges, following the rotational ripening of the fruits they eat. It may have been just this call of the wild that was the real reason Moses' cassowary failed to appear one evening. When I voiced concern that it had run off or been killed, Moses was unruffled. "You will see," he explained. "The cassowary is approaching puberty and so has gone to the great forests of the west to find her kinswomen and learn from them the ways of cassowaries. When she has learned what cassowaries must know, she will return." And so she did, about a month later.

In the classical version, the swan maiden is the quintessential woman by virtue of her knee-weakening loveliness. So, too, is Nambweapa'w. But as *her* story unfolds, the idealization swells far beyond good looks and fine figure. Maiden, wife, dowager—the three ages of woman—each is expressed in Nambweapa'w. As the ages progress, beauty and innocence give way to other qualities, which, for the Arapesh, are no less inherent in the sex. In the classical version, the restored swan maiden returns to what she was before. The Arapesh, who know better and whose existential problems are perhaps more acute, have turned this fairy tale into their own kind of morality play. After what the wifely Nambweapa'w endures in the second age—the pains of childbed and the drudgery of domestic captivity—for her to revert to maidenhood after recovering her skin would be silly (though her return to being a cassowary does imply that she recovers her penis-in-vagina maidenhead). Instead, after dispatching her husband, Nambweapa'w advances into the third age and completes herself as a culture heroine. Her foolishly selfish children—all but the youngest—do not honor the Edenic life she creates for them, and so she takes back the magic and *goes away,* leaving it to her children and their descendants, down to the present, to contemplate, yearn for, and regret what happened.

In life as in myth, Arapesh men struggle with themselves over mothers and wives. The myth offers no solution to the vulnerability men suffer by depending upon and, as a result, needing to dominate women (cf. Leavy 1994, 270). On the contrary, the drama is decidedly pessimistic about this and other nuclear relationships. But in casting the moral problems as narrative, as myth, as *culture,* the story reduces their psychical acuity, generalizes their importance, sustains their interest value, and enshrines their irresolution.

If Nambweapa'w the Cassowary Swan Maiden performs such valuable symbolic services, and if swan maidens in general are so popular in the world's folklore traditions, then why have many New Guinea societies either not adopted the motif or done so with little enthusiasm? It cannot be argued that they differ from Ilahita in that they lack beliefs about cassowaries; for while Ilahita's own cassowary beliefs may mesh especially well with classic swan maiden images, they are not unusual by New Guinea standards. On the contrary, the various widespread fantasies attached to this bird should have facilitated the adoption of swan maidens all across the island. Despite, however, the cultural treatment lavished upon cassowaries in many societies within the bird's geographic range, despite the widely recurrent use of cassowary images in symbolic representations of sexuality and gender—despite, in short, the preoccupation of the peoples of this region with cassowaries—they almost never appear as swan maidens. Neither, however, is some other creature widely preferred—because, in fact, very few of these societies have swan maidens at all.

One obvious reason for this comparative neglect is historical. Consistent with the Dixon-Lessa hypothesis, the New Guinea swan maiden motif entered the island with Malay traders and plume hunters, and its distribution coincides with the range of societies that have had direct or near-direct contact with these visitors (Lessa 1961, 163). Many groups would simply have been outside this sphere: the strength and duration of the diffusion impulse apparently petered out before the "swan maiden" reached them. So, for instance, in the central and eastern Highlands cassowaries are objects of symbolic interest (e.g., Bulmer 1967), often appearing in myth and ritual as strongly masculinized females (e.g., Herdt 1981, 131)—but not as "swan maidens." What about the other societies that were within potential reach of Malay influences?

Consider, first, the wider geography and history of the situation. From as early as the eighth century, and possibly long before that, the Birdshead,

Cenderawasih Peninsula, and Lake Sentani areas of western New Guinea lay within the outer fringes of various Malay trading networks (Swadling 1996, 53–59). Srivijaya, the Buddhist maritime and commercial empire based in southeastern Sumatra from the seventh through thirteenth centuries, traded bird-of-paradise plumes from early on, all the way to China and India (Swadling 1990, 78; Hall 1981). From the twelfth through seventeenth centuries, trade in the eastern archipelagoes was dominated by the rival sultanates of Ternate and Tidore, operating from adjacent islands near the west coast of Halmahera—which, itself, is near the west coast of New Guinea (map 4). These are the Moluccas, the fabled Spice Islands, where, starting in the early sixteenth century, Portuguese, Spanish, English, and Dutch powers variously sought to take over and control the trade in cloves and other exotic flavorings.[23] What little commercial interest these Europeans had in nearby New Guinea they were satisfied to pursue through Ternate and Tidore intermediaries, who for centuries had used vassals on the mainland coast and nearby islands to obtain slaves, plumes, trepang, and other prizes of the region.

For our purposes it is important to note that Moluccan activity on the New Guinea mainland, from its beginnings up until the mid–nineteenth century, appears to have been sharply confined to the Birdshead, coastal Geelvink (now Cenderawasih) Bay, the offshore islands of Biak and Numfoor, and other parts west of the Mamberamo River. From the archaeological record, Pamela Swadling concludes that from the time the Ternate and Tidore sultanates were established, "all direct Asian influence ceased on the north coast of New Guinea east of Cenderawasih Bay" (1990, 78). In the seventeenth century, at any rate, "neither sultanate had any real control over New Guinea, and certainly there was no control over the coast east of the Mamberamo River until a garrison was established at what became Hollandia (now Jayapura) in 1852" (ibid.; cf. Swadling 1996, 116–18).[24] So abrupt was the cessation of Indonesian influence eastward from this local region that one scholar, J. C. van Eerde, identified the line between Indonesian and Melanesian culture areas to be the Mamberamo River, which flows northward and enters the sea at the eastern extremity of the mouth of Geelvink Bay, at Cape d'Urville (Held 1957, 6–7).

This history contradicts the casual claim sometimes heard that Malays have been engaged in plume hunting in the Sepik hinterland since antiquity. References such as the following, by the biologist-adventurer A. J.

Marshall (1938, 192), confer a mythic aura on the history of Malay activity in the coastal and border mountain areas of the Sepik region. Here, Marshall (1938, 191–92) rhapsodizes about his coastal trek westward across the border separating the Australian and Dutch New Guineas:

> As time went on I became conscious of a vague excitement. Hollandia, that far-famed, remote, romantic centre of the old plume-trading days, seemed so unbelievably near. Journey's end! The boys, too, chattered expectantly. They had heard stories of Hollandia from their childhood. No man can say how long plume trading has gone on. Certainly long before Europeans ever saw the country, long before the first Portuguese, there has been a steady trade in plumes between New Guinea and the East.

While this passage may be literally correct, it misleadingly implies that Hollandia had been an entrepôt in the far-flung plume trade from ancient times; the same distortion is perpetuated by entomologist Evelyn Cheesman, who made a collecting expedition to the Hollandia-Aitape coastal area at the same time Marshall was there (Cheesman 1938, 36).[25] As noted, Hollandia was founded only in 1852; moreover, its site is 300 kilometers east of the mouth of the Mamberamo, which, all evidence indicates, marked the limit of Malay penetration in premodern times. Malays may have been going many places for many centuries, and taking plumes with them; but as regards the coast and mountainous interior of the Sepik region, their activities can be reliably dated from only the late nineteenth century.[26]

Why was the Mamberamo so formidable a barrier to Malay movements eastward? Part of the problem may have had to do with the difficulty of sailing around Cape d'Urville from the west, especially under the combined wind and current conditions during the six-month season of the southeast trades. Although the Moluccans were skilled seafarers, their routes mostly consisted of island hopping, coastal cruising, or the crossing of small, sheltered seas under virtual lagoon conditions. Use of the lateen sail—adopted from Arab sailors—would have enabled them to sail close-hauled to the wind. Even without this technology, it might have been possible to travel up and down the north coast of New Guinea, timing one's direction in accordance with the alternating southeast trades and northwest monsoons, were it not for the South Equatorial Current. Along northern New Guinea, this mighty current flows continuously from southeast to northwest, until Cape d'Urville, where it springs north, performs a hairpin turn, and heads due east as the Equatorial Counter Current.[27] For a distance of more than three hundred kilometers east of Cape d'Urville, the coastline's profile is that of a shallow depression tipped upward at its western end. The pressure built up by the current's driving at the coastline is suddenly released at Cape d'Urville, creating what sailors call a Venturi effect—an intense gush of wind and/or current rounding a headland.[28] Progress eastward beyond the cape would have meant sailing far out to sea and approaching the mainland from the north or northeast. By the same token, the islands of Biak and Numfoor, lying within the "shadow" of Cape d'Urville, could have been easily reached from the Moluccas and the Birdshead—as, indeed, they were. Also by the same token, the founding of Hollandia in 1852 was made feasible by the development of steam-powered vessels, which began plying the oceans in the 1830s.

If access by sea was not practicable, perhaps Moluccan hunters and traders came eastward by an overland route. Such a prospect is highly unlikely. Like most seafaring peoples, these Malays preferred riding to walking. Their routine was to establish a station on a beach nearest where the hunting or trading was to be had. Traipsing four hundred kilometers through extremely rough terrain and extremely hostile peoples would have required incentives far greater than any that would have existed at that time. It is clear from all accounts that the premodern demand for bird-of-paradise feathers and other New Guinea products, including slaves, was met sufficiently by exploiting territories west of the Mamberamo; there was simply no reason to venture farther east, and many reasons not to. Although plume hunting and trading were part of Hollandia's raison d'être from the start, the real plume boom occurred some years later, driven by changes in European women's fashions that began during the fin de siècle and crested in 1908. The heightened demand for exotic feathers was met by Ternatian Malays who had been actively working out of Hollandia since the 1880s, and who now begin vigorously to exploit the relatively untouched avian treasures of the Sepik interior (Swadling 1996, 213).

Interestingly, this profitable trade also facilitated the development of north-coast plantations during the German colonial period by providing a source of income during the seven or eight years it took for the palm plantings to reach maturity (Marshall 1938, 192; Fleetwood 1984, 10).

The owners of this enterprise were European, but they employed Malays as plantation laborers and as hunters and agents in the plume trade (Swadling 1996, 243). These were in addition to independent or freelance Malay businessmen and adventurers who attached themselves to Dutch and German interests in this part of New Guinea.

From 1852 onward, then, with the founding of Hollandia and, later, Aitape, a new era of Malay activity in New Guinea occurred. Moluccan traders and plume hunters once again ranged along the north shore. This time, however, beachheads were located much farther east than before. Under the aegis of Dutch and German plantation authorities, often in the pay of Chinese traders on the coast, Malays penetrated deep into the coastal mountains of what is now Papua New Guinea and crossed over into the northwest corner of the Sepik basin (Marshall 1938, 50).[29] They established regular routes and occupied base camps in the hinterland for months at a time (Marshall 1938, 198; Allen 1976, 57; Cheesman 1938, 37; McCarthy 1963, 161–62), long enough to establish relations with the local people and, in the nature of the situation, swap stories (Swadling 1996, 220–21).

At our historical remove it is impossible to know why most groups *within* the orbit of Malay influence did not acquire the swan maiden motif. All one can say is that conditions did not favor the transmission, either from the Malays initially or through space and time thereafter. In other places, attenuated elements of the swan maiden tale may have blended so fully with preexisting traditions as to be unrecognizable. Afek, for example, the androgynous, culture-bearing, husband-killing "Old Woman" of the Mountain Ok, the daughter of a cassowary, bears a slight family resemblance to Nambweapa'w (Brumbaugh 1990), as do the mythic "Great Mother" and ritual cassowary figures among the Yafar and Umeda of the Border Mountains of the West Sepik Province (Juillerat 1992; Gell 1992). Unfortunately, we can do no more than speculate about the history of possible connections among these traditions and Malay swan maidens.[30]

What we can say with certainty, however, is that the era of Malay forays into the Sepik hinterland was relatively recent and short-lived and that most groups in this large region were never visited or seriously affected by them. More than anything else, perhaps, this is why the swan maiden so rarely appears on the stage of Sepik mythology. This conclusion begs us to question Ilahita's exceptionally swift and enthusiastic capture of the Swan Maiden, once she came their way. What was the nature and urgency of this romance?

There is no indication that Malay patrols ever reached Ilahita, but rever-berations of their passage seem to have been felt via neighbors to the west, north, and northeast of their territory.[31] Keeping to our topic, the Malay swan maiden motif's chief local importer seems to have been the Arapesh, who would have assimilated it around the time of the intrusion of Middle Sepik peoples into the foothill and mountain region. I say this because the story told by the Mountain Arapesh—who regularly interacted with, and were culturally and linguistically indistinguishable from, Arapesh speakers living on the beach (Mead 1938)—resembles most closely the Oceanic standard and appears to be the immediate source of the elabo-rated Ilahita version. Other societies in the vicinity either do not know the story, recognize it as Arapesh property, or possess fragments clearly derived from Arapesh sources. A brief review of local variants will show the singularity of the Ilahita version—a singularity that, I argue, comes from this culture's very special, historically produced problems of male legitimacy and moral vulnerability.

1. The *Mountain Arapesh* version (Mead 1940, 376–77) is the only one in the vicinity that follows the Oceanic feature of giving the swan maiden's mother-in-law a place in the story. After the man captures the cassowary maiden by stealing her "apron" (i.e., rump feathers) while she is bathing, his mother tells him to build a house. She then assists the inexperienced daughter-in-law to deal with her first menstruation—brought on (as in the Ilahita story) by the husband tricking her into cut-ting herself and forming her vulva.[32] She bears (in order) three sons, a daughter, and another son. After accidentally finding her stolen garment, she runs away, telling her children to follow her after a certain bunch of bananas ripens. Upset by their mother's departure, the children reproach their father for not destroying the means of her escape: "'Why didn't you tell us to burn that grass skirt, or to throw it in the water. Instead you hid it in the village and now she has found it'" (p. 377).

Eventually, the three older sons go and find their cassowary-mother, calling her to a tree which they have climbed. In vain, she asks that one of them come down and go with her. They stay in the tree. After she departs, the three boys descend and return to the village. They and their father weep together.[33]

In mentioning the children's rebuke of their father, this version is one of the few in the whole wide world of swan maiden tales to raise the extremely obvious question of why the captor did not destroy the transforming garment.[34] Could any listener fail to wonder why the husband foolishly retains the one key to his wife's escape? Leavy (1994, 59) refers to a class of stories in which the husband trustingly (or remorsefully) offers the swan maiden her lost feathers; she grabs them and flies—and that's that.[35] In a minority of cases, however, for reasons of true love or self-interest, she declines her freedom (p. 291). Such stories contradict the essential wildness of the swan maiden and seem to be either euphemisms or the result of different tales being combined. In those stories, too, the swan-wife either knows all along that the husband has the magic garment or has had the initiative from the start.

Whatever the wrinkle, without the element of sustained secrecy and deception the psychology of the tale differs categorically from the cases we are discussing. Stories such as "Nambweapa'w" are more suspenseful and morally complex, first, because of the man's puzzling failure to destroy the garment, and, second, because of the storyteller's equally puzzling failure to notice the man's blunder, either editorially or (as in the Mountain Arapesh case) by having one of the characters put the question. This narrative conundrum is akin to a curious feature that will be seen again in Arapesh symbolic usage, namely, the *incriminating charter*—a paradoxical mythic image or scenario that by contradicting existing authority structures helps to sustain a sense of moral crisis and vulnerability on the part of those in authority.

Such puzzles emerge only if one applies commonsense standards of reasonableness to the behavior of mythic actors. But is this a valid procedure? If mythic phenomena are fantastical by definition, is it not absurd to challenge them on logical grounds? Furthermore, is the man's failure to dispose of the garment any more fanciful than, say, a cassowary stripping off her skin to become a woman? A critic might say that the only "failure" here is my own in not respecting the sanctity of the story. My response would be that a myth is a projective fantasy susceptible of interpretation at all levels; fantastic ideas are cognitively admissible through individual psychodynamic processes, mythologic structures, and genre cues calling for the suspension of disbelief—each of which provides a context of meaning and precedence; the man's failure to dispose of the garment,

while not overtly fantastical, is shielded from scrutiny by this psychocultural apparatus; finally, beyond contributing to a suspenseful story line
and certifying the man's foolishness, this detail projects disturbing ideas of
existential guilt, retribution, and abandonment. With little or no disguise,
the man's act crystallizes the (male) experience of male deception, vulnerability, and prospective calamity. Had the man sensibly destroyed the garment, logic would have been served—but only at the cost of morally
trivializing the story. As it is, the elements of self-incrimination and choice
guarantee the story's moral character and, because of chronically pressing
gender issues related to the men's cult, moral urgency.

The next three stories come from the immediate area and are more
or less close variants of the Ilahita version. Each is distinct, but a feature
common to all three, which sets them apart from "Nambweapa'w," has
to do with the precipitating cause of the Cassowary-Wife's departure. In
each version, she runs away because her husband beats her; in each, he
beats her for disobeying his orders by feeding seed yams to the children.
In the Ilahita story, the feeding episode has the Cassowary-Mother giving
tidbits of coconut to her last born, in return for his telling her a "secret"
(i.e., the hidden cassowary skin). There is no hint of disobedience, nor
is husbandly brutality invoked (as implied in story 2 below) to explain
Nambweapa'w's departure from and killing of her husband. Nambweapa'w's motives are neither mundane nor morally reassuring: she flees for
no reason but the opportunity to do so; she kills not because the man had
mistreated her—for all we know he was a loving husband—but because
he had *deceived* her, tricked her into joining his world. Discovery of the
cassowary skin meant that she had not been rescued that evening at the
pool, but captured; that womanly existence had not been self-fulfillment,
but self-abnegating captivity; and that her husband had all along been her
jailer. In the other versions the male audience can draw the comforting
lesson—one they know already—that a wife would not run away if she
is treated well; in "Nambweapa'w," the disconcerting message is that a
wife *would* run away, no matter how she is treated, if given the choice (cf.
Leavy 1994, 291).

2. At *Mui,* an Ilahita Arapesh village at the southern end of the dialect
area (Aufenanger 1972, 395–97), they tell a cassowary story that is a clear
cognate of the Ilahita version. The stolen item is a necklace, which the
man removes while the cassowary maidens are bathing in a river. The

woman's youngest son shows her the necklace's hiding place, after she gives him a piece of yam that the father had reserved for planting. Later, when the woman again disobeys her husband by cooking mamis he has set aside for planting, he angrily smashes the cooking pot. Unalo[36] dons her cassowary necklace and flees to join the wild cassowaries, but they reject her, saying she is a woman. She builds a village of her own, where her children join her. As in the Ilahita version, they bring their father and hide him under a leaf. The cassowary woman kills him with a palm wood sword. Unalo sends her children up a betel palm and causes a bee to sting each one as they descend to the ground, thus creating the languages "now spoken by the people around *Mui*." In the end the brothers and sisters intermarry, "and so now there are people everywhere." The story does not tell what becomes of the cassowary woman and, after having him reveal the secret of the necklace, assigns no special role to the youngest son.

3. A version collected by Stephen Likita (1980), then a high school student from an Ilahita outlier, *Auwi*, differs unaccountably from the one I heard repeatedly in the main village. In this just-so story the (unnamed) cassowary wife bears two sons, who reveal the hiding place of her cassowary skin after she feeds them some yams against her husband's orders. He beats her, and she runs away. The family is eventually reunited and all is well until, for some unstated reason, while the father is absent, the mother puts on her skin and frightens the sons. The father returns and realizes that the "cassowary" is his wife. He lies in wait and chops off her head, thinking this will restore her to human form. Instead, she dies. Disturbed, the father sends the eldest son up a betel palm to fetch some nuts. The boy slips and cries "Awi" as he is falling; hence the name of the settlement.

4. A swan maiden story from *Aupik*, an Abelam village adjacent the Ilahita Arapesh border, resembles "Nambweapa'w." This origin story has a man capturing a cassowary maiden by stealing her skirt while she is bathing (Akimoula 1980). They have two sons. The younger son cries for a yam that the father has reserved for planting. The mother gives in to the child and is beaten by her angry husband. She runs away to the mountains (no mention of retrieving her skirt or resuming her cassowary form), where she is joined by her sons. She magically creates a settlement, complete with a Tambaran spirit house and wives for her sons.[37]

These three stories illustrate variations on the Cassowary-Mother theme from within Ilahita's close neighborhood. Their genetic closeness cannot be doubted, and from what was said earlier it appears that they are all descended, one way or another, from a version that arrived on the coast and reached the hinterland by way of (what are now) the Mountain Arapesh.[38] Even within this narrow circle "Nambweapa'w" is not merely distinct but *significantly* distinct, confirming that its symbolic functions correspond, in part, to issues that are peculiar to this village—despite its belonging to a family of stories virtually worldwide in incidence. This is an important point, for it cautions against trying to snare *this* swan maiden without a finely meshed net of local cultural and historical circumstances.[39]

As stated earlier, some local villages, such as nearby Ningalimbi and the several Bumbita Arapesh villages to the west, do not have versions of their own but are aware of the story as belonging to Ilahita.[40] Beyond the first remove of surrounding societies, cassowary images occur that are either the remnants or received fragments of more complete cassowary maiden stories, or they are indigenous cassowary ideas of the sort that once combined with the swan maiden motif to form stories such as "Nambweapa'w."

5. From *Ariseli,* a Wom-speaking village in the mountains north of Ilahita and west of the Mountain Arapesh, comes a story in which a man captures a cassowary maiden by stealing her skin while she is bathing. He takes her to his village, and later he and the other humans obtain fire (for the first time) from her brother (Aufenanger 1975, 16–17). There is no mention of the cassowary wife leaving her husband.

6. West of the Bumbita Arapesh, the *Urat* tell a story (Bryant Allen, pers. comm.) of how night came to be. An old woman, who is secretly able to turn into a cassowary, does not think it right that there should be only daylight. She tells her son—her only child—about a cassowary she has seen regularly visit a particular fruit tree, suggesting he shoot it. She herself changes into the cassowary. When the arrow strikes her, she calls out, causing darkness to fall for the first time. She is not killed, but remains a cassowary and is not seen again.

7. In the *Nuku* area, some forty kilometers southwest of Ilahita, a story is told (Manari 1980) about a cassowary who gives birth to a human

boy and raises him for a time, before losing him to nearby villagers. The boy grows to young manhood, tampers with another man's wife, is driven away by the irate husband, and rejoins his mother. She induces him to shoot her. While dying she tells him how to dispose of her flesh in such a way that it will turn into yams and mamis. That is how these foods first began.

By now, certain details are familiar: the bathing scene; doffing the cassowary garment to become human; the cassowary as essentially feminine; the capture; the son being tricked into killing her; and the legacy of foodstuffs or other essentials. Missing from these short tales is an integration of these details with a psychodrama of masculine theft and deception leading to feminine abandonment and retribution—a drama that "Nambweapa'w" carries to its most intense, most prophetic extreme.

There is an old tradition in the West, and possibly elsewhere, that swans have the power of prophecy.[41] Legend has it they know when they are about to die and plaintively foretell the event with their proverbial "swan song." The Greeks held the swan sacred to Apollo, patron of prophets and oracles, his chariot drawn by seven swans. In the *Phaedo,* Plato (1961, 111) has the condemned Socrates gently chide Simmias for taking too gloomy a view of his (Socrates') impending death. "Will you not allow that I have as much of the spirit of prophecy in me as the swans?" asks the great teacher,

> For they, when they perceive they must die, having sung all their life long, do then sing more lustily than ever, rejoicing in the thought that they are about to go away to the god whose ministers they are. But men, because they are themselves afraid of death, slanderously affirm of the swans that they sing a lament at the last, not considering that no bird sings when cold, or hungry, or in pain . . . But because they are sacred to Apollo, they have the gift of prophecy, and anticipate the good things of another world; wherefore they sing and rejoice in that day more than ever they did before. And I, too, believing myself to be the consecrated servant of the same God, and the fellow-servant of the swans, and thinking I have received from my master gifts of prophecy which are not inferior to theirs, would not go out of life less merrily than the swans.

Although ancient and widespread in its own right, this tradition of prophecy never conjoined with the swan maiden story. When swans, Spenser's birds "of goodly hue," are depicted in relation to swan maiden stories, the qualities lauded are their beauty, grace, innocence, and whiteness—never their alleged soothsaying prowess. It is therefore a wonderful irony, or an exceedingly clever feat of bricolage, that Nambweapa'w's resemblance to a swan relies not on the latter's maidenly beauty, but on that separate tradition: her imagined powers of prophecy!

To an extent unforeseen in the classic swan maiden story, "Nambweapa'w" is a tale heavy with prophetic significance. The forecast of the hero's messianic return from America; Nambweapa'w's dying curse of mundanity on her New Guinea descendants; the ominous ordination that the theft and concealment of the skin will have unpleasant consequences—together, these plot elements generate a prophetic aura radiating beyond themselves and encompassing the story as a whole. "Nambweapa'w" is about what happened long ago, but it is also about what will happen in some indefinite future; indeed, its status as a charter myth means that some of its predictions have already come to pass, making it just a matter of time before the others do as well. Prophecies are strange birds, indeed. Like "Open Sesame!" and other so-called speech acts, prophecies are sometimes self-fulfilling, able to effect that which they signify. Construct them with cultural and psychological substance, repeat them often, mold them with the retellings, make them the arbiter of current events—and sometimes, as if by magic, they come true.

Chapter Five

THE WEB OF TRUE PROPHECY

Strange to say, the story of Nambweapa'w was unfinished when I first heard it. I say "unfinished." To be exact, the story was a prophecy in search of fulfillment. Not only did I not suspect this at the time, I would not have thought it possible that a cultural text could be unfinished or that a prophecy so constituted could be other than a narrative contrivance, a device to enchant the story with a shimmer of expectancy and magical causation. For me at the time of my first fieldwork, the last born's ordained return from America exemplified only the form of prophecy, not the reality. To the people of Ilahita, however, the story's owners, the expectation of the hero's return was real; its promise was genuinely predictive, not something recited merely as a fairy tale or idle abstraction. Simply stated, the villagers *believed* the story and assumed that I did too, now that they had told it to me. Although I did not "believe" the story, courtesy and method naturally obliged me not to try to disabuse them of their belief or of their presumption of mine.

Polite gestures are often misinterpreted, especially when the message is ambiguous or noncommittal, or when the receiver is motivated to perceive the gesture in a particular way. These distortions operated upon my deliberately cryptic response to "Nambweapa'w." My tactful acceptance was taken by some, possibly many, to mean that I affirmed the story—a heady endorsement, indeed, coming from a white American male. More important, the restoration of Nambweapa'w's magic was a promise in which the villagers fervently wanted to believe. Bihinguf's broad hint as to the significance of my response should have alerted me, but a few hours' fieldwork had not equipped me to catch even broad hints, let alone perceive that I had already entered into the villagers' calculations, just as surely as they had entered into mine. From the first day, the observer was equally the observed.

Bihinguf was a solicitous, somewhat smarmy bachelor of about thirty, the second-oldest bachelor in the village. He had been present at the poolside recitation. During a private chat the following day, he surprised me by silkily suggesting that perhaps I already knew the story of "Nambweapa'w," but was pretending not to. "We think that the Australians have the same story," he said, "because of the cassowary and the wallaby that are pictured on the kiap's badge."[1] Bihinguf deduced that if the Australians knew about Nambweapa'w, the Americans certainly would too, since they are directly descended from the youngest brother. Failing to grasp the import of this odd accusation, I guffawed and denied knowing the story, whereupon Bihinguf nodded agreeably and let the matter drop. Many years would pass before I came to realize that my possible familiarity with the story was a matter of some urgency to Bihinguf and to the others who had put him up to asking me about it. The strength of their interest prevented my denial from being taken as final on the truth of the story's prophecy and my ultimate involvement with it. At the same time, their convictions were protected by the notion, widespread in Melanesia, that white men know to guffaw and deny whenever mythic, millenarian truth comes close to falling into black hands.

The tale's foretelling of Ilahita's future covers more than the parting promise that the youngest brother will return, though that particular prediction, being explicit, does have the effect of suffusing the entire story with a prophetic flavor. Of special note, the revenge killing of First Man consummates the "prophetic" scenario of deception leading to revelation and thence to retribution. While the sequence unfolds as a dramatic imperative internal to the story, as myth it projects the more universal moral truth that deceit is inevitably discovered and retributed. This is not to say that all deceit is always found out; mundane deceit often goes undiscovered, which is why it is mundane and, unless the perpetrator suffers psychic pain, uninteresting. But in the ideal realm of myth and philosophic fiction, deceit—an essential, unstable disordering of trustful things—*must* be discovered and answered; why else would it be imagined? As a kind of New Guinea version of Dostoyevsky's *Crime and Punishment,* "Nambweapa'w" used the dramatic sequence to disclose the wages of moral error.

From this, one should not suppose that "Nambweapa'w" was a homily or that Ilahita folks sat around discoursing about the story's moral significance. Notions such as sin and guilt, prominent in the Judeo-Christian moral vocabulary, are either absent or differently configured in Ilahita. People there do not pass moral judgment on mythic heroes or scenarios, any more than we would condemn Yahweh for conspiring with Satan to torment Job or the Olympians for their deadly mischief on the plains of Ilium. What we might perceive, not incorrectly, as the "moral argument" in "Nambweapa'w" is cast in terms sometimes uncomplimentary of characters and their deeds, but always pragmatic in tone. Storyteller and audience do not consider First Man "immoral" for deceiving the cassowary-woman—anyone in his position would have done the same—but careless for allowing the skin to be discovered. Nor are the siblings judged "immoral" for disobeying their mother—were that so, we would all stand condemned—but witless for squandering the magical benefits she had provided.

And yet, because morality, in whatever terms it is locally expressed, is about choices and consequences, the actions in the story are indeed morally salient. They are also ominous, insofar as male auditors recognize themselves in the role of deceiver in relation to women and therefore as potential targets of the Cassowary's Revenge. Of such unsettling awareness there can be no doubt: it was a topic of male conversation; it informed many beliefs and fantasies; and, most of all, it sustained the entire, massive ideology of Tambaran secrecy. Behind its seemingly amoral narrative, Nambweapa'w's story posited masculine culpability, exposing as fraudulent the men's claims to ritual legitimacy and warning that serious consequences were in store for the men's past and continuing deceits.

The portentous element in "Nambweapa'w" affected how villagers thought about the story and how they acted upon and in respect of it. Accordingly, the case of "Nambweapa'w" exemplifies how, consciously and not, cultural actors engage with and modify myths and other folktales and how contingent circumstances can move cultural actors to defend against or preempt that which is foretold. It was the manifold seriousness of the story—its implications for action—that I failed to perceive in my conversation with Bihinguf and that he took for granted. This is an important point. The vicissitudes of belief and action that surround myths, their varied and changeable significances, are often overlooked by anthropologists and folklorists, who, following their own habits of inquiry, generally take these tales as they are, as things to collect and exhibit, as butterflies of culture.

This is the place to insert an important clarification. One of the main arguments of this study is that "Nambweapa'w" changed significantly between my first and second periods of fieldwork and that this change was prompted both by alterations in Ilahita's social circumstances and by the prospect of my return. Further, the change occurred not primarily in the text—a small but significant textual alteration will be discussed in the next chapter—but in the people's apprehension of the story. In the early incident described above, Bihinguf's mission consisted of sleuthing out whether the story's millenarian promise was about to be realized in my person. At the time, the deceit-retribution scenario so central to the story was irrelevant to the dazzling idea that I might be, literally or cryptically, the returning little brother. Would that millennia were so easily achieved! Years later, in preparation for my actual return, amidst other apocalyptic ideas and actions, village leaders knew better that they could not achieve the end of Nambweapa'w's story without enduring the middle. Revealing the cult secrets, killing the Tambaran, precipitating the Deluge—these were the men's enactment of the cassowary-woman's fateful recovery of her skin. Just as the mythic revelation cleared the way for blissful living, so the emulatory act of masculine self-destruction was meant to clear the way for my apocalyptic return. The parallels between myth and life were too tempting for the people to ignore. Besides, as those closest to him and present at his deathbed believed, Gidion had gone to fetch me.

In theory as in practice, observers tend to assume that traditional stories are whole by definition and do not point outside themselves, except perhaps to other stories. As products of culture, they are axiomatically not reducible to historical or environmental events (the "naturalistic fallacy"), primitive philosophizing (the "intellectualist fallacy"), or psychodynamic or cognitive phenomena (the "psychologistic fallacy"). This doctrinal horror of "reductionism"—a horror that is an enduring tradition in anthropology[2]—makes it difficult to conceptualize the commonsense fact that external phenomena *must* find their way into myths, albeit tailored to fit internal structural and narrative features. Because fieldworkers rarely observe this happening (e.g., du Toit 1969; Clark 1993; cf. Wagner 1996), knowledge of the process is meager, and it is easy to ignore or deny it in theoretical formulations. One result is that no broad agreement exists as to how myths interact with social and historical circumstances, or as to why myth varies the whole world round, but not nearly as much as experience does. Why are certain objects of experience and not others incorporated into myths?

Claude Lévi-Strauss may have touched the mark when he observed that myth, music, and mathematics are the most direct expressions of reality. As the most manifest of all abstractions, they come closest to exhibiting the pristine structure of Mind (*l'esprit humain*).[3] Submitted to these modalities, drossy experience becomes tidied and purified, distilled to a crystalline truth that is untouched by its vagarious expressions. The intense structuredness of myth is made possible through the liberal use of fantasy—lived life is never so structured as that which is imagined can be—which also renders the medium ideal for projecting wishes, fears, and other primary-process thoughts. That is why, as is often observed, myths are like dreams, with one important difference. Whereas dreams are constrained only by the dreamer's personal imagination, myths, as representations of collective imagination, must embody ideas of considerable importance and generality in the population of adherents.[4] Idiosyncratic or culturally dystonic fantasies do not make it into the mythic canon, or do not stay long if they do. Thus the reality that myth narrativizes, consists of the hopes and fears that recur with some frequency in the cultural group. If the message of a myth seems trivial, it is because one has not looked deeply enough. And inasmuch as the existential conditions of collective human life are not limitless in their variety, it is not surprising that certain mythic ideas recur across cultures or, perhaps, universally.

Taking Lévi-Strauss at his word, if myth reveals a superior kind of truth, can it be that "prophetic" myths may actually foretell the future? To my Ilahita friends the answer was plainly affirmative in the case of "Nambweapa'w," because they accepted its historical veracity and took as literal and authoritative the promise of the youngest brother's return. Such credulity is not permitted a rational outsider like myself, however, who would have to be crazy, credulous, or exorbitantly relativistic to accept the prophetic claim at face value. But if the prophecy is seen to be inadvertently introspective rather than prospective, and if the future is affected by the present, then to that extent it is valid to regard the mythic insight as authentically predictive—in its way, genuinely prophetic.[5] Similarly, the story of Nambweapa'w is genuinely prophetic, not by virtue of the parting promise—the explicit "prophecy" to which Ilahita auditors subscribe—but because the Cassowary's Revenge both reveals and conceals the moral reckoning that men nervously apprehend under the regime of the Tambaran.

Prophecy's truth, then, like divination's, arises from truthful insights into the present. Notionally, of course, prophecy refers to the future. In

European and other traditions, it is commonly understood to be a pre-science inspired by a divine or demonic intelligence always external to the ego. Prophecies emerge from dreams, visions, trances, and possession states: mentalities in which the spiritual sense supposedly hearkens to and transmits authoritative pronouncements reaching it, significantly, from "outside." At the next remove are specialist interpreters: astrologers, necromancers, tarot and palm readers—fortune-tellers of all kinds, whose spiritual gift or training enables them to read signs from mysterious sources of knowledge. Though frequently claiming to predict the future, these latter adepts are not usually dignified as "prophets." Operating outside formal religious channels of authority, they are often calumniated by those inside as pagans or devil worshipers.

And yet, orthodoxy aside, prophecy and those renegade forms are theoretically all very close; all are forms of divination. Indeed, in the Judeo-Christian tradition the power that prophets use to "foretell the future" arises from a more fundamental and etymologically older ability to reveal the will of God. Past, present, future—all are one to a Mind that encompasses everything, even temporality, within itself.[6] In its nontheistic version, prophecy implies insight into *the nature of things,* their occult essence and connectedness. As such, prophesying is an activity not so different from astrologically revealing causalities between human lives and astral bodies or tracing destiny in the lines of a hand. And, to repeat, the human practitioner is perceived to be the conduit—the medium—of such knowledge, not the source.

In Ilahita, too, individuals receive prophetic or divinatory knowledge from sources supposedly external to the ego. Dreams are said to be the wanderings of the sleeper's spirit on another plane, sometimes featuring encounters with spirits of dead persons who convey prophetic messages. Other dream images are conventional symbols that divine or foretell events in the life of the dreamer. For example, if a man dreams of himself carrying a large spear, it is a sign from a yam spirit or ancestral spirit— the two are practically indistinguishable—that a giant yam is ready to be harvested. When a person dies, sorcery is nearly always the presumed cause, and various divination procedures are used to consult ancestral spirits as to the guilty party. Prophetic knowledge, in short, may come in the form of an explicit, oracular message received from outside the ego, usually from a dead ancestor acting either on his own or on behalf of other entities of the spirit realm.

Another type of "exogenous" knowledge is compelling because it arises from *collective* experience, thus producing a mysterious magnification of the self. One man pulling on a rope produces a proportionate effect; a *hundred* men pulling on a rope produces an effect far out of proportion to any one of them, with the odd corresponding result that each experiences the strength of the hundred. Similarly, one man idly singing a Tambaran song hears his own voice and is entertained by it. When a *hundred* men sing in loud choral unison, individuals cannot hear their own voices: the voice of the one disappears into the many, only to echo back to each and every singer the illusion that his voice has the majesty of the hundred. This mysterious, transcendent, self-ish presence is the ultimate magic of the Tambaran, its Voice, whose singing materializes the stupendous power of the spirits.

Perhaps even more remarkable, because it combines the mysteries of collectivity and heritage, is wisdom borne of tradition, knowledge descending from a time beyond memory. Charter myths and just-so stories are obvious examples, but not all such knowledge is signified with full-blown narratives.

Once, for example, I watched while senior cult members employed a secret technique to excavate deep, narrow postholes for the new spirit house.[7] Marveling at the ingenuity of the technique I asked rhetorically, as one does at such moments, "Who ever thought up that idea?" A man working nearby took me literally, glanced quizzically at his fellows, and declared that no one had ever thought of that technique. The others nodded in agreement.

"Come now," I said, warming to the topic, "*someone* must have thought of it. It didn't just come from nowhere." My interlocutor explained that such ideas are received from tradition; they come from olden times (MP: *bun graun*), not from ordinary men. "I understand," I persisted, "but someone at some time must have invented it!" A couple more exchanges of this type followed, and then: "Let me ask you this," said one of the men, with friendly condescension. "Could *you* have invented this technique?" "No," I admitted, unable to avoid the trap. "That is true of us, too," the man said, resting his case.

This indigenous notion of inherited knowledge—*waf,* or "custom," if I may gloss it so—extends to many other ideas and practices. They amount to gifts or blessings or dubious bequests, things designed for human use or delectation but with sources mysteriously located either in the collective present or in the immemorial past. Myth is the example par excellence of inherited knowledge, because it is at once the purest manifestation of the form—quintessential custom—and a native theory of it. Myth dealienates the Other (the mysterious source) by personifying it, making it a veiled facsimile of the Self. Thus, all myths worth their salt are "prophetic" in that they penetrate to the "nature of things" and are able thereby to echo back to ego its own, inchoate intuitions—refined and enhanced, packaged and delivered, as it were, from "outside." Hence the uncanny, difficult-to-ignore quality of myth and its prophecies.

Most prophecies fail and are forgotten. Of those that succeed, many are lucky guesses; others predict outcomes so highly probable as to be trivial. The safest "prophecies" are retrodictive: created after the purported outcome, they invent or resignify prior events so as to imbue them with prophetic implication. Whether fraudulent or naive, such retrodictions often affirm personal religious beliefs and the interests of religious authority.

Another species of retrodictive prophecy is not religious in a strict sense, but rather it addresses broader metaphysical understandings about how and why things are as they are. Origin stories and other "charter myths" are of this type, in that they posit imaginary predeterminations. Nambweapa'w's prophetic curse—a mother's curse, the most powerful of all—ordains the ills of today. Symbolic plenitude and fittedness occur because the story is culturally embedded; which is to say, its meanings depend upon associations with other ideas held by the Ilahita. Just as one analyzes a dream by first eliciting the associations its reported elements have *for the dreamer,* so one analyzes a myth by first annotating it with ideas and images found elsewhere in the cultural repertoire. A successful analysis is one that retraces, mirrors, or otherwise recaptures the process by which meaning is created and sustained.[8] The associated ideas enrich the story qua myth by giving it a depth of implied, reflective meaning beneath the story line; they certify its nativity to the particular cultural tradition and comprise the framework of insight that enables mythic prophecy to be true, in its fashion. Contrary, then, to those who would hold that a text must be understood purely in its own terms, myths are quintessentially relational. Whatever Lévi-Straussian, Freudian, Jungian, or other universal elements they may contain, such tales must first be understood in local

103

terms. For it is by virtue of such local associations that myths prophesy in accordance with the nature of cultural things.

To interpret, therefore, Nambweapa'w's symbolic appeal, and the gripping, prophetic significance of her deeds, we must examine the story for elements that associate it with other ideas and conditions of Ilahita culture. We begin with the local setting of the story.

During walks in and around Ilahita it often happened that a companion would point to some landscape feature and say, "That place has a story" and then proceed to tell it to me. A cluster of boulders would be no ordinary rock pile, but a group of petrified humans who had once offended a bush demon. An improbable rod-shaped stone jutting up five feet out of bedrock would not be what it seemed, however improbably, but the culture-hero Baingap's lime stick, scarred by generations of yam magicians taking scrapings for their potions. As often as not, the speaker would be someone not very good at recalling traditional tales spontaneously or on demand; the landmark was what jarred memory. Such storied associations were clearly invested with sentiment, for it did not seem to matter that I might already know the story, perhaps had heard it from the same companion. I would hear it again. This may simply have been a way of making conversation. My suspicion, though, is that such stories are remembered, regardless of anyone else's presence, especially if the place is considered dangerous. Incantation, amusement, mnemonic—all three—the story renews the rememberer's membership in the imaginal landscape of myth and legend.[9] And vice versa: as relays in the transmission of an oral tradition these rememberings sustain the imaginal landscape itself (Young 1983; Barth 1987).

The most famous of all the landmarks belonging to Ilahita is the pool in which Nambweapa'w and her maiden companions were first espied. The story's vitality is helped by the fact that its opening scene is set right in the village—an ever-present reminder of Ilahita's First Lady. Many people pass by the site practically on a daily basis. It lies alongside a busy path (nowadays a vehicular road) connecting Balanga ward with its garden lands, the neighboring ward of Nangup, and Arapesh and Kwanga villages to the south. One can easily imagine generations of parents and grandparents, prompted by the sight of the pool, telling Nambweapa'w's story to youngsters and visitors or to each other.

The effect of this re-cognition is magnified in the case of "Nambweapa'w" because the place and the story are proudly claimed by the entire village, not merely a local clan or residence group. Everyone in Ilahita has the right to tell the story, and, it would seem, everyone does. The villagers do not doubt that Nambweapa'w's pool is a landmark of global importance, for it is the spot where *all* people began. Indeed, one woman in my original escort group wondered aloud how Ilahita would feed and shelter the throngs of international visitors who would surely come once the story of Nambweapa'w became generally known. This gentle boast was my first encounter with a notion recurrent in Ilahita, namely, that all the world was interested in their village because what happened there could (and, in the beginning, *did*) affect all humanity.

Taking me to the pool was thus their way of introducing the village, displaying its most famous and distinctive feature. A short time earlier I had explained to them that I was there to find out all I could about Ilahita—its stories, customs, and language. My new friends took me at my word. Nambweapa'w, the Cassowary-Mother, was *theirs*. Her story was what the village was about; it was necessary for me to know it, if I was to understand Ilahita. In the quarter century that has passed since that introduction, events and my own reflections have confirmed the prophetic truth of their claim.

A moment ago I mentioned that particular landscape features attract symbolic attention because they are unusual. Nambweapa'w's bathing pool stirs the mythic imagination in part because of the rarity of such bodies in this part of the Sepik hinterland. More than a landmark, the pond is a geographic curiosity. The only comparable formation in the area is a small lake far away in the mountains above Maprik, which Ilahita did not know about until fairly recently. Local water catchments do occur, but on a much smaller scale, such as where a stream makes a bend or encounters a boulder or log and the eddying or damming action creates a small pool.

These pools, along with other anomalies, such as boulder clusters, gigantic or oddly shaped trees, steep declivities, or swampy spots aglow with luminescent, decay-eating fungi, are nearly always assumed to be inhabited by some kind of spirit entity. The most colorful and exotic of these are *maolinipunemb* (MP: *masalai*), named bush demons who often figure in stories told about these places (cf. Mead 1933; 1940, 341–42).[10] Masalai mischief ranges from inducing miscarriages to causing earthquakes and severe weather. Shape shifting is within their power, as when one leaves its lair to assume an animal disguise,[11] engage in petty thievery, play disappearing tricks on twilight travelers, or impersonate a husband visiting his wife's bed. Masalai, in short, are tricksters—capricious, amoral, lustful, impish, and playful in a nasty sort of way.

Masalai who inhabit watery places may, it is thought, traffic with spirits of the ancestral dead—lordly beings who cannot leave the water and whose character is opposite that of masalai.[12] To be exact, these are the spirits of deceased men (not women or children) who have been dead for some time but who were known in life by descendants who are still living. The latter proviso is necessary because ancestral spirits represent only the second of three successive states undergone by persons after death.[13] These should be described in some detail, as background to Nambweapa'w's pronounced association with the afterlife—or, perhaps more accurately, Otherlife.

Ghosts. During the time a corpse's flesh is decaying, its ghost is considered to be highly dangerous. Thrust from life, the spirit of the dead is forgetful of normal manners and terrified by its new condition. Toward the living the ghost is wrathful and envious, yet it desperately longs to be with them again. Erratic, in effect situationally insane, a ghost is liable to kill the living, randomly or for reasons susceptible of divination. In the immediacy of an imagined encounter, male ghosts and female ghosts are feared equally; gender niceties do not apply when you wake to an icy hand grasping yours in the night or when an apparition crosses your lonely jungle path at twilight. In more dispassionate moments of divination or ethnographic conversation, however, ghostly phenomena are described as having gender differences. When attack by a male ghost is suspected, the act is often interpreted as revenge against the person who, physically or by sorcery, caused its death. The ghost knows who the culprit is, but the wherewithal to take revenge is provided by a living magician, usually a surviving kinsman. Consequently, attacks and accusations involving putative male ghosts occur at an emotional distance, that is to say, between estranged or enemy parties—actions which, paraphrasing Clausewitz, are a continuation of war by other means.

Although, in theory, female ghosts may be enlisted to avenge their own deaths, in practice the reasons given for their attacks are nearly always otherwise, for the victims are nearly always close family members. The charitable explanation is that the lady ghost kills in order to reunite with the spirits of loved ones left behind. As a mother, the ghost would naturally wish to have her children with her in death. As a *woman,* however, now with ghostly strength and awareness, she is imagined to desire revenge for the tricks and wrongs dealt her in life. Her situation is not unlike that of Nambweapa'w upon recovering her cassowary skin and the otherworldly powers that go with it. In both cases, the impulse for revenge settles on the deceiving husband. No ghost is more dangerous to a man than that of his newly dead wife; pitiful it is to see the double burden of sorrow and fear that oppresses a man when his wife dies, especially if they had been together for a long time.

During this transitional stage of ghosthood, when not scaring people or causing nightmares, the spirit (male or female) haunts the water shrine of its mother's patriclan. Undoing the accumulation of flesh that occurred during gestation, childhood, and adolescence—a process mystically sponsored by a person's mother's clan—the dead flesh dissolves into the maternal waters from whence it came. This image fits with local descent ideology, corresponding notions about the body, and recurrent mythic associations between femininity, birth, death, and watery media (Tuzin 1976, 1977). Familiar, intimate, and yet disturbingly ego-alien, the moral and affective "maternal" conditions in which the newly dead find themselves were tellingly summarized by one informant, who compared the ghost's bizarre behavior to that of a newborn child: bewildered, agitated, and violent—but in the ghost's case, also possessed of superhuman power.

Ancestors. When the bones are dry, the spirit flies to take up permanent residence in the water shrine of its patriclan, its transit visible as a light streaking across the night sky—in our terms, a meteor.[14] The change in status from free-ranging ghost to water-bound ancestral shade finalizes the return of living, pseudosolid flesh to its aqueous elements[15]—back to the water-filled hole from which the flesh emerged in the first place. Death, then, is a reversion to the watery place that precedes birth; death, in other words, like birth, is about women.[16]

More will be said about the symbolic nexus of water, women, birth, and death. For now I need only observe that Nambweapa'w's associations with a pool, in the beginning, and a flood, in the end, beyond contributing to the narrative, signify her spiritual union with the dead and the unborn. Unlike men, whose powers owe themselves to technologies of magic, cult initiation, and ritual hygiene, her more awesome powers spring from her essential being. For living Arapesh males, Nambwea-pa'w—primal mother, quintessential woman, timeless avenger—is the ultimate nemesis.

Although dependence on a watery medium restricts the ancestors' mobility, there is a way for them to go abroad from their shrines, for example, to attend funerals and Tambaran ceremonies among the living. At such times they harbor in ground-crab holes. These small excavations occur commonly in sheltered spots around the village, typically in the cramped space formed just inside the place where the sloping thatch of the A-frame houses meets the ground. The animal digs a vertical shaft ending in a hollowed-out cavity and locates its nest on a shelf carved into the wall of the shaft. When, during heavy storms, some water finds its way into the hole, it bypasses the nest and flows into the lower chamber. There it stays: absorption is retarded by the dense, clayey soil, and evaporation is minimized by the narrow diameter and shaded mouth of the shaft. Even during prolonged dry spells, water persists at the bottom of many of these holes and is therefore available to ancestral spirits whenever they require temporary accommodation in the village.

Picture, then, a humanish spirit, tiny in size but mighty in implication, nurturantly suspended within a water-filled vessel, animated and yet not living, in a state adjacent to life, where breathing is not possible or necessary. Evoking not only death and the afterlife, but birth and the *prelife*—specifically, a being in utero—this image condenses the Arapesh atmospherics of death, birth, water, and femininity.

In another story that draws upon this association, a pregnant woman finds herself—never mind how—hanging stranded from a cloud. Her husband, unable to rescue her, digs a hole in the ground in order to catch the drippings of her bodily decay. This happens, and at length the fetus itself drops into the hole, there to complete gestation in these waters of maternal death. In due course a baby boy is "born" from the hole and grows up to be a handsome hero, with superhuman powers acquired from having incorporated his mother's ghostly essences.

The vitality of the birth-death-water-woman association is confirmed in other mythic and ritual contexts (Tuzin 1977). In "Nambweapa'w" it informs the significance of the pool at the beginning, the flood at the end, and the otherwise inscrutable detail of the *ground-crab hole*. Recall that when the youngest son threw his grass spear in search of Nambweapa'w, it pierced a ground-crab hole next to where she was sitting.[17] In view of the associations just reviewed, no more efficient image than this could connect Nambweapa'w's with death, birth, water, and, in this particular instance, maternal and (by association) sibling incest.

The ancestral dead are thought to take a benign interest in the affairs of the living, in particular the welfare of their descendants.[18] Men apply to their dead fathers for assistance in magical endeavors, confident of a positive response. When the cause of a death or illness is under investigation, it is the dead who give signs in answer to the diviner's questions. Their messages are sometimes occult and open to interpretation, but never false. The dead uphold conventional morality, but with a flexibility that, recognizably human, puts the interests of living kith and kin before those of any larger collective. Their politics and sentiments are similar to what they were in life, but now they assist their survivors with deathly power and insight. Whatever traffic may occur among themselves and with other creatures of that realm, their orientation is mainly toward the living.

Power. When all filial connection expires and there is none left alive who knew him in life, the spirit sheds personal identity and merges into a reservoir of power. The nature of this power is not specified, but from it flows the mysterious energy that animates all preceding conditions of life and death. Although this stage is the one least understood or talked about, some generalities are possible.

To begin with, this ancestrally derived spiritual force—if I may call it that—is at once remote and near. It is a repository of supreme moral values, the consciousness operating from which bestows prosperity, fertility, war success, and, when necessary, punishments on the living. Strictly speaking, the dead at this ultimate stage are not "ancestral," insofar as they are depersonified, anonymous, and preside unitarily over the entire village. They are the pure virtue remaining after all social and historical contingency has fallen away. Links to the living occur via the filial ties of ancestral spirits proper, who obscurely answer to that more remote agency. If a member of the living violates a taboo or prescription—invariably, it would appear, a Tambaran rule—the sentence of death, disease, or disfigurement originates at this highest level but is administered by the cognizant Tambaran spirit, who authorizes and empowers a living sorcerer to do the actual deed. If calamity befalls the entire community—famine, drought, epidemic, earthquake—blame is not assigned to spirits of the dead (of any stage), but to the largely amoral acts of a masalai.[19]

The diffuse character of this spiritual force does not lend itself to being identified with particular landscape features. The watery habitat of the preceding stage seems no longer to be binding, and people are generally unclear as to precisely where these most senior spirits reside. Once, when pressed on the question, a circle of ritually sophisticated men speculated that they live beyond the village, beyond the gardens and sago groves and water shrines, in the deep forest. On the whole, the issue was not as compelling to them as was, for example, the question of where ancestors or ghosts are to be found or avoided.

The idea of a deep forest habitation is intriguing to our discussion, however, for that is also the abode of cassowaries, various minor sprites and masalai, and, significantly, Tambaran spirits during the ritual "off season." The latter are brought or summoned from the forest when needed, installed in a house built especially for them on one of the village's ceremonial plazas, and rudely chased back to the forest when the initiation or other cult event is completed. Tambaran spirits are thought to collaborate with both the water-bound ancestral spirits and those of the higher level (forest?) category. Indeed, the name of the highest Tambaran grade, *nggwal,* is the generic term for the individually named cult spirits who are seen to be clan patrons, *and* it is the name given to that group of cult spirits. In the latter sense, the capitalized Nggwal is the apotheosis of clan spirits, which, conversely, are the forms Nggwal adopts in direct dealings with humans. During its season Nggwal becomes what the Tambaran is all the time and in all seasons: the mystic totality into which the people, the clans, the cult, and the village society—all are merged (Tuzin 1980).

The point is that the dual sense of "nggwal" and "Nggwal" closely parallels the dual sense of ancestral and postancestral dead.[20] Those of the first term are still implicated in life and history, having finite careers of their own; those of the second are abstractions that transcend such limitations. But neither Nggwal nor the transcendent dead are totally unbound, fully abstracted; for each in its way—ways so similar as to be interchangeable and confusable—exists by and for the *village* community.

Arapesh ideas about spirits of the dead and other imagined creatures are sometimes fragmentary and ambiguous, but they agree on the fundamental otherness of that realm and on the presumption that its diverse inhabitants communicate and are aware of each other's activities. Spiritual otherness is typically projected onto parts of the landscape where humans normally do not go. Except under unusual and temporary circumstances, spirits do not enter the village, and when living folks enter *their* realm—in watery areas or in the deep forest, or where natural forces have wrought something "unnatural"—they do so with feelings of creepiness and unease.

On the other hand, it must be remembered that "the Other" is an oxymoron, a projection of the same Ego that produces the Self. That culture and the human psyche incorporate both Self and Other is manifest in Arapesh theories about dreams and trances, in ritual practices, and in the presence of otherly formations within village precincts. Nambweapa'w's pool, a giant, masalai-harboring ficus tree near my house, a salt spring adjacent to another hamlet—such local anomalies indicate that this mystic power of the Other is also attractive to the Self, who shelters in its presence and is spiritually enlivened by its proximity. The Other is of no use to the Self if it is too far away. By the same logic, when Nggwal builds his great house, he prefers to locate it alongside a gigantic tree—a tree that has a "story."

If I have carried on at some length about Arapesh ideas concerning death and the Otherlife, it is to make the important point that these "off-text" associations irradiate the story of Nambweapa'w with cultural and emotional significance. The Cassowary-Mother's powers and her affinity with water and with the forest are clues that she belongs to the spirit world; other details specify this as an involvement with death.[21] The ground-crab hole is one clear example; so, too, is the fact that Nambweapa'w instructed her children to seek for her in the grass fields by *blowing a conch shell* and calling her name as they walked along. Thus, at twilight on the day of a funeral, members of the immediate family gather in the hamlet of the deceased. There they hold a moving ceremony that involves blowing conch shells and then calling the name of the dead person into the surrounding jungle. If an answer—"Mwein?" ("What?")—is "heard," it is a message to all, but especially the husband, that the uxorial ghost harbors no ill feeling. Such responses are often "heard" by survivors, presumably by a trick of the ear prompted by their desire for reassurance. To my knowledge, this instrument is only used to call out to the dead. No other sound-making device is used for this purpose, and I am not aware that conch shells function in any other context.

Nambweapa'w, then, by virtue of these associations, has an affinity with death. As she trips between life and the Otherworld of death, she marks the main turning points of the tale. Her voluntary demise near the end of the story repeats, but with greater finality, the earlier abandonment of her family, when she departed for the world of her true nature. Whether that world is some other *place* or is the world she carries with her and embodies in her cassowary form is hardly relevant. What matters is that that world is wherever she is, and when she departs, by dying or by abandoning her human family, that world goes with her.

Recalling the symbolic associations of death and water, the mythmaker's choice of *water* as the medium that rises up and carries off the obedient, beloved son signifies that he is following his mother to the land of the dead. His departure in a blaze of moral indignation is coupled with Nambweapa'w's equally moralistic death, linked and yet separated by the venal, self-centered acts of the siblings. Mother and son leave the living and the mundane; or rather they *create* the mundane as a residuum by taking with them the knowledge and power that made existence idyllic.

But of course the story does not say that the son died, only that he went away. Death is converted into abandonment. For the surviving siblings, the loss is the same. But denial of the finality of mortal loss permits the consoling hope and expectation, stated explicitly at the end of the story, that the little brother *will return*. Part of the story's perennial fascination lies in that prophetic promise, which unites mythic past and mythic future and defines the present as an unfortunate, mundane interregnum. Hence the Revivalist notion that this unhappy interlude could be made *prelude* to a glorious future that would begin immediately. But I am getting ahead of myself: alerted to the possibility that the story is, among other things, a lightly disguised examination of death and its meaning for life, let us consider "Nambweapa'w" more carefully.

The reasons for the story's popular appeal are plain to see. Like all good myths, "Nambweapa'w" unites the faraway with the near-at-hand: it is about the first people and about how things of today began and what they mean. It is an entertainment of magic and enchantment, woven with primordial strands of fear, violence, abandonment, and deep nostalgic longing. It is also a tale of suspense, centered on the theft and recovery of Nambweapa'w's animal skin, her husband's duplicity, and the revenge that is hers on discovering she had been tricked. The stack of skins, with one too few, leads to Nambweapa'w's temporary undoing; the stack of spears, with one too many, leads to her husband's permanent undoing. The structural symmetry fulfills the listener's expectation that a plot premised on a deception must proceed to a revelation of the deception, with retribution proportional to the insult. But in this case, does the punishment fit the crime? For that matter, are Nambweapa'w's self-sacrificial death and society's fall from its idyllic beginnings appropriate penalties for the breaking of a food taboo? From somewhere deep within the Ilahita psyche, the judge nods yes to both questions.

Is it reasonable to observe that the punishments are excessive? Judging from the murmurs of Arapesh listeners, and their occasional startled laughters, they, too, are impressed by the severity of Nambweapa'w's revenges. For scholars who treat myths and other cultural products as literary texts complete unto themselves, however, this protest would be irrelevant: the punishment, like the myth itself, like Adam's navel, *is as it is*. The issue of severity, because it is absent from the text, does not exist except as the observer's moral or aesthetic imposition. Nor (to continue the contrary argument) should it surprise us that the punishments are extreme: mythic punishments usually are, manifesting the fantastical nature common to the mythic genre. This position, then, maintains not one but two relativisms, both of which blunt the analytic probe: the relativity of the *text*, which prohibits the exogenous questioning of moral and aesthetic anomalies; and the relativity of the genre, which shields mythic reality from contradictions based on the facts of life and everyday understandings.

Rather than explain away the extreme punishments by relativizing them, I would argue that such excesses are not random or emotionally neutral, but are part of the "myth-work"[22] through which psychocultural meanings are variously revealed, concealed, and constituted in the narrative mode. The myth-work occurs when the tale is first created—a forgotten or denied moment that, in itself, has a paradoxical, distinctly mythic character—and also in the retellings, when, consciously or not, off-text associations permeate the listener's meaningful engagement with the story. In this light, the exorbitant aspect of Nambweapa'w's reprisals may indicate that the offenses in question are far more serious than they might appear. Anomalies in the surface structure, in other words, help to resonate deeper, more occult significance. The exaggerated deception-discovery motif, for example, enlisting other polarities such as gender and age, sparks the arcane idea that these moments of encounter between illusion and truth illumine the junction of life and death. To characterize the junction between life and death is to know what life and death *are*— surely a metaphysical achievement worthy of a myth of human origins.

Some of the off-text associations of "Nambweapa'w" have already been examined. For example, the seemingly trivial and unnecessary detail of the "ground-crab hole" serves to connect "Nambweapa'w" with collateral notions of death, birth, and femininity; likewise, independent beliefs concerning cassowaries confer phallically aggressive femininity on this particular "swan maiden." By knitting the story into the fabric of Ilahita imagination, such strands furnish both information and credibility for the prophetic insights of "Nambweapa'w" into local cultural problems. There is nothing mysterious or deeply unconscious about these associations; unless elicited under questioning (by me), they simply exist as parts of an implicit, natively accessible background to the narrative momentarily commanding attention. Without this background, though, the story would fail to evoke the audience's interest or sense of recognition. Let us identify a few more of the strands connecting Nambweapa'w with her Ilahita descendants.

• Nambweapa'w has several direct associations with the Tambaran, some more fully integrated than others. For example, in the secret story of "Kamba'wa," which tells of an important Tambaran spirit by that name, the protagonists are a group of young boys who accidentally discover the spirit during their play (Tuzin 1980, 205–6). After netting and killing a large cassowary that they intend to feed to Kamba'wa, the boys panic and run away from the carcass, suddenly fearing that the cassowary is actually a masalai. That night, the dead cassowary appears to them in their dreams. She is not a cassowary, she declares, but Nambweapa'w! The boys should return and eat her body; for the power of her flesh will make them great yam growers and love magicians. This the boys do; but they do not live to become great, because the men find out about Kamba'wa and seize it, killing the boys to ensure their silence.

"Kamba'wa" is the slender justification for Nambweapa'w's inclusion in certain Tambaran contexts. The facade of the Nggwal Bunafunei spirit house features a handsome lintel, carved with a recumbent Nambweapa'w and her human consort at opposite ends, separated "paper-doll" fashion by their alternately sexed children. Protruding from the right front (facing) of the house is a colorful effigy in wood and plant materials of a cassowary, which represents Nambweapa'w and is also referred to as the "left foot of Nggwal" (Tuzin 1980, 193). Among the secret sound-making devices that represent the "voice" of Nggwal, one consists of a slitgong, the opening of which is covered with broad taro leaves. A bamboo tube is inserted into the covered chamber, and the operator vocalizes deep booming shouts into the tube, in imitation of Nambweapa'w. The effect is, indeed, a reasonable imitation of the thrumming sound made by a cassowary. The coital imagery of a stiff pipe inserted into a slitted vessel, which occurs also in the pipe-in-drum configuration of another of Nggwal's voices (Tuzin 1980, 242), explicitly supports the professed purpose of this rite: the renewal of all life forms.

The Tambaran not only draws upon Nambweapa'w's creative potencies, it invokes her as a means for subsuming themes of death and old age. In the dimly lit interior of the spirit house of Nggwal Walipeine, the "old men's Tambaran," standing inconspicuously to one side by itself, is a small figurine representing "Nambweapa'w" in her human form. No official explanation or function attaches to "her" presence, only that "she" belongs there. It is probably significant, however, that the figurine is positioned so as to face the inner sanctum of the Nggwal Walipeine house, which is a chamber built in the center of the floor area. Resembling an inverted, elongated tub, the chamber's outer walls consist of panels exquisitely painted to represent lacy broad leaves. Their predominantly white coloration befits the whiteness of old age and the pale ashes that proverbially dust the skins of old persons, as they sleep close to the hearth. Within the chamber are hidden the sacred drums and pipes that are this Tambaran's "voice." These paraphernalia, along with the men who operate them from within the chamber, are said to be First Man from the story—ancient, decrepit, cowering beneath the taro leaves moments before Nambweapa'w does him to death. The Tambaran's message is that this is the oblivion that soon awaits old men as they enter this final grade of the cult.

• Nambweapa'w changes state by removing or putting on her (cassowary) skin. A similar image occurs elsewhere in the Ilahita mythic canon, only there it involves a man, and the skin in question is the one he wears as an old man. The man is Imoina, whom the narrator identifies as Baingap's younger brother, grown old in the years since Baingap's departure (Tuzin 1980, 250–53).[23] For amusement, Imoina occasionally tricks his young wife by doffing his wrinkled skin and presenting himself to her as Imoina's handsome "young friend." The wife eventually suspects that something is amiss and sets their young son to spy on him. The truth is reported to her. The next time Imoina plays his game, she denounces him to his (young) face. Imoina, angrily ashamed at being exposed, impulsively throws his lime stick at the woman, striking her on the breast. To Imoina's regret, she turns into a parrot and flies away, calling in the raucous, scolding voice that is now its signature.

• The alternating sexes of the primal children is convenient as regards the nuptial pairing that Nambweapa'w mandates later in the story; it is also the preferred birth ordering among latter-day Arapesh, who, until very recently, practiced sister-exchange marriage. According to my 1969 sociological census, approximately half of extant marriages had been formed in this manner. This comparatively high frequency was achieved with the help of liberal adoption practices within the agnatic group. Children were shuffled about to correct naturally occurring sex imbalances within the nuclear or extended family; alternatively, requital could be deferred until the next generation, allowing a man to surrender a child, rather than a sister, to the group from whom he acquired his wife. Of the 30 percent of marriages that were not sister exchanges, most involved wives who had been widows, divorcées, or war captives or were of poor character or physically deformed. Such women were usually added to households as secondary wives or as first wife to a man who was grossly undesirable himself or had lost his father at a young age and was without an exchange contract when he entered adulthood. The custom of bride-price was known to exist among some other New Guinea peoples—Ilahita men had heard about it while working on the coastal or island plantations—but was considered morally offensive because it treated women as objects to be bought and sold. As one man put it, "Women are important. They are not like anything else you could give in exchange. A man should have to give a woman in order to get a woman."

Logically, this exchange principle implies the equation sister = wife. Men realize, of course, that the equivalence is notional, not real, and yet many of their usages appear to embody recognition of something more literal—a cultural flirtation, one might say, with the incestuous overtones of the exchange. A sister is given and "comes back" as a wife.[24] When men talk or litigate about a sister or daughter, it is almost always in reference to the kinswoman as a marriage-exchange object, reminding one of the cartoon fox who hungrily eyes the barnyard hen as already plucked, roasted, and on a platter or the king who beholds his infant not as the puking, colicky thing it is, but as heir to the throne.

Likewise, the Ilahita sister-exchange pattern permits an easy, idiomatic inversion of marriage and incest categories: a man hungry for marriage beholds his sister and sees in her a wife; a man wishing his line to prosper beholds a daughter and sees in her both the wife of his son and a vehicle of immediate political alliance. By a parallel logic, one does not eat one's own pig—"That would be like eating your child"—but gives it in exchange for another's pig, which *can* be eaten. Eating one's own yams is quite allowable, but the previous reasoning still applies, in that people go out of their way to exchange them. The seeming redundancy of exchanging yams instills the mundane act of eating with the charisma of the Gift, the sentiments of commensality, and the peculiar spiritual efficacy that surrounds the joint estate of an exchange partnership. Yam and pig exchanges are therefore the de rigueur core element in all ritual feasts.[25]

Exchanging like for like resolves what Annette B. Weiner (1992) calls "the paradox of keeping-while-giving." In Ilahita marriage practice, men "keep" their sisters by substituting wives for them. Indeed, traditionally, a preadolescent girl was sent to join the household of her fiancé, "as a sister," there to complete her growth and, by virtue of living with the family and eating its yams, absorb the spiritual essences upon which a harmonious, prosperous marriage with that family depends. The implication is fairly explicit: to be a wife, a woman must first be a sister.

"Nambweapa'w" capitalizes upon the incestuous core of sister-exchange marriage. The mass marriage ordered by the Cassowary-Mother imagines a mythic moment when the absence of other people requires sisters actually to become wives, collapsing the sister-wife equivalence gently upon itself. With a tidiness unknown in normal exchange transactions, all sisters become wives, while the Cassowary-Mother becomes a very special wife to her sisterless youngest son. The pairings are not only logical and expedient, they lead the characters into a blissful, though short-lived, existence in which all needs are magically fulfilled. In itself, primal incest is not unusual; it occurs in many of the world's myths of origin, and, along with the arguably universal incest taboo, has received a good deal of anthropological attention. What makes this instance native to Ilahita is that the incest theme utilizes the device of the "(long) line of alternately sexed children," the culturally ideal arrangement to which all

117

responsible parents aspire, naturally or by adoption. Integrating the story with its home culture, the mythmaker conjures up the incestuous spirit from within conventional sister exchange and redeploys it to formulate and authenticate primal incest in Nambweapa'w's creation saga.[26]

• Meanwhile, the sibling incest sets the scene for the less explicit but unmistakable incestuous tie between Nambweapa'w and her youngest son. Storytellers differ slightly on this detail: some ignore the implications of the sibling marriage arrangement for the sisterless youngest son; others aver that, because the youngest had no one to wed, Nambweapa'w clasped him to her or looked after him, or, less commonly, married him. Whatever the euphemism used, the incestuous implication is clear enough and is, in my view, fully intended. My impression is that storytellers, along with their audience, find the idea of mother-son incest a little too raw and uncomfortable to exhibit openly, whereas they do not seem to mind addressing sibling incest, if the story calls for it. Father-daughter incest appears in no stories that I have heard; though rare in actual behavior, it nonetheless occurs with much greater frequency than do the other types.[27]

The maternal incest in the second half of the story is enhanced by another tale that also unites this theme with a magically produced, idyllic village. The story[28] goes that the brothers Wilitin and Amilawen hunt for birds every day and bring them to their elderly mother.

Wilitin, the older brother, only manages to catch black and drab-colored birds; Amilawen always brings birds of paradise and others of gay plumage, which the mother prefers. Wilitin is jealous and secretly drowns Amilawen in a water-filled hole he prepares for the purpose. Suspecting foul play, the mother finds Amilawen's body and revives it with stinging insects.[29]

During the next several months, while hiding the young man from his older brother, she fashions a rope. When it is long enough, she attaches one end to her vulva [or, depending on the storyteller, to the rear of her house] and sends Amilawen away, playing the rope out behind him. After many days he runs out of rope and encircles an area with the last segment. He sleeps. In the morning he wakes to find that an attractive village has sprung up within the circle of the rope. In each house is a beautiful, obliging maiden. He marries them all. A year later, his mother follows the rope and joins him there, where they all live happily together.

In due course, Wilitin discovers the rope trail, follows it to the enchanted village, and there beseeches his little brother to give him some of his wives. Amilawen magnanimously gives his brother two desirable women—in the guise, however, of sprouted coconuts. After some minor mishaps confirming Wilitin to be an envious oaf, he arrives home with the two coconuts, which turn back into women. They replace the tree kangaroos he has had as wives until then, which is how men came to have human women as wives.

As in the story of "Nambweapa'w," it is the unsympathetic older brother who is ancestral. His misdeeds stem not from a wicked nature, or even from ill-will, but from dunderheadedness; his character winds up abject and dependent. The smarter, appealing, helpful younger brother, on the other hand, is the one who goes away, enjoys special favor with the mother, achieves sexual and material fulfillment on a grand scale, and pursues a blissful existence in an Other place.[30] He is brought back from the dead; more precisely, his mother's labors effect his "rebirth" from a water-filled hole. He is then dispatched by her to an Other place—a magical place, which, attached to her private parts, amounts to a remote womb. The action may not be identical to that in "Nambweapa'w," but the two stories plainly occupy the same psychological and existential domain: a fantasy realm bounded by envy, greed, discord, regret, nostalgia, sexuality, death, (re)birth, return, and motherhood. Along this subnarrative dimension the two stories iterate and complement one another; they provide overlapping imaginal contexts for one another, have doubtless imitated and plagiarized one another. In sum, they draw strength and validity from their mutual association. Nor are they the only entities that enter into this cultural alliance: many other ideas constituted in myth and other media contribute to the peculiar reality in which Nambweapa'w is embedded and from which she draws prophetic insight into this-worldly affairs.

• In the last chapter I discussed the local folk notion that cassowaries are females who lack external genitalia. In "Nambweapa'w," this anatomical peculiarity might well have spoiled the First Honeymoon and ended the story right there, were it not for the mythmaker's use of it to make a major statement about male procreative power. Thus, to equip the lovely cassowary-maiden to be his wife, First Man tricks her into wounding herself, forming a vagina. We must assume that what followed is pure, paradigmatic male paradise: an artful bondage in which Nambweapa'w is persuaded that the captivities of childbirth, motherhood, sexual slavery, food-getting drudgery, and all the rest are her salvation. Until she recovers her cassowary skin.

The ideas culturally associated with the story's early scene are several. To begin with, the wounding evokes a concept pervasive in Tambaran ritual practice: that female procreative power can be appropriated to male ritual purposes, but only if done surreptitiously with the use of tricks and illusions. By deceptively coopting feminine powers, men accomplish the simultaneous ritual inclusion and exclusion of women. The Tambaran's pseudoprocreative deeds depend upon this maneuver (Tuzin 1995b), confirming that gender-directed secrecy and deception are inherent in the cult's ritual efficacy. It is therefore highly consistent with Arapesh understandings that the origin of women's procreative ability would have come about under conditions of male trickery and manipulation—rather than, for example, spontaneously or as a result of undisguised surgery.

In another sense, First Man's self-serving deed usurps female procreative power; at least, it represents the male's taking credit for it. Similarly, the story of "Olafen" (from *olaf*, meaning "house post") describes how women first learned to deliver babies *per vaginam* (Tuzin 1980, 168–69). The knowledge was given to the woman of the story by a spirit living in the carved effigy post of a Tambaran house. The storyteller is careful to explain, however, that it was the woman's own husband who deserved credit, for he was the one who had carved the house post. The kindly Tambaran spirit was none other than an aspect of the husband himself.

This notion of males creating, controlling, or otherwise taking credit for female procreation occurs also in beliefs associated with the semiwild palm sago, an important food source whose stupendous fertility renders it an ideal symbol of feminine reproductive potency. That is to say, it is men who, through ideas and practices of myth, cultivation, tenure, extraction, and exchange, bring the wonderfully feminine icon of palm sago under their control (Tuzin 1992). As part of the same set of associations, men harbor the notion that the resumption of menstrual cycles after the postpartum lactation interval—a three-year period of sexual taboo—is caused by the resumption of sexual intercourse between the parents. The men explain that the husband's penis "wounds" his wife's parts, causing the periodic bleeding to resume.[31] According to Beverly Tuzin (pers. comm.), women do not subscribe to this notion and are privately amused that the men claim control over a process that, the women perceive, happens quite naturally.

• When Nambweapa'w took her children into the forest after killing the husband, she caused rain to fall and ordered her sons to sleep sheltered inside a palm, her daughters inside a wild banana plant. During the night, the plants turned into a Tambaran house and a menstrual house, respectively. In the morning, the children emerged to find themselves in the midst of a beautiful village. In addition to its chartering of gender-specific house types, the sequence is associated with death. Thus, the banana plant (*ha'awin*) and palm tree (*bufwin*) specified, both known for their watery interiors, are referred to as alternative "doors of the dead," portals through which spirits pass between the two worlds.

A similar image appears in a vision reported by the Revivalist prophet Samuel (Tuzin 1989, 200–1). Samuel was cradling his aged father when he died. At the moment of death, Samuel "saw" his father's spirit rise from the body and walk away. Samuel's spirit followed the father's spirit as it entered the base of a wooden cross and emerged into the world of the dead. The vision continues from there. Likewise, again, the story of "Olafen" (above) mentions in passing that a Tambaran spirit goes in and out of a spirit-house post, carved to represent the spirit himself. Ambiguously, the spirit lives inside the post and also uses the post as a door to traverse between this world and the other. In general, Tambaran spirits range freely and are not "captive" within the post carved in their image.

One could extend this association further and observe, on evidence of design details and ritual significances, that the men's cult house is symbolic of a tree (Tuzin 1980, 156).[32] Though no one ever voiced this equation to me in so many words, the interpretation is nicely consistent with the notion that when initiands crawl through the front door of the house on hands and knees to confront and be mauled by the giant spirits dwelling within, they are entering into another world. Emerging through the rear door, the young men are marvelously unscathed and yet, it is claimed, utterly transformed. Indeed, by dint of the powers with which, as initiates, they are now embued, they have become like spirits themselves.

At an even deeper occult level, ritual access to the house's inner sanctum, in which are hidden the sacred flutes and drums, is achieved through a door. This door is itself camouflaged within a mosaic of hundreds of bark paintings that covers the outer wall of the inner sanctum. The paintings, one for each initiation partnership, are arranged in order of genealogical proximity, with the result that the whole is a massive chart replicating the entire descent structure of the village. Thus, the ritualized expression of Ilahita society, exhibited in the house's outer sanctum, mediates between the undisciplined outer world of women and mundane things, and the secret, inner world of spiritual truth, power, and purity. Ritual activates these spiritual spaces, and ceremonialism enables men to pass—like spirits of the dead—between them, by means of *doors*.

Unlike cult houses in other parts of the Sepik and elsewhere, Ilahita cult houses are not used as men's residences. Only on the night before a battle did the warriors sleep inside the cult house—inside the spirit domain, there to inhale, absorb, and rub up against powers that should serve them well the next day. For the most part, however, it is hallowed as the house where men may enter but only spirits may dwell, their mysterious presence made visible by hundreds of paintings, scores of sculptures, and those most sacred pipes and drums that sound the "voice of the Tambaran." Like the core of a nuclear reactor, the cult house manifests a potent reality, one far different from the ordinary; behind its dramatic facade—inside the "tree"—lives a world spiritually brilliant and powerful, right in the heart of the village.

• If, at times, Nambweapa'w is a lovely maiden or a loving mother, at other times she displays her savage, cassowary nature. In the casual killing of her husband and in the fierce or threatening way she sometimes treats her children, she is definitely a lady to be feared. Whence this aspect of her character? In a society in which maternal nurturance is the expressed ideal, on what basis would listeners relate to, or accept as credible, the dark side of Nambweapa'w's personality?

The associations relating to this question bear a distinctly Kleinian[33] cast, in that they project murderous, cannibalistic propensities onto maternal figures, specifically, old women. Insofar as actual old women are probably the gentlest, least threatening segment of adult society, one must suspect that the horrific appetites assigned to them in cultural fantasy are displacements. To anticipate a later argument, the primary object of these attributions are women of childbearing age, the actual, functioning mothers, who, like Nambweapa'w at that stage, are ostensibly naive and powerless. To imagine them otherwise, one must consider how children, sons in particular, experience them. Fearful fantasies developed in childhood toward actual mothers become elaborated in adult culture, by which time, as a matter of psychodynamic convenience and distancing, the "mother" has grown old. All the power and malevolence attributed to mothers, as fantasized and to some extent experienced by young boys, is displaced onto the *grandmothers* whom these mothers become, just as their sons become the adult men who tell these stories. Not all mythic mothers are negatively depicted. The mother in "Wilitin and Amilawen" has tender qualities, though Wilitin might disagree. Neither are all ogreish characters female. Still, from the men's point of view the power that goes with old age is problematic in the postmenopausal woman—the hag, the crone— for it departs so radically from the relative powerlessness she had had previously. She is, after all, almost dead.

Consider, for example, Epelini'w, another dangerous old woman of Ilahita imagination. Though Epelini'w lacks most of Nambweapa'w's socially redeeming qualities, it must be admitted that she does love her son, albeit to apparently jealous extremes. The lack of a husband implies that Epelini'w, like the later Nambweapa'w, is a widow, causing the story to focus initial attention on the emotionally hazardous mother-son attachment. The old woman's name derives from *epelin,* meaning "fingernail" or "toenail." She is one of the ogresses in Ilahita's literary canon.

> Epelini'w had a single child, a son, on whom she doted. The boy grew to manhood and married. Soon afterward, he went away for the day, leaving his new wife in the care of his mother. Epelini'w killed the daughter-in-law and ate her body, leaving not a trace. When the son returned and asked after his wife, Epelini'w lied and said she did not know where she had gone. The son married again, and Epelini'w secretly killed and ate that woman as well. The same thing happened a third time.
>
> With his fourth wife, the man was not going to take any chances. In preparing to leave to attend a festival, he dug a deep hole in the floor of his yam house and hid his wife there. He covered the hole with stone slabs, a layer of dirt, and piles of yams. Before leaving he told his mother to guard her.
>
> Instead, Epelini'w began digging with her long, sharp fingernail to get at her, with her usual cannibalistic intent. But she broke her fingernail on the stone. Hearing her cry and thrash

about in pain, the hidden woman realized that it was Epelini'w herself who had been killing the wives. Later, she told her husband what had happened, and the two of them waited for a chance to destroy the evil old woman. An opportunity was soon offered to the wife. While they were out working together, she speared Epelini'w with the sharpened bamboo pole hook used to harvest breadfruit. She burned Epelini'w's body. Some blood splashed on a leaf, away from the fire, and grew into a boy-child and a girl-child. The two children insinuated themselves back into the village. Having Epelini'w's murderous nature, they immediately began killing and eating first one old man, then another. The villagers eventually caught on to the children's crimes and moved to kill them. The children escaped to a hole in the top of a tall tree and taunted those below by noisily eating the meat of their latest victim and vowing thenceforth to prey upon villagers from their treetop lair.

The villagers chopped down the tree. As it fell the children leapt clear of their attackers and escaped in opposite directions. The girl ran south to the Wosera, where she instituted the *maolimu'w* witchcraft associated with the women there; the boy fled north to the Wom, where he instituted the *ma'akw* sangguma sorcery associated with the men there. Nowadays, Ilahita looks to the Wosera and the Wom as experts in these deadly arts, but it was Epelini'w of Ilahita who actually started them both.

The associational web spun by "Nambweapa'w" exceeds that of any other story in the Ilahita repertoire, proving its cultural importance and robust, dynamically evolving character. With its unusual length and detailed imagery, the narrative fairly bristles with evocations of other cultural, social, or psychological ideas. These filaments of meaning integrate "Nambweapa'w" with Ilahita cultural ideology and by so doing substantiate its prophetic authority. The next chapter completes my account of this story's success in predicting and directing the future, including entrapment of myself within its web of mythic significance. Meanwhile, I would ask the reader not to forget the idea of maternal menace represented by Epelini'w, in cultural sisterhood with Nambweapa'w in old age. Later in this study, this theme will be taken up again, not only as further encoded in myth, ritual, and other cultural constructs, but according to its possible sources in experience. For it is the social and behavioral circumstances leading men to fear women—first their mothers, then their wives—that integrate "Nambweapa'w" with problems of gender in Ilahita society and with the forces underlying the life and death of the Tambaran.

Chapter Six

MILLENNIUM

It is said that between 1502, when Spanish adventurers first landed on the New World mainland, and 1519, when Hernán Cortés and his companions entered the brilliant capital of the Aztec empire, comets, lightning bolts from the blue sky, monstrous births, and other freakish events occurred in the Valley of Mexico. Montezuma II and his advisers took them to be signs of impending doom. They were right—apparently so, or in effect. As news of ship sightings and landings arrived from the coast, thoughts nervously turned to the fabled Quetzalcoatl and to the mythic promise that the white god would someday return from the east to reclaim his kingdom. The legend of those portents and divinations comes down to us as perhaps the most famous case in history of prophetic fulfillment or, if you will, pseudoprophetic coincidence.

But was it truly as the chroniclers say? Never mind whether genuine prophecy was pronounced in the halls of Montezuma: were there queer happenings at all, and were they actually taken to be dark omens and harbingers of Quetzalcoatl? Against scholars who maintain "that these portents in Mexico were artfully devised in the 1530s or 1540s on the ground that simple people find catastrophes easier to bear if it can be argued that they have been foretold," historian Hugh Thomas (1993) accepts that some or most of the unusual events occurred.[1] They were probably unsensational in themselves and "might have been forgotten had the Mexican empire subsequently prospered" (p. 43). But because imperial calamity ensued instead, the portents were later remembered and became legend. Thomas's interpretation (p. 43) is that "given that rumours of atrocious happenings in Panama and the Caribbean had reached Tenochtitlan, gloomy conclusions were instantly drawn [from the unusual events]; that though they may have been temporarily forgotten, both the portents and the interpretations were recalled in 1519; and that clever Mexicans and friars, writing later of the Mexican empire, were happy to link those memories" with the tendency, common in sixteenth-century

Europe, to impute prophetic significance to natural anomalies. By an Or-
wellian paradox, the same events that validate prophecy by fulfilling it
undermine prophecy by historicizing it, thereby inviting skeptics to
charge that a given prophecy was invented, rigged, or confabulated after
the event it supposedly foretold. To an outsider or a later observer, the
whole matter can become quite convoluted, the more so when the observer is the subject of the prophecy—and its target.

As in Old Mexico, sixteenth-century Europe, and most other places,
auguries in Ilahita occur frequently during times of social and cultural
upheaval. Some events are immediately perceived to be portentous; others
pass relatively unnoticed until some later development discloses their
meaning, retrospectively. Even under normal conditions, people attach
divinatory meaning to anomalous objects and events. For example, the
call of a night bird during daylight hours is understood to herald death;
the persistent fluttering of a butterfly nearby signifies that a visitor is about
to appear; a muscle twitch means someone is talking about you. The
seriousness with which such signs are taken varies with person and circumstance, just as it does in our own culture: sometimes the augury is
a playful, acknowledged superstition; at other times it triggers paranoid
delusions that have ramified consequences for individuals and the society.

This divinatory impulse was intermittently frenzied around the time
we arrived in Ilahita in early July 1985. So it continued until the following
January, when interest receded, only to resurge weakly in March–April
1986. The decline occurred for several reasons: disappointment that the
Christmas and New Year season had not brought major millennial happenings; cumulative fatigue, sapping the people's ability to sustain the
manifold intensity of the Revival; the rise of competing issues, especially
the heating up of a decades-long land dispute with the enemy village of
Mamilimbi; warnings by external Church authorities that legal measures
were at hand to punish continued Revivalist "cargo" activities; and, perhaps not least, disappointment that my visit was not turning out as the
Revivalists (or, in their way, the traditionalists) had hoped it would. Despite these setbacks, the March–April resurgence might have picked up
steam, were it not for a dangerous gastrointestinal malady erupting in
early May, just before the long-awaited judgment in the land dispute went
catastrophically against Ilahita in the National Court of Justice. Both calamities, coming together, caused the Revivalists to pause and ponder
their divinatory significance.

Prior to the postholiday recession, however, excitement ran very high. Villagers behaved as if reality's gears were temporarily disengaged. Distinctions of past, present, and future dissolved into a magical solution of mania and paranoia in which outrageous, delusional things were affirmed by persons I knew (or thought I knew) to be levelheaded. Credibility was suddenly judged by a mythic standard. It was as if a group of Australian Aboriginals had awakened in the Dreamtime, able, like Alice, to believe in as many as six impossible things before breakfast. As mentioned above, past events were recalled or invented, to be (re)interpreted in the light of current expectations. More radically, past events were *brought into* the present: the lifting of time barriers enabled current events to be seen as fulfillments on a cultural scale of explicit or implied prophecies handed down in myth and legend.[2] This appears to have been the encompassing use made of "Nambweapa'w" toward the revelation of cult secrets, the murder of the Tambaran, and my timely return to the village. The cultural associations discussed in the last chapter, which gave "Nambweapa'w" expression of the mythic past, now gave the story direction of the mythic present.

To understand the mythic formulation of these events, we return to the explicit prophetic sequence in "Nambweapa'w"—the flood-borne departure of the youngest son, with the storyteller's promise that he would return. I wondered upon first hearing the story, even before my curious conversation with Bihinguf, whether the young gallant's having gone to America was a detail improvised on the spot for my benefit. Probably not, I decided, since reference to the hero's American destination did not draw any particular reaction from the others in the escort group. Furthermore, bits of information previously obtained from administrators in Maprik suggested that the inclusion of "America," though obviously of limited antiquity, reflected a pro-Americanism substantially preceding my arrival in Ilahita. "Be sure to tell them you're American," Mike Neal, the assistant district commissioner, had advised in his Sydneysider's twang, "the people loooove Yanks."

So they did, apparently. Announcing myself as an American produced a gratifying shiver of enthusiasm among the people who first gathered around me and my gear; and from then on, my nationality was favorably mentioned whenever a villager introduced me to someone new. Surely though, I remarked to myself, Americans are not so very different in looks and manner from other white types to which the Ilahitans were by then accustomed—Australian, New Zealander, English, and German, none of which received similar commendation. The people's persistent pleasure in the fact of my being American therefore always struck me as distinctly odd and exaggerated.

Their attitude is probably traceable to World War II. Men who as wartime youths had spent time near troop concentrations on the coast or in the islands reported that American soldiers were generous and friendly toward New Guineans, not like the aloof Australians. Amazingly, some of the American soldiers were black skinned, like the New Guineans; yet they fought, worked, and ate right alongside their white comrades. There were no black men in Australian army uniforms. These perceptions may have been based on rumor rather than on direct experience. Whether or not the Ilahitans actually saw or interacted with American troops—two claimed to me they had, but the details were fuzzy—they returned home after the war to spread the news of American largesse and black-white fraternalism.

Were these wartime impressions the source of Ilahita's felt kinship with America?[3] Did they inspire the mythmaker's notion that Nambweapa'w's son went there to father the white race? This seems a plausible interpretation, in my view, considering that Ilahita had no knowledge of America prior to World War II and little or no contact with Americans after the war. Nor does this narrative detail appear to have been borrowed from some other Cassowary-Mother story or story fragment, since it is not present in any other version known to me. In fact, "Nambweapa'w" appears to be the only story of any kind from the immediate area in which one of the characters departs for another *country,* as opposed to somewhere in the vicinity: the forest, the grass fields, a mountain unvisited but visible in the distance, or the place of the dead. This general pattern is hardly surprising, since other countries were not known to exist until fairly recently.

If the story's detail concerning America dates from knowledge acquired around the time of World War II, another source is almost certain to have been the contact these Ilahita men first had at that time with New Guineans from the coastal Madang area (map 4). There, cargoistic incorporations of white men into the local cosmology have been going on since at least 1871, when the Russian explorer Baron Nikolai Miklouho-Maclay arrived on the southern Madang coast. In that region the relevant myth is the widespread story of two brothers, Manup and Kilibob, who were supposedly brought into being by the creator god, Anut (Lawrence 1964, 21). The brothers fall out after Manup's wife steals one of Kilibob's arrows and forces him "to tattoo its incised design on her pudendum" (Lawrence 1964, 22). Manup tries to kill Kilibob, who flees in a large canoe. The roles may be reversed between versions; but it is always the younger, smarter, more virtuous brother (usually, the one named Kilibob) who departs, leaving behind the expectation he will return. According to Lawrence (p. 65), "Maclay may have been identified as Kilibob or Manup." Thus,

> Yabob informants told [Lawrence] that their forbears believed
> that the first European ship they saw belonged to Kilibob, who
> was at last returning as their myth had prophesied. (Their idea
> was supported by the belief that Kilibob was light-skinned like
> Europeans.)

Another tale, this one from the northern Madang coastal area, is highly reminiscent of the closing scenes of "Nambweapa'w"; it is about Ambwerk and his younger brother Tuman (Burridge [1960] 1970, 165–72). The story goes that a child is killed and is buried by its mother, who is without male protection. The mother marries and gives birth to more sons. She returns to the first child's grave, to find salt water and fish being produced from the putrefying body.

> The woman takes a small fish, and some water, and makes a meal
> of them for her family. They find it good. More than that, a son
> quickly develops into manhood—a circumstance that occasions
> the curiosity and envy of the husband's brother and his family.
> Letting them into the secret, the woman warns her relatives by
> marriage that they must not shoot the *ramatzka* fish. But the warn-
> ing goes unheeded, and the ramatzka is shot. The earth rumbles,
> and the sea rises up to divide brother from brother. (Burridge
> [1960] 1970, 165–66)

Ambwerk, the older brother, "stupidly" violated the injunction and is identified as the black man. Tuman, the innocent and obedient younger brother, is identified with the white man. Tuman, moreover, went on to perform great technological feats and to father (or materially to endow) the white race. "'And that,'" according to Burridge's informant, "'is why

white men have all the good things of this world and we have only yams'"
(p. 171). Blacks have only themselves to blame for a life of deprivation
and servitude; and yet there is a promise that the descendants of Tuman
will someday return to give the people what the white man has. The
white man is not a stranger: "He is a brother—one who will help, or
who could be constrained to help, because as a brother he ought to help"
(p. 176). Hence the mythic rationale for cargo aspirations (Burridge
1969, 64–74).

Ever since the late 1930s, when Ilahita men first began to be recruited
as laborers on the coastal and island plantations, they have looked to
peoples of the coastal Madang area as sources of powerful magic and prestigious dances and as cultural mentors in how to understand and deal with
Europeans. There are still men living who know about, and indeed claim
to have met, Yali, who led a major cargo movement in the Madang area
soon after World War II (Lawrence 1964). In view of this history of contact and cultural emulation, it would appear highly likely that "Ambwerk
and Tuman," "Manup and Kilibob," and other cognates,[4] together with
their use in interpreting the problematic relationship of blacks and whites,
were the source of ideas and images that found their way into the prophetic ending of Nambweapa'w's story.

Beyond adding more background to "Nambweapa'w," the point of this
brief side trip to Madang is to reconfirm the fluid nature of living myth—
a feature paradoxically at odds with the illusion of profound permanence
that marks the genre. Thus, it should not be supposed that the comparative recency of the "America" reference, or the probability that certain
key story elements were borrowed not long ago, detracts from the cultural
authenticity or full mythic standing of "Nambweapa'w." On the contrary,
this part of the history is proof, again, of the spongy resilience (better,
opportunism) of Ilahita's mythic tradition; and, more specifically, it is a
fresh, within-living-memory trace of America's assimilation to the preexisting metaphysical category of "the Other."[5]

With America's mythic standing already certified in Ilahita's creation
epic, was my arrival as an American suggestive of the foretold return of
the little brother? Quetzalcoatl in New Guinea? The idea seemed uncom-
fortably close to something from a Rider Haggard quest adventure,
though I admit that it did cross my mind. If a messianic thought occurred
to any villager, the reality of my workaday presence would have starved

it before long. No magic or miracle from this American. When, during my stay, the Mount Hurun "cargo" movement arose and swept through the area from its center east of Maprik (Hwekmarin et al. 1971; Gesch 1985), no mystic link was offered between my presence and that millenarian prospect. As it happened, only two men from Ilahita[6] subscribed to the Mount Hurun movement—there was a substantial cash membership fee—and they were mercilessly ridiculed for their gullibility. Having been disappointed by previous cargo enthusiasms, the villagers were not about to go that route again. So, while the entire Maprik area seemed to be reveling in the hope that "Sydney" was about to appear on the top of Mount Hurun, Ilahita busied itself with Tambaran activities. "Sydney" did not come, but the Tambaran did; and Ilahita glowed proud and smugly superior over the outcome of events. By all appearances, cargo thinking had lost all appeal and credibility.

Eventually, fieldwork came to an end. I left Ilahita, sorry to lose the people who in three years had become, and who described themselves as being, my family. I left Ilahita, promising to return.

The circumstances of my return, thirteen years later, were told in an earlier chapter. Relevant here is the suspicious coincidence of that event with the collapse of the Tambaran, the supercharging of Ilahita's atmosphere with millenarian expectations, the death of Gidion, and the coming to life of Nambweapa'w's old tale of retribution and masculine woe. It was not so much my original arrival in Ilahita that had stirred apocalyptic thoughts (at least not for long); it was my *return from America*—possibly even from the dead—amid the agitated conditions of the moment, that created all of the commotion.

Let me pause to observe that while the idea of someone—namely myself—returning from the dead, or from some equally remote, mythic place, may violate practical rationality, it is not unprecedented among the Ilahita, their neighbors, or, indeed, many peoples in the Melanesian area. Accounts of "first contact" frequently record that indigenous peoples initially took the white men to be spirits or ghosts, possibly the people's own ancestral dead. Such perceptions occurred among the nearby Bumbita Arapesh, and still do (Leavitt 1989, 1995), and among the Balif Arapesh, just to the north of Ilahita (Macdonald 1995). They also occurred in several instances from New Guinea and the Pacific islands, cited by Marshall

Sahlins (1995, 177–89; also Schieffelin and Crittenden 1991; Williams [1923] 1977, 342; Webster 1984, 72).

Sahlins cites these cases in rebutting Gananath Obeyesekere's dubious argument (1992) that, contrary to historical tradition, the Hawaiians did not perceive Captain Cook—*returning* on his third voyage—to be the god Lono. Indeed, claims Obeyesekere, the alleged apotheosis of Captain Cook not only violates universal "practical rationality," but was a European invention, an Enlightenment myth.[7] Obeyesekere notes (pp. 20–21) that he is addressing a mode of thinking, not a mode of thought or the rationality of belief. But this caveat sets his argument at cross-purposes with Sahlins's thesis, which largely concerns the cultural logics of the case; it also renders his claim moot, for one must doubt whether at this remove Obeyesekere can determine, in his terms, the parol of contemporaneous Hawaiian thinking in respect of Captain Cook. More to the point is Andrew Strathern's remark on the matter, which probably echoes a common observation among New Guinea ethnographers. Referring to the claim that Highlanders during the contact era of the 1930s readily shifted from seeing the white strangers as men rather than spirits, Strathern comments: "One may wonder a little about this, since in Hagen and Pangaia the idea that the Europeans may be spirits continues to be entertained along with the normal working assumption that they are probably people" (1984, 108).

So it is in Ilahita. When a trigger-happy patrol first passed near the village back in "German times" (ca. 1910), the people assumed they were ghosts, and the word *dowank* ("ghost"; MP: *daiman*) is still used to refer to white men, though not to their faces. The strangers might have been perceived as masalai or tambaran, but their human form and white skins indicated they were "ghosts." The point is that the white men were quickly assigned to the preexisting category of "the Other" (Leavitt 1995, 179); and, given a cosmology so restrictive that it placed the end of the world at the visible horizon, it is perfectly understandable that this should have been the cognitive response.[8]

This category, as I attempted to show in the last chapter, includes a variety of sentient beings that are not ordinary, living humans. As a residuum "the Other" flourishes without being cognized as such or designated by a vernacular term, while the alleged interactions among its members serve to maintain its unitary character. Members of that category are denizens of an imagined spatial dimension with many gateways to our world—at masalai places and "doors of the dead," for example—but normally invisible to us. This is a realm separate from, and yet frequently engaged with, everyday reality, as in the experiences of dreaming, life crisis, ritual, and, as in the present case, in the experiences of myth.

Following the distinction drawn by Obeyesekere, it does not require much for the "mode of thought" embodied in this construct to generate a corresponding "mode of thinking." In conducting my sociological census—a massive job lasting about six months—I had saved Ilifalemb for last. It was the ward farthest distant from my house (map 2). Because by that time I was practiced in asking the right questions in the right way, I was not prepared when the Ilifalemb folk reacted sullenly to my routine, innocuous inquiries. When I mentioned this to a friend who had in-laws in Ilifalemb, he offered to ask around. He learned that word had circulated in the ward, from sources unknown, that I was an agent of the dead; that the information about family relationships and property tenure I was collecting was to be used to take the land away from the people when the dead returned. With the support of some villagers who knew me well, I met with ward elders and vowed that I was not sent by the dead to harm them. They must have accepted my disclaimer, for I met no further resistance to my census activities.

This mode of thought also lends itself to cargo "thinking." When administrative officers on patrol stayed the night in Ilahita, they always used the rest house specially maintained for that purpose. On one memorable occasion, though, a young officer on census patrol was accompanied by his new wife. Fresh from suburban Australia, she disliked these typically ramshackle, rat-infested, and, for newlyweds, rather unprivate residences. Accordingly, during the three nights they were in Ilahita, the visitors slept in a tent they pitched in an overgrown, grassy area out behind the rest house.

To my surprise, this action produced a rustle of alarm throughout the community. At least six times during the first two days, individuals or small groups furtively besought me to explain why the kiap and his lady would shun a comfortable rest house in favor of a cramped little cloth house. It was not just that the people were curious; they were troubled, even incensed, by the kiap's behavior. Were they offended that the visitors apparently did not think a rest house made of bush materials was good enough for them? Believing this to be the explanation, I commiseratively agreed that the couple's behavior was puzzling; I should know, having slept in the rest house for an entire month without discomfort. Newly-weds, I added unnecessarily, often like to be by themselves. My response did not satisfy the inquisitors, however, and I began to wonder why everyone was making such a big deal out of the kiap's sleeping arrangements.

On the third day of the visit, counterquestioning on my part finally revealed the true object of concern. The people did not care that the couple preferred the tent over the rest house, nor were they at all offended by the choice. Their actual question was not "Why a tent?" but "Why *there?*" Unbeknownst to him (or me), the kiap had pitched his tent in an overgrown cemetery! The worry was that the couple, exercising power or influence over the moldering dead, were using the tent as a blind for nefariously extracting cargo from the graves during the night. My skeptical response—namely, that the heaves and moans heard coming from the tent probably had more to do with honeymooning than with grave robbing—did little to allay suspicions. The next day the kiap and his bride moved on, never knowing how close they had come to provoking a possibly violent incident.

I offer these incidents to show that a certain mode of thought prevails in Ilahita and that a relatively minor anomaly is enough to precipitate it into a mode of *thinking* that eagerly accepts the possibility of an Other-worldly cause. Many such cases came to my attention during fieldwork, and I have no doubt that those were only a tiny fraction of actual instances in Ilahita during that period. Every time this casuistry is deployed, it renews the reality of "the Other" and reconfirms that creatures of that realm may intervene in the everyday affairs of the living. It is in this manner, as we saw in the last chapter, that ghosts, masalai, and tambaran are often invoked to explain odd occurrences.

These examples indicate that whites are also, and perhaps especially, liable to being categorized with "the Other": first, because of the original and lingering identification of whites as spirits of the dead (*dowax*), which automatically places them in the more general category; second, because by virtue of their evident material comforts, whites appear to lead a charmed existence; and, third, because much of what whites do—albeit decreasingly—is puzzling and mysterious to village onlookers.[9] From the first, mind-boggling encounter, whites have been typed as spirits, a metaphysical understanding that no disclaimer or demonstration can disprove. As the generations turned, however, as interactions with whites have grown more routine and diverse, and as the people's own experiential universe has widened, this irrefutable understanding has steadily given way to the working assumption (see above) that whites are people. Practice, not theory or theology, will eventually eliminate the old understanding, and the "working" assumption will be the only assumption there is. As of the mid-1980s, that time had not yet come. Under the fevered millenarian expectations of the moment, it was by no means clear which of the two assumptions was the "working" one. The situation changed day by day, as rumor swirled around the Revival, and the gates swinging between this reality and the other seemed ready to fly off their hinges.

In the light of this fluid metaphysical situation, the prophetic aura of my return was intense enough to cast a retrospective glow over my earlier fieldwork, revealing (or creating) significances that had not been apparent at the time. Consider the following points. I had been young in 1969, unmarried for the first six months of fieldwork, and eager to learn about Ilahita's language, stories, and customs. My competence in these matters was less than a child's, and yet I was adept and experienced in other ways quite mysterious to the villagers. My purpose, explained in the opening minutes of fieldwork, was not to govern, judge, punish, cure, teach, or preach to the people of Ilahita, but simply to live among them. My announced plan was to stay in Ilahita, not simply for a night or even a fortnight, but for a long time. In all of these respects, I was a visitor unlike any the village had ever known. And, to the best of their knowledge and mine, I was the first American ever to visit Ilahita.[10]

I suggest that these features of myself and my first fieldwork in Ilahita were remembered and became portentous during the subsequent years, culminating in the expectation that something apocalyptic would occur because of, or in obscure association with, my return. Not only these original features: my rumored death two years after leaving the village, and then, in 1984, Gidion's death and his deathbed declaration that I would return, followed a few weeks later by my letter announcing precisely that—all became matériel, so to speak, for a prophetic framework that would encompass the apocalyptic events anticipated by the Revivalists. The mythmaker's prediction seemed to be coming true. The identification of this American with the mythic youngest brother in "Nambweapa'w," an idea too fatuous to entertain at the time of first fieldwork, emerged as the consuming theme of the expected and actual *return* to Ilahita. The prospect of my imminent return may not have been the only factor in the Tambaran's fall, but it was an important one, because nothing of a wondrous nature could occur without prior elimination of that supposed Satanic abomination. The irreversible way to do that was for the men to expose the cult secrets to the women, thereby risking Nambweapa'w's revenge. They were gambling with very high stakes: their identity, their spiritual livelihood. Sometimes their disappointment and frustration showed, as the return fieldwork ground on, month after month, no more miraculous than before. Indeed, the return visit was decidedly less miraculous, considering that the first sojourn now enjoyed the lustrous distortions of memory.

The linkage of "Nambweapa'w," my return, and the Revival's millenarian aspirations is confirmed by a detail, which, apparently minor in itself, assumes major significance in this discussion. The Ilahita Arapesh, like other Sepik peoples (Bateson [1936] 1958; Harrison 1990), attach great importance to personal names. The ideas and bestowal practices surrounding names are highly ramified (Tuzin 1976, 135f.), starting from the premise that personal names, especially heirloom names owned by patriclans, are spiritually charged. Names embody a person's essence; heirloom names are vessels containing a lifetime's spiritual allotment from the ancestral pool. At death, the name returns to that pool for reconsecration, before being rebestowed on someone newly born. Because, in addition, each of the five Tambaran initiations involves the placing of one or more new names, persons—males, in particular—acquire and shed numerous names during a lifetime. More than any other marker, a name captures the individuality of the person. Persons from the same community should not use the same name at the same time, for this would be metaphysically troubling, and it would confound marriage and ritual exchanges and other procedures presupposing the uniqueness of the person.

Within a few weeks of first arriving in Ilahita, I was given an Owapwi clan name, Walimini. It was a token of friendly acceptance, an appellation also easier for people to pronounce and remember than the one shown on my birth certificate. "Walimini" belongs to one of the Owapwi Tambaran spirits and is bestowed at initiation on the tallest Owapwi man in the group being initiated.[11] The preceding "Walimini" had discarded the name upon converting to Christianity; hence its availability for my use. Within days the Sao'um clan, on whose land I was living, in a gesture of friendly rivalry toward the Owapwi, gave me the name "Kafumbwili," which also connotes tallness, and also happened to be available. Beverly, whom I married and brought to Ilahita six months later, was given a name borne by no other woman of the village: "Nambweapa'w."

Names carry rights—implied ownership of one's self being the most precious—and they carry obligations, in that each is a locus on a grid of ritual and economic exchange relationships. For me, however, those legal-istic entailments were apparently suspended, and the names were never more than tokens of hospitality, signifying a kind of honorary membership in the Owapwi and Sao'um clans. Gidion's clan, the Mano'um, did not give me a name; but more than anyone else, Gidion treated and referred to me as "younger brother," and the others of his clan treated me accordingly.

Upon my return in 1985, Councilor Kunai ceremoniously announced that "Walimini" and "Kafumbwili" would no longer be my names; that my age and importance meant that if people wanted to call me by an Ilahita name, it should be "Baingap." The designation was further appropriate, Kunai declared, because the large boulder formation across the clearing from my house was "Baingap," after the culture hero who had placed it there. Previously, Gidion's house had stood atop Baingap's stone; nearby in the same quadrant was the dwelling and yam house of Soweapo, another man of the Mano'um clan. Now, however, both sites stood empty and forlorn. With Gidion dead and Soweapo removed to a bush hamlet, my house was alone on the clearing, making it my job to "look after" Baingap. Besides, Kunai added, with a significant glance, "as you know, Baingap is a great name."

Kunai was right. Baingap's importance in Ilahita's mythic canon rivals that of Nambweapa'w, whose name Beverly continued to use during the return fieldwork. Long ago, the story tells, my illustrious namesake had lived in Ilahita with his unnamed wife and young son.

> Whenever they needed food Baingap would go alone to
> fetch it. Only he knew the secret of how to get the food. When
> he was gone, his wife and child had to go hungry. When he re-
> turned, he would bring yams and meat of the pig, cassowary, wal-
> laby, tree kangaroo, and bandicoot.
>   Baingap got the food by going to the foot of the mountains,
> where, at the base of a waterfall, he collected special types of
> leaves. He put the leaves in two separate bamboo tubes and filled

them with water from the cascade. From one bamboo would later come yams, from the other, meat.

Eventually Baingap's wife grew weary of having to depend on Baingap for all her food. She told her son to follow him and see where he got the food. The boy did so and returned to tell his mother how it was done.

One day Baingap left the village for the day. By afternoon, his family was hungry. "You know the secret of the food," said the mother to her son, "go fetch us some." So the boy did exactly what he had seen his father do. But instead of the water in the bamboo turning to food, it boiled up, spilled out of the bamboo, and turned into a great torrent that swept the boy away.

In another part of the forest, Baingap heard the noise and guessed what was happening. Seizing his spear, he started running to the place. At intervals he would pause to catch his breath, and his heaving caused stones to spring up around him.

When Baingap arrived, he saw his son in trouble and tried to halt the flood by putting his spear across its path. But the waters were too strong. They caught Baingap. As he was being swept away, he called to his wife. He sent her to fetch a length of sprouting bamboo. When she returned, Baingap spat into the bamboo, saying to her that this was the secret of the food. He told his wife to keep the bamboo that she might eat, and that he and the boy were leaving with the waters. As he left, Baingap sang to the people of this area that they would thenceforth eat yams and meat.

The water swept Baingap into the country of the Kwanga, and as he passed he sang that they would eat banana and meat and some yams. He did this in the Kwanga language. The flood eventually carried him down to the Sepik River, where Baingap sang that the people there would eat only fish. Finally, the waters subsided and Baingap was left near the boundary of the Abelam and Sepik peoples. There he remains to this day, while we in Ilahita still follow his instructions. We still have the bamboo containing his spittle. It is the secret of our food.

Baingap's story may lack the dramatic sizzle and magicality of "Nambweapa'w," but it is impossible to miss certain thematic resemblances between the two stories and their respective protagonists. Staple foods are chartered; cultural groups in the area are differentiated because of events originating in Ilahita; a child is instrumental in betraying the father's secret to the mother; the revelation of the secret produces calamitous results and the end of an Edenic subsistence arrangement; finally, the morally superior hero is swept away on a flood, removed to a place where he continues to live, to this day. Baingap affirms what Nambweapa'w denies, namely, the traditional (Tambaran) ideology that males hold priority in the moral and procreative sphere.

The complementarity between Baingap and Nambweapa'w is more than logical, more than substantive: the two actually end up in the same story together, triply paired as husband–wife, eldest son–mother, and youngest son–mother. That is to say, in all versions of "Nambweapa'w" recorded during my first fieldwork, none gave the name of the First Man. Usually the storyteller would state, without being asked, that the man's name was unknown or forgotten (e.g., Tuzin 1980, 1). At some point during the following thirteen years, however, his name was remembered, or, at any rate, a name became attributed to him; for in the versions collected during my return visit, his name was routinely given as Baingap! The deceiver, the victim of Nambweapa'w's revenge, was no longer merely some nameless, no-account man, but Baingap, the hero par excellence of Ilahita tradition. By so naming him, the storyteller moved an important step closer to admitting that Nambweapa'w's victim was none other than the masculine principle, embodied in the Tambaran. Furthermore, by the local logic of filial succession and replacement, the revised story implies an identification between Baingap and the youngest son, to whom attention shifts after the old man is killed.

An additional twist, suggested by Ilahita naming practices, arises from the identification between "father's father" and "son's son." By this measure the young hero in "Nambweapa'w" stands in the position of Baingap's grandson. Such a view is consistent with their relative ages and also with the Ilahita notion that the eldest child, male or female, is the parent surrogate (Tuzin 1991, 124). The death of Baingap redefines the eldest child—the Ilahita ancestor—as "father" of the other siblings, especially the youngest. Having toppled his father, Baingap, the youngest son—now Baingap himself, by virtue of *grandfatherly* succession—goes on to achieve moral superiority over his Ilahita eldest brother, now "father." By virtue of these shifting, cross-generational identifications and successions, which are confirmed in naming practices and other institutional usages (Tuzin 1976, 1991), the story is oedipal with a vengeance!

This interpretation reevokes the incestuous overtones of the relationship between the youngest son and Nambweapa'w. It is recalled that the Cassowary-Mother compels each son to marry the sister behind him in birth order; mother and youngest son are paired, because there is no younger sister for him to marry. By the kind of symmetrical recentering Ilahita mythmakers like to employ, Baingap the elder is to the young, powerless Nambweapa'w what Baingap the younger is to the old, powerful Nambweapa'w.

That two or more characters can share the same identity in a single story should not alarm the reader, once it is understood that mythic narrative, in Ilahita and elsewhere, is often decentered and quite capable of shifting points of view. The effect is that of the museum guide showing you the skull of Charles II, displayed next to the skull of Charles II as an old man. The story of Nambweapa'w lends itself to this maneuver, in that it appears to be a composite of two distinct, rather differently toned stories, linked together by the incident of the revenge killing. The first half of "Nambweapa'w" is a rendition of the standard Oceanic "swan maiden" tale, while the killing and its aftermath make up a partner narrative that, among other things, integrates the "swan maiden" with a variety of ideas indigenous to the Ilahita Arapesh.[12]

A question arises. In honoring me with Baingap's name, *which* Baingap did my Ilahita mentors—in this instance, Kunai and his inner circle of Revivalist cronies—have in mind? Ostensibly, it was Baingap the culture hero, the one with the "great name" whose heavy breathing had produced the rock formation across the clearing from my house. Perhaps because his mythic role has collective import, Baingap's name is not owned by any particular clan, nor did I ever hear of anyone using it for himself. With one exception: Kunai, my nominator, was frequently called "Baingap" during the return field trip. He told me that this was a mistake and that his real name was not "Baingap," but the Abelam variant, "Baingarap." It may be that he had been using the name "Baingap" up until my return, then passed it on to me and appropriated, to take its place and yet retain the boastful implication, the Abelam equivalent.[13] It is equally likely that Kunai was establishing a tactical affiliation with me, an identity for more than merely "the name's sake."

Be that as it may, "Baingap" made good sense as a name for me. Like the culture hero, I took a great interest in Ilahita culture for its own sake; and, although I was active in the social life of the village, my identity was not bound by any of its categories. It might even be said that the people had assigned me to a kind of creator role—creator in the sense of redeemer, in that they explicitly saw me as having rescued their customs by writing them down, putting them in a book, and letting the people in America know about them. Rescued, mind you, not for eventual reinstatement, but as an archive, a museum of themselves and their fathers, which their children and grandchildren could enjoy and take pride in from, so to speak, a safe distance.

This raises an important point about the cultural process underway in Ilahita at that time. Judging from their attitude toward my ethnographic work, most of the Revivalists were not interested in obliterating the Tambaran from memory, but in memorializing it.[14] The Tambaran stood for Ilahita's past greatness—in retrospect tainted, to be sure, but nonetheless glorious. Those who led in the destruction of cult paraphernalia understood the cultural and emotional enormity of the deed. Theirs was a violent repudiation of all that had formed their identity, all that their fathers had lived by, all that they had grown up fearing and loving and believing in. Such an investment is not easy to liquidate. Never mind that the whole enterprise had been ruled over by Satan, a theory the Revivalists eagerly accepted; despite Christian missionary injunctions, one does not simply forget one's self and begin a totally new life and identity "in Christ." Based on native insight into the way symbols operate in Ilahita, the Revivalists wanted to remember, but also redefine the value and relevance of, those traditions, putting them safely at bay from the self. It was an act of emotional distancing, blunting the sinful allure of those traditions and yet preserving them in collective memory. It was a daring self-secularization in which life and practice were transformed into heritage and reminiscence.[15] The maneuver placed the Tambaran astride the poles of a fine ambivalence between attraction and repulsion, sustaining a contradiction that, for today's adult generations, mirrors the present cultural and spiritual condition. Once again, a moral and cognitive dissonance was cast in the form of an "incriminating charter," in this case the promulgation of a "heritage," a cultural enshrinement that ironically indicts today's modernist ideology and deprives it of unquestioned legitimacy.

In flattering me with the name of the culture hero Baingap, the Revivalists recruited me to their project. Or, perhaps more correctly, they modified their project to take advantage of my return. In the interval since the first fieldwork, my supposedly commanding knowledge of the Tambaran and other Ilahita traditions had become legendary—wildly overrated, especially among young adults who had grown up hearing about it. The prospect of my return therefore may have inspired the idea of blending a "heritage" element into their otherwise forward-looking millenarian program. An accommodation of this sort may have been unavoidable, in that my vocational interests as a student of Ilahita culture needed to be reconciled with the apocalyptic, *countercultural* hopes pinned upon my returning from America.

That reconciliation was achieved, in a mythic manner of speaking, by inserting Baingap as a named character into the story of Nambweapa'w. As the First Man—not merely an ancestor but the Grand Progenitor, the father of all ancestors—Baingap displays the same historical transcendence as does Baingap the culture hero in the title role of his own story. As with all fathers, his identity is transmitted to his children. Of those many children, the two most interesting are the unnamed eldest and youngest sons: the eldest, because he is the ancestor of the Ilahita Arapesh and thus would be seen as having a partisan attachment to the traditions the Revivalists seek to extirpate; the youngest, because of his intimate relationship with Nambweapa'w and her retribution and because he went away to America *so that he may return,* presumably to champion the Revivalist cause.

Now, in Ilahita ideology, the statuses of eldest and youngest siblings, especially same-sex siblings, are explicitly complementary. Whereas opposite sexes are complementary around procreation, and opposite generations are complementary around nurturance, opposite siblings are complementary around the theme of authority and precedence. As the pure form of this theme, their relationship supplies the metaphor for the complementarity of super- and subordination elsewhere in the society. The Tambaran's initiation structure, for example, operates through a highly elaborate dual organization; of the eight oppositional levels that make up the latticework of this organization, four are metaphorically derived from the elder brother–younger brother relationships.

In cultural ideology, eldest sibling and youngest sibling are seen to replace the parental generation, according to a stepwise succession that combines elements of primogeniture and ultimogeniture. Thus, from the time a couple's first grandchild is born, their spirits are increasingly fused into one. Eventually, the eldest child of either sex succeeds to that unitary parental status, but in the normal course of siblings dying in birth order is ultimately succeeded by the *youngest* child.

> It is a tontine . . . destined to be won by the last born. The reward is the exalted position resulting from the elimination of all who were above him in the [genealogical] hierarchy, corresponding to which members of the next generation would esteem him (or her) as the "'last'" father (or mother). (Tuzin 1991, 124–25)

This actuarial pattern may help to explain the curious fact that, despite a prevailing ideology of primogeniture, the youngest sibling is nearly always the smartest, most attractive, and most virtuous of the offspring. Many myths, including "Nambweapa'w," depict the youngest brother in these terms; and to a remarkable extent youngest brothers excel in politics, exchange, and other activities favoring entrepreneurial energy and flair.

In various jural and ritual modes, then, the cycle of identity and succession is father/mother > parent > eldest child > youngest child > father/mother > parent, etc. Those born in middle position are eliminated from consideration, except, as sometimes happens, when they are temporarily clumped with either the oldest or youngest of the line. By this logic Baingap's insertion into the story of Nambweapa'w signifies his identification not just as the named First Man, but also as the eldest son and the youngest son. And by the logic of name spirituality, all of these identifications were bestowed on me with the name "Baingap." The honor was not without cost, for it cinched my recruitment to Nambweapa'w's vengeful saga and raised feverish expectations that I had returned to fulfill the Revivalists' millenarian program.

It isn't easy being a messiah. Even Jesus complained (John 4:48) about His followers' tiresome need for "signs and wonders" as a condition of faith. But whereas Jesus could deliver such signs and wonders, I could not. My failings did not deter many Revivalists from continuing to expect or suspect such acts from me, or to resent or despise what they increasingly saw as my refusal to help them. These negative attitudes were perhaps no less strong among our closest friends among the Revivalists, those who stood to gain the most from our miraculous benefices. But because they were close friends, and because they potentially had too much to lose by estranging us, they dissembled their hostility, putting both parties in an uncomfortable position. Instead of being confronted openly with our meanness, we were subjected to recurrent, gratuitous expressions of impatience and frustration. This hurtful treatment would have been more baffling but for occasional things whispered to us by movement turncoats: persons who had fallen out of belief, or who had fallen victim to the rough, fast-moving politics of the Revival, or who had been ejected for alleged moral or religious crimes. Though as outcasts or apostates their motives were suspect—they wanted to turn us against their persecutors—what they confided did make sense of what was happening around and to us.

On one occasion, a disturbing allegation came to my attention. Bato'w, a young woman from Nangup ward, where the Revival was more or less headquartered, was electrifying the community with feats of prophetic insight, soothsaying, and miracle working. Church authorities were gathering evidence that she was perpetrating illegal "cargo" schemes, and her defense was a cause célèbre among the Revivalists, who saw her as their inspired champion. I had had very little contact with Bato'w when, at the height of her fame, she accused me of stealing money from a graveyard. Shades of the hapless kiap from earlier in this chapter! Supposedly, Bato'w had caught me in the act. When I tried to buy her silence by offering to make her my accomplice, she refused, demanding that I stop stealing from the graves. An angry delegation of her followers came to me with Bato'w's accusation. My denial in the face of such compelling "evidence" took them by surprise. With the help of friends who spoke up in my defense, the confrontation was soon defused, and the posse withdrew in confusion. I heard no more about my fabulous grave robbing, but there can be no doubt that the incident was added to the store of anxious speculations surrounding our presence in the village.

The overt hostility triggered by the Bato'w incident, while exceptional, illustrates the volatility of the situation and the ease with which the seemingly paranoid hysteria gripping the village could seize upon the anomaly of our white presence. Far more common, especially among our closer friends and neighbors, were projections that included us in their fantasies or ploys that were calculated to flush us out. The trick was to find the key—the right word, phrase, or insight—that would cause the largesse we controlled to be showered upon privileged persons in our circle. A few examples should confirm our psychological salience in the people's spiritual imagination and, related to this, illustrate the mediation of individual fantasy in coordinating our presence with the fluidities of Revivalist belief during this period.

Our nearest neighbors were Wa'akea and her family. She was in her late thirties, a reserved, rather shrewish mother of six living children. Before, we had known her and her husband, Salalaman, as an appealing couple, happily married with a four-year-old (who died soon afterward) and an infant; the young family lived a few hamlets away with Salalaman's aged parents. Wa'akea and Salalaman were both sweet, ingenuous, and unassertive. By the time we returned, they had become active, self-important leaders of the Ililip cell of the Revival movement. Wa'akea was one of twenty-four female tok profet in Ilahita, which meant that she had the "gift" of spiritual insight—a socially useful ability to ferret out Satan's agents, expose marital infidelities, find lost objects, identify thieves and other malefactors, and relay divine instructions (including punishment prescriptions) to individuals and the community.

Parenthetically, nearly all of these revelations were prejudicial to men, who, if they were Revivalists, were hauled before the congregation to be shamed and made to confess their domestic sins at peril of being ejected from the community of the blessed. It is said that the Holy Spirit favored women as Its vessel because they were untainted by the satanic evil of the Tambaran.[16] "The women now rule with their own Tambaran," philosophized the traditionalists. The inversion was nearly total. Although men certainly participated in the Revival and most of the preachers were men, the zealots of the movement were women. They were the most assertive, vocal, and histrionic members of the congregation, far more likely than men were to lapse into trance or fly into hysteria. In all essential respects, the women now formed the ritual collective in Ilahita. They, not the men, were organized and unified. In their periodic, mass prayer meetings that drew from many surrounding villages, men were strictly forbidden. Said Mangas, the middle-aged traditionalist from chapter 3 who was becoming homicidal over his wife's insubordination, "When I think of all those women, together, in their secret meeting, it makes me very afraid."

Subsequent to my first fieldwork Salalaman had gone to Bible school at the SSEC field headquarters at Brugam, some fifteen kilometers west of Ilahita. His theological sophistication was well below that of others with similar experience; and it may have been his lack of charisma and corresponding lack of success as a deacon, combined with his low social standing by traditional measures, that pushed him toward the heterodox Revival movement. Before, a rather dull but amiable person, Salalaman was now bumptious and occasionally strident. He was also less friendly toward us—more guarded, given to heaving loud sighs while commenting on the heat or on the hard work that filled their lives compared with the easy existence white people enjoyed. While the invidious comparison may have been merited, the complaint about hard work was ironic coming from Salalaman, who was one of the least industrious men of his generation in the village. Before, he had passively fantasized a better life for himself, thinking he deserved one, but lacking the imagination, energy, or opportunity to improve his lot. The Revival answered strongly to these needs; hence his unshakable commitment to the cause, even when it meant defending ideas and practices that were bizarre by local, decidedly extreme, standards.[17]

Most people in our part of the village knew that I was interested in hearing dream reports. Accordingly, it was not unusual when, early on the morning of March 17, 1986, Wa'akea and Salalaman came to tell me about a dream Wa'akea had just experienced. Not so usual was their breathlessness: both were noticeably excited by what they had to tell me and eager to get my reaction. They studied my face closely as Wa'akea gave the following account, changed here to the third person.

> Wa'akea looks from her house to the Elaf plaza and sees that a big yellow airplane is parked in front of the Tuzins' door. She goes to investigate. Tuzin is there. Wa'akea asks him why the airplane is there. He replies, "It is for you. Come inside and bring Beti [her infant daughter], Leslie, and Albert, but not the other children." Wa'akea protests that she wants to bring all of her children, but Tuzin says "No." They get into the airplane. Two white women, whom Wa'akea does not recognize, are already in the airplane. The airplane takes off with Tuzin as pilot and flies over [the neighboring friendly village of] Ningalimbi and then on south toward Ambunti [on the Sepik River]. It circles back and starts to descend. Wa'akea asks Tuzin if they are going to land now and collect the other children. He says, "No, we are going to continue flying around for a while." Wa'akea awakes.

The dream leaves little to the imagination, as to the wishful place Wa'akea created for me in her millenarian fantasies. The meticulous interest she and Salalaman showed in my reaction must be understood in the context of Arapesh dream theory, which holds that dreams are literal experiences of the sleeper on the spiritual plane. Like many beliefs positing spirit phenomena, the Ilahita are not entirely consistent in their adherence to them and tend to be selective according to whether they are otherwise motivated to believe. In this case, the compulsion to believe would have been very strong. But for me to have probed Wa'akea and Salalaman on what *they* understood the dream to mean would have only intensified their conviction that I was hiding precious knowledge; it would have come across as a ploy to discover how much they already knew before deciding how much to tell them.

From their demeanor, and in the light of many other encounters of similar strange type, including with these two individuals, this much is certain: they thought that Wa'akea's dream was about something real, that I was implicated in some fashion resembling my role in the dream, that Wa'akea's "airplane ride" meant preferment for her, and that confronting me with the dream might trick or induce me into admitting—perhaps only to them—the secret of spiritual and material fulfillment. Indeed, their conspiratorial air suggested that, as far as they were concerned, the dream was my way of declaring myself to them; their coming to me with the dream was in the nature of offering a countersign, signifying, so to speak, that my "message" had been received. The entire episode was full of knowing looks and sly smiles on their part, while I struggled to look innocent and unaware of their extravagant signaling. My handling of this ludicrous exchange could not have fooled them; on the contrary, I fear that it confirmed that I was hiding something and that I was not ready to acknowledge openly the bond that the dream certified.

Wa'akea's conjuring of an airplane is understandable. For her, it is the ultimate "cargo", it has a natural skyward affinity to heaven above, and it requires a pilot, this being a common metaphor for Jesus in missionary sermons. As to the dream machine's size and color, it so happens that a big yellow vehicle *was* often parked in front of my door. This was the big yellow flatbed truck that Ililip had recently bought, hoping to make money hauling goods and passengers. I made a substantial cash contribution to its down payment and for long periods was the only person available who was able to "pilot" it. The people acted as though, responding to their need, I should put aside my notebooks and spend the year as their driver. Their importunities could not be completely refused and consequently I spent more time than I could afford on the road to Maprik and, occasionally, Wewak. As to the two white women aboard the dream flight, I cannot comment, since Wa'akea did not recognize them and could not describe them in any detail. Wa'akea's concern over leaving three of her children behind is of particular interest, in itself and for its reappearance in a dream experienced the very evening of the day she and Salalaman came to me with the "airplane" dream.

That evening, Wa'akea and Salalaman were sitting together at their house. Wa'akea complained that she was tired of eating taro and that Salalaman should process a sago palm. Salalaman retorted that he was weary of processing sago and that they should eat taro. They went back and forth in disagreement, tempers mounting. In a henpecked huff, Salalaman took his Bible and went to the evening church service. Wa'akea put her children to bed, except for her daughter Dokas, the eldest (age twelve), and prayed to be rid of her annoyed feelings toward Salalaman. Then she and Dokas went to the nearby house of Tambwiliwa (Gidion's widow) to sleep, while Tambwiliwa went a few steps away to her adult daughter's house to sleep. Wa'akea and Dokas prayed and slept.

But Wa'akea does not sleep; she dies. She sees herself lying on her back on a table, like the one in Tuzin's kitchen area, with a white cloth over her. Salalaman and their children are standing by the wall of the room. A door opens. God is there, beckoning her to come. [In answer to Beverly's question, Wa'akea describes God as tall, white skinned, and bearded—a conventional description, which also happens to fit the ethnographer.] Wa'akea goes to God, knowing that He is going to take her to Heaven. Salalaman says, "You can't leave. Who will take care of the children?" Wa'akea answers, "You can take care of the children. I am going to Heaven." But Salalaman and the children are too strong in their insistence, and she comes back to them. Wa'akea awakens.

The powerful stock image of the "door," with connotations of a different reality revealable from behind it, along with the cultural significances already discussed, is very common in Revivalist dreams and visions. Of more specific interest, it is noteworthy that Wa'akea's concern in both dreams about leaving her children draws upon patterned domestic conflict that arose in the aftermath of the collapse of the Tambaran. Wa'akea was terribly weary and resentful of her maternal role, but as a dedicated mother she felt guilty over wishing to be free of her children. The pain of perceiving herself as a bad mother, and the prospect of public censure if others were to join in that view, generated its own resentment, which she vented against Salalaman and her children, making family matters worse and herself more beaten down and shrewish. This conflict involving the maternal role was repeated in many Revivalist households, and it is interesting to see it displayed with such clarity in Wa'akea's personal dreams of escape from domestic captivity; an escape not to the great forest or the grass fields, the Other places to which Nambweapa'w fled, but to Heaven.

Returning to the question of my recruitment to the Revivalist project, the following dream and associated vision by Wa'akea confirm that the link is through dead Gidion. The dream occurred on the morning of March 29, 1986, which was the day following Good Friday. As before, Wa'akea was sleeping in Tambwiliwa's house, this time with Dokas and her infant daughter, Beti. She was moved to remark that, just as she was retiring to bed the night before, after praying, she had noticed the lamp being extinguished in our house. She stirred early the next morning, saw that the dawn was breaking, fell back asleep, and dreamed.

> Wa'akea is sleeping in Tambwiliwa's house, but is awakened
> by a loud rapping on the door. The door opens to reveal Tuzin
> standing there. He puts one leg over the threshold, half stepping
> into the house. He is holding a flashlight, and Wa'akea can see
> Gidion standing behind him. They tell her to get up and go back
> to her own house. They are plainly excited about something, and
> Wa'akea knows that this means they have something for her. She
> awakens.

Immediately upon awakening, Wa'akea carelessly swallowed, causing herself, according to local belief, to forget all but the portion of the dream stated above. She was sure that there was more and that what she was forgetting was the most important part. Urgently she prayed, hoping this would restore her memory or guide her to whatever Gidion and I had brought for her. As luck would have it, during her prayer Dokas touched her on the back and broke her concentration.

A short time later, after participating in an ad hoc prayer group convened to ease a neighbor woman's splitting headache, Wa'akea proceeded to the morning service in the Ililip chapel, located in a nearby hamlet.

There was an initial hymn, followed by a group prayer. Wa'akea's prayer was interrupted, however, by a clear vision of *me*.

> Tuzin is standing in front of Tambwiliwa's door, prancing[18] and holding high a fat bundle of kina notes bound with a rubber band. He is offering the money to Wa'akea. She is excited and wants to go to the house for the money, when, much to her annoyance, another hymn starts up in the congregation and the vision quickly fades away. Wa'akea is back in the world of the ordinary. She knows that if she rushes back to Tambwiliwa's door, Tuzin will not be there. She knows that she has missed her chance.

Wa'akea was by no means the only person to feature me in her dreams and visions. On the contrary, from the fraction of experiences actually reported to me, I estimate that there were times, especially during periods of agitated millenarian expectations, when my nightly rounds were very heavily scheduled. The recurrent images and thematic similarities between these accounts, which the people took as proof that they were all glimpsing the same spiritual reality, was in fact the predictable consequence of the feverish reporting and comparing of visionary experiences among members of the Revival community. They were indeed drawing upon a common reality, but it was a reality that existed neither "out there" nor "in there," in some profound spiritual sense: it was a reality emergent from the intense, even obsessional communicating and mutual emulating of personal fantasies within the tightly knit community of believers. Let me offer additional examples, to show that Wa'akea was not alone.

• In July 1985, immediately after our arrival in the village, Salalaman had a dream in which a tall white man with a beard carried him away. This person told Salalaman to look down under the ground. There he saw many tin-roofed houses of unfamiliar design, with flowers and pretty decorations. Salalaman editorially wondered whether the tall white man was in fact me.

• In another dream, Salalaman sees God, who is a tall, bearded white man ("like Tuzin"). God beckons to him to come through an open door, but warns that if he goes through the door, he cannot come back again. Salalaman decides not to go, so God tells him that he must go forth and spread the Good News about the Bible.

• Hengewen, a friend and kinswoman of Wa'akea and the wife of the Ililip pastor, had this dream.

> Mo'otawa [an educated, popular young man of Ililip who has just returned from a prestigious job in Wewak] and Tuzin are gathered in Hengewen's house. She senses that the time is about dawn. Tuzin hands around navy biscuits, and Hengewen notices that [Tuzin's nine-year-old son] Gregory is also present. He, too, receives a biscuit. Tuzin gives Hengewen sixty toea, saying, "Take it, there is more to come." Then he gives her six exercise books, such as are commonly used in area schools. The lined pages are apparently blank. Tuzin produces a bottle of yellow fluid, similar to the antiseptic wash used at the Mission clinic. Half of it he pours into another bottle and gives to her. She understands that he intends for her to drink it. Tuzin says, "I am giving this to you, but not to Balif [a village seven miles north in a different Arapesh dialect area]. They do not come to see me, and so they will have sorrows, and fighting will erupt among them."
>
> But then as Hengewen looks at Tuzin, he changes. He is himself, but he is not. Hengewen asks, "Who are you? Are you Tuzin?" In a voice not his own, he answers, "No, I am not Tuzin. I am Gidion." To her horror, Hengewen is now looking into the face, and hearing the voice, of Gidion. She is afraid because she knows that Gidion is dead. Her fear awakens her. She searches for the 60t and the liquid given to her in the dream but cannot find them.

The nightmarish transformation of myself into the dead Gidion may be (but probably is not) a novel touch. At the least, the detail is a graphic personal depiction of a group fantasy. That fantasy goes as follows: I am allied with Gidion in an exciting millenarian project involving Ilahita. Having vowed in life that I would return, Gidion in death went to fetch me in the land of the dead or in America, the two places being the same in this context. By the other rules that govern manifest forms in that realm, Gidion and I are now one and the same—or, masalai-like, are able to change into one another at will. For many New Guinea peoples, these notions would be familiar as applications of the idea that whites are dead people, indeed are ghosts or ancestors of the people themselves. For the people of Ilahita, specifically, the fantasy fulfills the prophetic scenario of Nambweapa'w's beloved youngest son departing on a flood to America, from whence he will return.

Other features confirm that Hengewen's dream is a pastiche of images constantly barraging her from the limited Revivalist repertoire. In this respect the dreams are akin to Ilahita traditional narratives, which often appear to have been confected of mixed, matched, and lightly embroidered modules, taken from a relatively small set of such units. In Hengewen's account a corresponding dream module would be, for example, the miraculous fluids. In red, yellow, or colorless form, this elixir shows up often in Revivalists' dreams and visions and in Bato'w's bogus miracle working. According to Salalaman, drinking the liquid would make one's eyes clear and one's moral vision pure enough to attract and retain God's blessing. Unfortunately, something always happens to prevent the dreamer from drinking the mysterious water. In one dream recalled by Salalaman, an angel filled a bottle with this liquid and started to bring it to Salalaman, but then turned aside. (Angels, Salalaman offers, are white men and white women.) On waking reflection, Salalaman blames the disruptive acts of those who condemn the Revivalists and seek to bring them to court for causing the angel to turn aside at the last moment. To his way of thinking, until those reprobates accept the Revival and submit to its truth, the water will remain undelivered, undrunk, and just out of reach.

Dream- and hope-driven fantasies of the preceding sort dominated Revivalist thought and action during the year of our return. I say "action" advisedly, for most of what the Revivalists did was dictated by their spiritual program. Gardens, coffee groves, children, and pigs were neglected by householders who spent hours every morning and long into every night in church. The health of bodies, minds, families, and civil society was sacrificed to the exhausting incessancy of expectation, disappointment, and scapegoating. Earlier I used the simile of disengaged gears to describe the irreality into which the Revivalists plunged themselves. The killing of the Tambaran enacted the Cassowary's Revenge, and the people now eagerly looked to my return—the return of dead Gidion's "little brother" from America—as the instrument of their reward. Their strenuous pretendings and imaginings were more than wishful thinking, though they were certainly that; they were also a traditionally accepted technique for bringing about the desired result. In ritual ceremonies and in magical healing, for example, material procedures were designed as iconic of, and therefore *precipitating of,* effective processes occurring on the spiritual plane.[19] For all kinds of reasons then, the Revivalists' mythic interpretation of my return was culturally appropriate and powerfully motivated.

Although the Revivalists largely controlled Ilahita's metaphysical agenda during the 1985–86 period, not all villagers thought as they did. A sizable, heterogeneous minority consisting of non-Christians, SSEC Christians, and members of a small, more tradition-friendly Christian sect known as the New Apostles, were scathingly critical of the Revivalist beliefs and antics. The presence of these skeptics, neighbors quick to ridicule or to bring legal action, is what forced the Revivalists to be so secretive. From their vantage point as inside outsiders, these nonbelievers sometimes offered acute insights into Revivalist phenomena.

One such instance occurred during a fortnight of unusually intense Revival activity. Rumors had been flying, and every hour, it seemed, new revelatory dreams and strange happenings were being reported. I was sitting at my house with a small, age-mixed group of traditionalists, listening to them reflect bitterly on the excesses of their Revivalist neighbors and kin. It was well past midnight. From its location in a nearby hamlet came the very audible sounds of the chapel service still in progress—songs and group prayers, punctuated by noisy hubbubs indicating that someone had been seized by the Holy Spirit.[20] Eventually, the clatter would subside, and the congregation would disperse to their beds, where decent folk should be at that hour of the night. Before that, however, the group I was with would themselves retire, so as to avoid unpleasant encounters with Revivalists coming stoked and belligerent from their meeting.

My companions poked fun at the Revivalist belief that these phony outbursts conveyed divinely inspired truth; they recalled howlingly erroneous claims and predictions issued by Revivalists during trance. Our talk then moved to the question of why Revivalists have so many dreams and visions that seem to confirm their beliefs. Do such experiences have any source other than God and Satan? I was interested in how these men might attempt to deny the validity of dream-based revelations, given the traditional notion that dreams are true and veridical experiences of the sleeper's spirit. A couple members of the group dismissed the reports as outright lies; others were willing to believe that the dreams had occurred and therefore had difficulty in justifying their reluctance to accept the religious and cargoistic claims based upon them. Fahien, however, a man in his mid-thirties, stepped outside the register of traditional thinking about dreams and penetrated to the heart of the matter. "Listen," he said,

> we are sitting here tonight discussing a topic. It could be any
> topic. Then later tonight some of us might dream about this
> topic. I think this is what happens with the Revivalists. They at-
> tend chapel in the evening and stay there until late at night. They
> talk about God and think about God. They know that someone
> has lost something or is in some kind of trouble. They wish for
> things. After chapel, they go home and go straight to bed. Then,
> they dream about what had earlier interested them, and they sup-
> pose that it is God telling or showing or giving them something
> that will solve the problem. You see, their dreams are relevant
> not because God is their source, but because they are continua-
> tions of the ideas from the evening, ideas they fell asleep thinking
> about.

One must admire Fahien's explanation. Correctly and succinctly, in my view, he identifies autosuggestion, group suggestion, wishful think-ing, doctrinal understandings, and the continuity of waking and sleeping thoughts as elements in the constitution of validatory dreams and visions. Going beyond the traditionally assumed literalness with which dreams are regarded—a literalness central to Revivalist ontology—his interpretation addresses the crucial interpenetration of public and private fantasy. But just as, on further analysis, Wa'akea's and Hengewen's dreams would yield more deeply private significances—symbolic associations antecedent to the public issues we are discussing—so the Revivalist debates and discus-sions are conditioned by antecedent cultural understandings about dreams, myths, and causal relations and by the interpreted significance of current events, such as the murder of the Tambaran and the provocative coincidence of Gidion's death with the announcement of my return from America.

Much of Nambweapa'w's story has now been told. We have traced her kinship with other swan maidens featured in folk traditions scattered throughout much of the Old World. Upon arrival in Ilahita in the last century, this swan maiden was modified and deployed so as to dramatize a moral dilemma brought about by the coincident adoption of the Tam-baran cult. We have seen that Nambweapa'w's performative success and the prophetic power of her story rests on a synthesis of images and associations drawn from a wide array of Ilahita cultural ideas. How much more indigenized can a story be than to have risen so quickly from alien narrative to Creation Epic in the space of only a few generations?

The rapidity of her cultural advancement is due to the importance of Nambweapa'w's symbolic work, in conjunction with the powerful livingness common to oral traditions such as hers. With each retelling, Nambweapa'w's story remolds itself to changing circumstances, churning itself into a remarkably coherent jumble of older and newer meanings.[21] The detail of the youngest brother's departure "for America," with its millenarian overtones, dates from the period of World War II. But it was apparently not until my first arrival in 1969 that the significance of a mythic connection with America began to be realized. And it was not until the announcement in 1984 of my *return,* that the significance of the original visit was realized. Prophecy works that way—by remembrance and revisitation. Today's events fold back upon memories of yesterday and, by a Proustian alchemy, transfigure them. Isolated fragments from the past become realized as significant objects of intentional meaning, animated and integrated with the present. At the core of this process of remembering is an aesthetic illusion: both for individuals in their ways and cultures in theirs, it is the illusion of the self finding itself in memory. An image at once familiar and not, this illusion is the source of the uncanny in dreams, myths, prophecies, and other modes of aesthetic imagery. It was, after all, none other than the Titaness Mnemosyne, goddess of memory, who by Zeus gave birth to the Muses.

Invoking creation myths for expressive purposes is culture's way of "remembering" and, under unusual circumstances, re-creating itself. Metaphysical problems require metaphysical measures. During the tumultuous period surrounding the death of the Tambaran and the rise of millenarian Revivalism, Ilahita did indeed seek to re-create itself. Bringing Nambweapa'w's prophecy to fulfillment by destroying the Masculine Deceiver and construing my return as the return of the Last-Born, the Ilahita mythmaker cleared the way for a radically different future. This was no easy task, for it required facing down and overcoming the masculine fear embodied in the tale of the Cassowary-Mother. This aspect of her story, the dark side of Nambweapa'w, the side she shares with the ogress Epelini'w, is her final chapter.

Chapter Seven

FEAR IN THE HEART

Ethnographers usually collect myths in order to illustrate a figment of cultural imagination or to test and explore the cultural salience of observed social or psychological phenomena. Only recently have some ethnographers begun to treat myths, the origins of which are apparently remote in time and fantastical in nature, as actively affecting immediate behavior or the indigenous interpretation of current events (e.g., Sahlins 1983, 1985; Young 1983; Glasse 1995; Clark 1995).[1] Once this livingness is better understood, the next step will be to conceptualize how myth may contribute to developments at the level of society and culture. Meanwhile, phrases such as "mythic domain," "mythic thinking," and "mythic consciousness" continue in use, presupposing a separation between mythic pseudoreality and the commonplace reality governing mundane affairs. Nineteenth-century scholars, such as J. J. Bachofen and F. Max Müller, speculated that myths are culturally enshrined memories of (pre)-historic events and processes, by implication far removed from immediate realities. There is clearly something to this. As Susanne Langer says, "All knowledge goes back to experience; we cannot know anything that *bears no relation* to our experience" (1953, 390). Likewise, mythical knowledge must originate in experience of some kind.

The difficulty with the "myth as cultural memory" notion, however, is that it does not adequately account for why culture bothers to remember the remote past at all or why these supposed memories, by definition, are filtered through the mythologizing lens of fantasy. Bronislaw Malinowski ([1926] 1948) applied a more modern understanding to the phenomena by observing that some myths function as "charters" authorizing present-day social arrangements and entitlements: totemic categories, status hierarchies, property tenure, ritual prerogatives, and the like. Thus was myth objectified and neatly inserted into the conceptually manageable field of social action.

The myth-as-charter notion is now an anthropological staple, its utility proved many times since Malinowski articulated it. But, of course, myths function in nonideological ways as well; the relationship between myth and human affairs can be seen in a light that preserves its subjective, indeed aesthetic, quality. This view is partly contained in analyses treating myths as psychological or sociological projections, expressive of contradictions embedded in the psyche or the social order. Left there, however, especially in the context of an oral tradition, the approach retains the objectivist reading of myth and neglects the dialectical nature of the projective process. Describe them as you will—whether in classic historical, sociological, or psychological terms—once they are objectified it is difficult to appreciate the fact that myths act upon, as well as are acted upon by, contingent events (Sahlins 1983).

My treatment of "Nambweapa'w" and its slew of associations, including its implicit, untoward adoption of me, was a demonstration that living myth abides in the interactive flux of texts, contexts, occasions, and audiences. Myths, it is true, emerge from sources in thought, experience, and social action and are molded by cultural understandings; but as changeable objects of collective fantasy, they also react upon the realms from whence they come.[2] This reaction alters the source of projected images, which in turn changes the counterprojection, and so on. The interactive pseudodomains cycle through one another with each retelling, coevolving until the myth either dies or is canonized—death by another name—in a written form. If living myths are objects, they are objects paradoxically devoid of inertia, changing, like subatomic particles, at the instant of expression.

Through this dialectic, Ilahita mythology helped to propagate men's anxieties about their supremacy in ritual, politics, and the household. Behind the strict secrecy of the cult, the violent rhetoric against women, the illusions devised to trick and mystify women as to the Tambaran's true nature—behind this elaborate misogyny, one could clearly detect that the men's assaults were preemptive, expressing fear and imagined vulnerability on their part. We know that Nambweapa'w—the fierce, phallic, abandoning mother; the mother who kills the decrepit deceiver-father with his own spear; the mother whose magic is of the dead and the wild—virtually pinpoints this anxiety within men's intuitions about maternal power and aggressiveness. We know also that "Nambweapa'w" arrived in Ilahita at about the same time as the Tambaran, but from the opposite direction, indicating a possible coevolutionary relationship between them.

As we are about to see, "Nambweapa'w" and the Tambaran do indeed play upon the same dread-of-woman idea. And yet this thematic correspondence, because it belongs to the same order of fantasy, says little about the independent sources of the anxiety; we cannot use one to interpret the other. Recalling Langer's injunction, we must ask to what experience the fear and imagined vulnerability common to "Nambweapa'w" and the Tambaran relates. This question must now be addressed, beginning with the evidence that these distressing feelings exist at all, independently of their ritual and mythic representations. One does not have to look far.

Several stories held secret by the Tambaran tell of times past when certain paramount cult objects were discovered or invented by women, children, or, in one tale, dogs (Tuzin 1980).[3] The men were terrorized by the devices—usually weird sound-making instruments such as bullroarers and voice pipes—until they found out the truth about them. Discovering they had been tricked and that the eerie sounds came not from frightful monsters lurking just out of view but from bits of wood and bamboo manipulated by women (or children, or dogs), they killed the original owners, seized the devices, and installed them among the central mysteries of the Tambaran (Tuzin 1980).

Whatever the source of these mythical constructs may have been,[4] the men's mythically "remembered" victory triggered a real and intractable fear, one that the men discussed among themselves in the form of an anxious question: What if the women found out about their primal ownership of these ritual goods and claimed them back? Retaining the devices by force would not do, since their coercive effect depended on cult outsiders not knowing their true nature. The end of secrecy would mean the end of women's credulity and men's legitimacy, such that it would be silly for the Tambaran to persist in these ritual antics after the women found out the truth about them. Thus, although expressed as an image of women seizing back the cult paraphernalia, the men's fear did not go so far as to contemplate a ritual role reversal: a Tambaran operated by and for women and against men, such as the Revival eventually brought to pass. Rather, they envisioned an apocalyptic collapse of male authority and of the social order in general.

No such apprehension attached to children and dogs, the other "rightful owners" remembered in myth. To fear rebellion from those powerless quarters may have seemed ludicrous, though no more so than the idea that dogs secretly used to put on paint and feathers to dance the night away. The men's refusal even to imagine the possibility of dogs or young boys claiming back their ritual rights has two somewhat contradictory implications. First, the elision directs the men's attention to the moral and practical hazards in their relations with *women*. Second, it obscures what may be a psychologically more primitive insecurity on the men's part, one that fears not only women, but dogs and children and everything over which men have dominion, including themselves. Pervasive and insidious, this fear is about the prospect of losing masculine identity; about the loss of potency in the most general sense; about castration, literal and figurative. The fear of women is unrealistic because it unconsciously carries something categorically larger and more weighty: anxiety over the prospect of oblivion, a prospect mythically expressed as a calamitous Deluge.[5] The double-layeredness of male insecurity should be kept in mind as we examine its parts more closely, beginning with the relatively explicit fear of women and of what they might do if they found out that the Tambaran had been duping them these many years.

That this anxiety preyed on men's minds is shown by its presence on their lips. That the concern was also chronic is confirmed by the curious fact, overlooked by writers on the subject of "myths of matriarchy" (e.g., Bamberger 1974; Gewertz 1988), that *the men keep telling these stories to themselves.* As was wondered in the case of First Man and his wife's cassowary skin, why did the men of the Tambaran preserve the incriminating charter? If the secrets were lethal to the men's interests, why did they not simply stop telling them, burying the secrets, once and for all, under six feet of amnesia? Or, better yet, why didn't the mythmaker concoct a set of tales *justifying* the men's seizure of ritual prerogatives from the women, such as characterizes "myths of matriarchy" among the Mundurucú, Mehinaku, and other South American groups (Murphy and Murphy 1985, 115; Gregor 1985, 112–13; Hays 1988, 99–100)?[6]

The answer is that the Ilahita men cleaved to these stories in order to cope with felt vulnerabilities arising from social and psychological circumstances. Naming or narrativizing an existential fear is no cure for it. So long as the conditions generating the fear survive, the stories will be retold. Nevertheless, named fears are less terrifying than unnamed ones, and the ability to project these fears as pictures, stories, and ideologies is a large part of what separates us from the beasts. In Ilahita, at least until recently, the cult stories serviceably objectified the moral contradictions with which the men lived. The retellings vented, but at the same time regenerated, the psychical discomfort that some (perhaps many) men experienced over this moral dilemma.[7] The stories, in a phrase, sustained a modus vivendi, predicated on a chronic moral crisis between ritual and domestic values. That is, so long as the Tambaran kept its secrets.

This brings us to that fateful day in September 1984, when Ilahita's ethnographic present became its past. We now know in some detail what happened during the ensuing months, with the Tambaran dead, custom repealed, and the women ecstatically seizing control. But what of the immediate impact? After generations of male foreboding over this prospect, what *did* happen when the women were told that the Tambaran was a lie? Judging from recollections Beverly and I gleaned from men and women a year or so afterward, the event was not the shocker the men had expected it to be. Indeed, somewhat to the men's chagrin, the women were yawningly indifferent to the particulars of this institution from which they and their foremothers had been excluded.

Furthermore, women were now at liberty to admit to us, and to concur among themselves, that they had always assumed that the men were lying when they spoke of gigantic people-eating monsters, adolescent initiates being turned into flying foxes, and other improbabilities; it is just that they did not know, and did not particularly care, what the truth was behind the men's fictions. Finding out what had actually been going on excited them about as little as being shown a urinal would excite a grown woman in our society: a male thing, a male "secret"—so what? We always figured it had to be something like that. On the other hand, cutting straight to the gender politics of the Tambaran, the women were impatiently skeptical of the ritual excuses that had mandated their exclusion and wrathful at having been duped. Although some women voiced pity over the ordeals and disciplines that the cult had imposed on the men, even they were not impressed by the claim that all this was borne of cosmological necessity. In general, the women's view was that the men's ritual understandings were variously irrelevant, hostile, and fraudulent; mostly, though, they were unimpressed.[8]

Ironically, this may have been the reaction men feared the most. "We are willing to be wicked," said Molière, "but we will not be ridiculous."[9]

Psychoanalyst Karen Horney ([1932] 1966) opined that the male's wide-spread dread of woman originates not as a fear of castration, but as "a reaction to the menace to his self-respect" brought on by a boy's feeling that "his penis is much too small for his mother's genital," and that she will reject and deride him for his phallic inadequacy (p. 91). So it was with the Tambaran men of Ilahita, who dreaded the shame and embarrassment that would be theirs if the women found out about the deceptions. Fear of ridicule was indeed paramount in the men's defenses, as it has been in other New Guinea men's cults (Hays 1988, 106). "Nothing we could say would make the women understand [about the Tambaran]," as one man expressed it. "They would laugh at us." Events were to prove him correct: the women did not understand; they did laugh—and then they retaliated. Correctly, the man intuited that the secret men's cult is about men's secrets: insecurities and fantasies peculiar to their sex. These anxieties are rooted in the fragility of masculine sexual self-esteem, therefore undermining confidence in power wielded in the name of masculinity—the very essence of the Tambaran. Only the powerful can be ridiculous, and only men can have small penises, which is why men so often construe both their power and their vulnerability in phallic terms.

As usual, the Ilahita have a story to cover the subject, one that was touched on in chapter 4:

> There was once a man whose penis was so long he had to carry it coiled over his shoulder. [The audience laughs at this ridiculous image.] This organ he would send on long underground excursions in search of women. One woman, annoyed at having the thing penetrate her when she bent over, hacked it to pieces with her ax, causing the man at the other end to die. Ever since then men have had short penises.

The reassuring, counterphobic point about this little story is that short penises are not ridiculous, long ones are—like the ones we used to have.

In view of the Tambaran's elaborate gender-inflected ideology and sexual cum procreative imagery (Tuzin 1995b), it is not surprising that the male ritual mystique would be associated with the penis and that a threat to the one would also be a threat to the other.[10] Hence the men's urgent identification with the Tambaran and their perception that its demise would be a calamity of apocalyptic proportions. Long ago, I asked one of the sharpest, most knowledgeable cult elders what the truth was about the Tambaran—the true truth, that is, the reality behind all of the tricks and illusions. Cutting to the quick, he replied that the Tambaran is "what men do," implying an ontological barrier impenetrable to women so long as tradition lasted.[11] For him, the alignment of personal and collective male purpose, and the coincidence of male virtue, necessity, and reward, was complete. For him, the great fear was the prospect of the end of tradition, for that would spell the loss of masculine identity, the revelation of phallic inadequacy, and the end of existential meaning (cf. Murphy and Murphy 1985, 256). He lived to see the day.

It is not surprising, either, that cult orthodoxy obfuscated these primordial fears, though not with uniform effectiveness. The intrusion of women would offend the Tambaran, it was claimed, thereby jeopardizing village peace and prosperity; relaxing the rules, it was feared, would entail the catastrophic loss of spirit patronage. Only the most junior initiates believed that this was the whole of it, however. One would hear men talk and make speeches about how women are the bane of the solidarity men require for war, ritual, and social transactions. Men who were somewhat senior in the cult, while perhaps not doubting the cosmological and sociological imperatives, also recognized a measure of duplicity and self-interest in the cult's orthodoxy and correspondingly feared reprisal. One man went so far as to admit privately that the Tambaran was unfairly punishing to women, but that "if we told [the women] now that for all these generations they had been deceived, they would make life unbearable for us. There is nothing we can do" (see Tuzin 1980, 302). Of course, there *was* something the men could do, and thirteen years later they did it. My informant was dead by then, and the reprisal he feared went ahead in his absence.

These fears, though consequential for the men and for this study, presupposed the cult; they existed because the cult existed. That the men feared exposure was simply an artifact of their having inherited an institution that violently excludes women and spends a good deal of its energies on deceiving them. But what of the fear(s) that are in some sense anterior to the cult, fears to which the Tambaran itself is a response? What primitive fear sustains the belief that men and their works would be grievously harmed if women were involved or even knew about it? Part of the answer may lie in the above-mentioned fragility of masculine sexual self-esteem, a fragility that is perhaps not unique to the Arapesh. There is more to it than this, however, judging from ideas and behaviors of a more local kind.

One obvious place to seek insight into the men's fear of women might be the realm of male fantasies about feminine sexuality and alleged pollution and, in particular, the harrowing dangers of menstrual blood. Among the Arapesh, however, in contrast with attitudes reported for many other New Guinea societies, the men do not evince inordinate fear of the feminine principle as such, or its manifestation in menstrual blood or vaginal secretions. Indicatively, once the men were satisfied that Beverly—undeniably feminine—understood and respected the need for cult secrecy and would not betray the Tambaran to the women, they did not object to her presence at secret events. That is to say, there was nothing in her femininity that would impair their ritual works. Nor did men hesitate to accept food from Beverly, even though she might have been menstruating and unaware of the danger she posed to men while in that condition. It was not women in general they feared; it was *their* women.

As to the polluting effects of Ilahita women, while the men did indeed avoid contact with menstrual blood, they did not do so with any of the horror reported for some other areas of Melanesia (e.g., Allen 1967; Herdt 1981, 246–48; Meigs 1984, 111). During the early years of marriage, a menstruating wife may retire to the local girls' sleeping house, but that is more to enjoy the local equivalent of a pajama party than to avoid polluting her household. Later, after she has outgrown her taste for this diversion, it is sufficient for husband and menstruating wife to separate their sleeping mats, lessening the chances of inadvertent contact or sexual temptation during the night. It is true that an older man with a nubile daughter in the house, needing to safeguard his health and magic, will typically remove to his yam house, next door, there to sleep and take his meals. But the danger in this case has only partly to do with the daughter's femininity: it is equally the result of her sexuality being youthful and unrelieved, which is the "hottest" sexuality of all. Young men are "hot" for the same reason; hence the strength of young warriors, which also endangers the health and spiritual vitality of old men and the success of their magical projects.

Despite these modest precautions, daily intercourse with women (sexual and otherwise) does take its toll on a man's physical and spiritual vigor, as female contaminants accumulate in his blood. Periodic penile bloodletting enables a man to cleanse his system of these factors. Though men jokingly refer to this as the "male menstruation," the procedure is masturbatory and quintessentially masculine (Tuzin 1980, 74–77), an assertion of male power and spiritual autonomy. There is little in it to evoke Bruno Bettelheim's theory (1954) that penis cutting strives to emulate female anatomy and procreativity, still less that it signifies an inordinate fear of women. If there is any emulation or fear component at all—and I am not saying there is—it concerns the youthful, virginal, *male* condition, the potential menace of which is more realistic to the older men than are any powers attributable to women. Also telling of a relatively friendly attitude toward feminine sexuality, cunnilingus is recognized as a not uncommon form of lovemaking and, according to some older informants, has always been so (Tuzin 1995a, 265).

In summary, Ilahita men are only moderately worried about feminine essences; certainly, their anxiety in this regard is disproportionately slight in comparison with the traditional fear associated with the women's finding out about the Tambaran. Perhaps, then, a better place to seek illumination might be in the male's *experience* of females, beginning with the mother. During my first fieldwork, problems in the mother-son relationship were detectable but overshadowed by the effects of ritual controls on this and all other relationships; by the time of my return, the death of the Tambaran and the altered state of gender relations had yanked these problems into stark visibility. To open this issue, let us consider independent testimony from a rather unusual witness.

Rosa was in her early twenties at the time of my 1985–86 fieldwork—a big, strapping woman with large thighs and breasts, large facial features, and a large, jolly manner. She was from near Mount Hagen, far away in the Western Highlands Province. There, she had met and married Ambonas, an Ilahita man who was working in the Hagen area as a driver. Ambonas dressed her in finery and brought her home to Ilahita, where he built her a handsome stilted house. Across the small clearing stood the humble groundhouse of Afwiliwa, Ambonas's first wife, and their three sons, ages five through twelve. Next to the sexy, brazen, blooming Rosa, Afwiliwa at thirty-three looked withered, frumpy, and terribly old-fashioned. Rosa spoke excellent Melanesian Pidgin, Afwiliwa's Pidgin was halting. Communication was out of the question anyway, even if language had not been a barrier. Everyone knew: Afwiliwa hated Rosa.

Lovestruck in the same way Ta'af had been, Ambonas made no secret of his preference for Rosa. He paraded her as a trophy wife, favored her with store-bought goods from Maprik and Wewak, and always took sides with her against the unfortunate, hard-working Afwiliwa. This was a mistake on his part. Afwiliwa, dignified and generally uncomplaining, was not above reminding Ambonas that, as his first wife, she was entitled to greater respect. Further, she had come to Ambonas as part of a sister exchange, which, as we know, gave their marriage a ritual sanctity far beyond anything the homewrecking Rosa could claim. Afwiliwa had custom and local sentiment on her side. Whereas his brothers were reluctant to tell the increasingly defensive Ambonas how to manage his wives—his noble father would have set him straight, but he had died shortly before Rosa came on the scene—the other wives of the group empathized with Afwiliwa and rallied loudly in her support. Poor Rosa, whose only crime was to be young, attractive, and a little bit spoiled, was made to feel like an outsider by the other women. Some teenage girls found her glamorous and kept her company on that account; but among the older women, Rosa did not have any friends. She was also homesick.

One afternoon, on a day when the village felt more deserted than usual by people working in their gardens, I strolled through Rosa's hamlet—it was near my own—and noticed her sitting alone in the shade of her portico. We exchanged greetings and a few pleasantries, which led to my sitting down for a little chat. The chat stretched into a remarkable conversation lasting about two hours; remarkable because Rosa had a perspective on Ilahita that was informative and unlike any that I had previously encountered. It began with my asking Rosa to tell me about the customs of her Mount Hagen homeland. She eagerly obliged, in tones of great nostalgia and in terms that, in her narcissistically bruised, disgruntled state, repeatedly drew invidious comparisons with conditions in Ilahita. Climate, flora and fauna, foods, settlement patterns, house styles, and degrees of "bushiness" were covered, all to Ilahita's disadvantage. When Rosa perceived that I was not rushing to defend Ilahita against her criticisms, she became more confident and extended her complaints more pointedly to the way Ilahita family members treat each other. What upset her the most, she said, her voice brimming with emotion, was the way mothers here treat their sons. "They think nothing of beating them when they are small," she observed, "and when the boys are older, their mothers all the time curse and scream at them—ah, it makes me very sad! Ilahita mothers treat their daughters well enough, but their sons they do not value at all. It is not like that in Mount Hagen."

Rosa had brooded on this difference for some time. She had even worked out a theory to account for Ilahita's pattern of selective abuse. It is because boys here are not required to help their mothers at their work the way girls are from an early age. In Mount Hagen, she averred, boys and girls equally assist in weeding and sweeping the gardens and in other chores that, in Ilahita, are treated exclusively as women's work.[12] Ilahita mothers treat their sons as worthless because, as far as the they are concerned, they *are* worthless. And because they have no household responsibilities, boys are unruly and defiant of maternal authority, which angers their mothers even more. Rosa added that, with sister-exchange marriage now a thing of the past, a boy is costly in the money the family must raise for bride-price, whereas the marriage of a daughter brings money and other goods to her natal family.[13]

Granting some amount of exaggeration and bias, Rosa's anthropological assessment is remarkably astute, especially for the modern period. Sons and mothers behave pretty much as she describes, locked in an unhappy embrace of bitchiness and sassiness. The strict sexual division of labor leaves boys with too much time on their hands, at least until they are big enough to do men's work, and impedes the formation of sympathy and respect for their mothers.

One day, for example, soon after her husband had left for employment in West New Britain, Falafu'w was in the garden with her fourteen-year-old son, August. When she told him to do something, August twice ignored her and went on playing with his catapult. Falafu'w shouted angrily at him. August then turned the formidable weapon on her, striking her three times in the torso before scoring a massively bleeding wound on her scalp. In the father's absence no other man jumped forward to discipline the strapping youth; and in fact it was generally agreed that the father would not have done so either, had he been there. On another occasion, Maufena discovered that her fourteen-year-old son, Anias, had stolen K10 from her. This time, the father was present and was called upon to hold the boy down while Maufena kicked and pummeled him until his face was swollen and bloody beyond recognition. The father later claimed he had felt sorry for the youth and rueful of his role in the beating but was cowed into participating by the furious Maufena. In several other cases serious enough to require medical attention, it was an adult son who beat his elderly mother, sometimes in conjunction with beating his wife, the two women having sided against him. Such attacks by sons against their mothers *never occurred* during my first fieldwork.

This comparison does not imply that mother-son relations were formerly untroubled or free of ambivalence. What is clear in retrospect is that the Tambaran—that most woman hating of institutions—actually helped to protect the maternal relationship by displacing and diffusing much of its negative affect. That is to say, in its time the Tambaran deflected to itself what would have been, and what has become in its absence, raw emotional vectors within the nuclear family. Let me explain.

Traditionally, a boy's alienation from women, especially his mother, was the avowed goal of the first three Tambaran grades, entered at approximately the ages of five, nine, and sixteen. In numerous ways the Tambaran encouraged young boys to stay apart from women, to consider themselves superior beings compared to them. Mothers reacted to this juvenile abuse as mothers anywhere would—with hurt and anger. But at least they had the consolation of knowing that the rejection was impersonally the result of the Tambaran's turning their sons against them. Mothers knew that for boys to become men, this is what must happen, for the Tambaran was the defining business of men. What men do is what men are.

Also in those days, fathers took a hand in mitigating the extreme misogynism of the Tambaran. Feeling "sorry" for their wives, who went "hungry" while they feasted, men would often bring back pieces of meat, explaining that the Tambaran had eaten its fill and had kicked this bit aside, saying that it could be given to the women. Fathers would counsel their sons to respect and obey their mothers, even as the Tambaran thundered the opposite lesson with respect to women in general. The important point is that ritual tyranny was not only not laid to the account of the father, it was actually combated by him. This paradoxical effect is a feature of secrecy itself, within a close relationship, as was noted in passing by Georg Simmel (1950, 330n) in his famous treatise on secrecy:

> For however destructive [a secret] often is for a relation between
> two if one of them has committed a fault against the other of

which both are conscious, it can, on the contrary, be very useful for the relation if the guilty one alone knows of the fault. For, this causes in him a considerateness, a delicacy, a secret wish to make up for it, a yieldingness and selflessness, none of which could ever occur to him had he a completely untroubled conscience.

For women and children, the harshnesses of their exclusion came from the Tambaran, that mysterious lord to whom men were obscurely accomplice but also subordinate in their own fashion. For men, the tyranny was mandated by the force of tradition, personified by the Tambaran, and, more immediately, by the exigencies of inherited obligations toward ritual exchange partners. In that moiety-based system, the entire apparatus of ritual enforcement operated through indirection. Just as men did not eat their own pigs or marry their own sisters, but gave them to other men in exchange for their pigs and their sisters, so men called upon their inherited Tambaran partners to subject their sons to the rigors of initiation. Despite the considerable cost in labor and resources, that call was always answered, for it was the partner's prescribed way of repaying the debt of his own initiation. To disown the obligation would have been to incur opprobrium and Tambaran-sanctioned sorcery from the cult membership. Although all men participated in this system of ritual severities, each could unhypocritically sympathize with his sons and wives and daughters, for he was never the one inflicting the hardships. So long as these exchange obligations were honored, the validity of the Tambaran was upheld and the men could enjoy moral distance from their acts. But there were times, too, when this false consciousness broke down and men alone or in groups would glimpse the truth that the Tambaran—what men do—is what they themselves do and that the illusions played upon women and children were all that prevented this truth from being generally recognized.

Although the structure of the cult united fathers and sons as members of the same moiety, that solidarity counted for little compared with the hierarchy of five initiation grades that separated them by degrees of ritual rank and secrecy. Fathers exercised ritual authority over their sons surreptitiously, by prevailing upon the intervening exchange partner to undertake the elaborate initiations in which the sons were celebrants. Unbeknownst, then, to the young man it was his own father who invoked the Tambaran—the wild, the Other—against him, and by so doing exercised his will over the intermediatory junior initiation partner as well.

Apart from these formal ritual structures, the principle of indirection traditionally pervaded a man's strategy for controlling his son. Ilahita listeners of "Nambweapa'w" would always smile in recognition at the hapless First Father who, unable to control his six-year-old son, resorted to donning his wife's cassowary skin and frightening the saucy child into good behavior. The father's difficult task—the difficult task of many fathers in many societies—was to dominate the son without injuring or estranging him or losing manly dignity. Duplicity and disguised intimidation provided the solution: the First Father employed the cassowary skin; his latter-day descendants, the Tambaran.

The importance of the Tambaran as context and mediator of the father-son relationship is clear when viewed next to the paucity of alternatives. Unlike some New Guinea societies, where fathers live separately in a men's house and rarely interact with their juvenile sons, Ilahita domestic life was traditionally based on nuclear- and extended-family households. And yet, to a considerable extent, the father *was* absent. The exigencies of war and high-level, protracted Tambaran involvements caused fathers and sons to be separated; so did hunting and gardening because the one was too dangerous, the other too heavy for boys to be of use. The fact is that other than the Tambaran and the shared masculinity that it exalted, fathers and sons had little in common. Even the father's right to control his son through corporal punishment was constrained by his wife's brother—the boy's mother's brother—whose responsibility was to safeguard the boy's flesh, especially against the father. Even a justified paternal spanking could bring avuncular retaliation in the form of a broken lime gourd, speared pig, or felled coconut palm. The result was that fathers and sons were curiously distant from one another. And, as if glamorizing the technological and jural aspects of the separation, the Tambaran obscured the father in a cloud of religious mystery and ritual danger.

This distance between fathers and sons was not unfriendly. On the contrary, there was much positive sentiment between them, sometimes verging on the maudlin. But that attachment hung largely on the son's idealization of the psychologically remote father, not on everyday, companionate interactions that are productive of realistic filial bonding. Across the divide, a man rarely acted directly to impose discipline on his son but relied instead on the Tambaran or the boy's mother to do so.[14] For the most part then, fathers were benignly unpracticed in the art of governing their sons, which is why the Tambaran was so important and its loss so devastating to the delicate balance of power between father, son, and mother.

Today, all of that buffering indirection is gone, as the baby with the bathwater. Fathers must deal with their sons directly, and yet without the Tambaran to support them—morality, magic, mystery, and masculine society, all rolled into one—men can no longer apprehend their own authority, let alone impose it effectively on their sons. Because there is no Tambaran, there is no need either for men to mitigate against it, and the situation between sons and mothers has become rather Hobbesian. Changes in the marriage system, generational conflict arising from educational and economic opportunities available to today's youths, and the loss of traditional disciplines and male functions associated with war, ritual, and exchange—all have contributed to a parental sense, strongest among mothers, that boys these days are a lot more trouble than they are worth. Parental behavior accords with this assessment, causing boys to act all the more delinquent. And so on.

Modern conditions have created a serious rift between fathers and sons. The "distance" lodged in the former relationship has turned from benign to antagonistic. Without the Tambaran, fathers lack the male solidarity and ritual terrorism that they formerly relied upon to help them control their sons. Corporate restraint is giving way to individual freedom (chapter 3), and young people are making the most of it. Even personal magic, which men formerly retained as insurance that their sons would respect and protect them until the end, has lost its leverage. Thus, the end of competitive yam growing has sent the value of gardening magic plummeting; the shotguns that have replaced pig hunting nets do not need magical lures; beauty magic, essential to the success of ceremonial costumes, died with the Tambaran; even traditional love magic—surely an item of timeless utility—has been displaced by perfumes and colognes available at local trade stores.

Feeling powerless in the present situation, at risk of being thrashed by an adolescent or adult son who does not like being told what to do, most fathers throw up their hands and withdraw into a state of sulky disapproval over unruly behavior that includes theft, drunkenness, rape, and brawling. Without the guidance of the Tambaran and its social-control apparatus, men do not know how to be fathers. At the same time, some traditional-ists derive a dark satisfaction from the delinquency of many of today's youth, for it vindicates their warning that the death of the Tambaran would spell dire consequences for the society.

Modern conditions created new frictions between mothers and sons, to be sure; but more significant, they permitted older troubles to surface.[15] Never mind that a husband mitigated against the severities of the ritual system, he also did his part to suppress wifely defiance of the Tambaran, if only out of concern for her safety. The pervasive secrecy of the cult meant that his obscure alliance with the Tambaran was something his wife could neither trust nor fathom. Instead, she endured a free-floating resentment, which perhaps comes closest to capturing the generalized sense of subordination she experienced as a woman in that society. To describe that state as one of chronic anger and frustration is perhaps to give greater definition than is justified. And yet, once in a rare while, those emotions would erupt, as when an incident would trigger an out-burst of insubordination against immediate male authority or, in the man-ner of blasphemy, against the Tambaran itself. Those were dangerous lapses, punishable not just by a swift beating by the husband, but by the prospect of death to herself or a loved one through Tambaran-sponsored sorcery (Tuzin 1980).

Under these circumstances, it is not surprising that the woman's frus-trated anger settled upon her sons—those other males in her life who were not fully under the protection of the Tambaran or, for that matter, their benign, remote fathers. The spasms of cruelty that Rosa described were a continuation into the modern period of behavior that I observed nearly twenty years previously, when boys were still valued as future gar-deners, hunters, and custodians of the Tambaran. Ironically, this maternal behavior propagated its own tragedy by giving boys an experience of women that was consistent with the grim lessons of the Tambaran. Never mind that the boys may have grown up to be caring husbands, men who were not always happy with what the Tambaran required of them; the morbid thoughts seemingly forgotten from childhood found outlet in the violent imagery of the Tambaran. It was to those tyrannies that wives responded. Like mothers before them, wives would vent their frustrations upon their sons, and so the cycle was repeated: men punishing mothers, in the guises of wives.

The perceptions of Mother that arise out of mother-son conflicts may have predisposed boys and young men to accept Tambaran doctrines concerning women, at least until marriage and the softening effects of domesticity and heterosexual intimacy. On the other hand, the emotional turbulence Rosa and I have been describing does not come from nowhere, but is a continuation of problems in the mother-child relationship at an even earlier stage. I refer to the period of early childhood, before gender differentiation is clearly established; when personal identity is being formed and the presence or absence of essential trust in primary relationships is setting the trajectory of future stages of development. One way to begin this topic is to ask, Why do young children cry?

The return fieldwork (1985–86) was part of a comparative project examining the acquisition of cultural knowledge in middle childhood. My associates, Stephen C. Leavitt and Karen J. Brison, had arrived the year before, and were pursuing doctoral research among the nearby Bumbita Arapesh and Kwanga, respectively. On one occasion in this collaboration, we conducted "cry surveys" in our respective field sites. The object was to find out what sorts of circumstances produced tears in children between the ages of 3½ and 5 and what sorts of responses the crying engendered from caregivers.[16] The results were mutually consistent and relevant to an understanding of how maternal images form in childhood experience.

In each of the three settings, by far the most frequent cause of crying was hunger or appetite on the child's part, most of it in the form of "impatience crying."[17] A typical sight around any hearth during the predinner hour—it even figures significantly in an early scene of "Nambweapa'w"—is the mother preparing food, trying to fend off the family toddler who cries and whines for a foretaste of the meal. Sometimes, to silence the youngster, the mother relents and gives him a tidbit. Usually it is a piece of coconut, which is one of the few items that can be eaten raw and that a child of this age is permitted to eat. Invariably, this capitulation comes after the mother has several times refused the child's importuning, saying that he or she should wait for dinner and not pester her while she is preparing it. In most instances, however, the mother does not yield. Tired and hungry herself after a long day in the gardens, she often ends the siege by yelling sharply or striking the toddler. The scene is repeated day after day, month after month, until children are old enough to control their appetites or fend for themselves in the predinner food quest.

To appreciate the nutritional and psychological import of this pattern, consider the following facts. More than 85 percent of the Ilahita diet consists of carbohydrates—tubers, sago, other vegetables.[18] Protein accounts for about 8 percent of the diet, with fat comprising a mere 5 percent. To obtain adequate nutrition from such a regime, one must consume the food in large quantities, something adults are able to do but young children are not. As it is, the Ilahita, notwithstanding the pride they take in their food, are borderline malnourished. Far worse for the children in question, who are weanlings: a category that is at special nutritional risk in many societies. The risk is psychological as well, in that their objective hunger is sharpened by the spectacle of a younger sibling noisily, greedily nursing from the breast that was so recently his.

At a level of 5 percent of caloric intake, compared with an average of 35 percent among Americans, the fat content of the Ilahita diet is dangerously close to basal minimum. All the more so for young children, for whom fat is important in myelination, connective-tissue formation, and the like. In addition, fat is the satiety factor in the diet, contributing more than its share of the psychological gratification (immediate and postprandial) of eating. The Arapesh, like many other New Guinea peoples, hunger for fat and will consume it with gusto when, on a rare occasion, a pig or other animal is slaughtered.

During the developmentally crucial eighteen months following weaning, Ilahita children are hungry most of the time. Yams, taro, sago, breadfruit, and most of the other foods take considerable time to prepare; once cooked, they are highly perishable. Leftover roasted yams may be eaten the following morning, but that is largely the extent of casual eating. Traditionally, bananas were used in the actual weaning process, but were tabooed immediately afterward, for the remainder of childhood. For weanlings, there is little or no snacking during the day; and yet they are in as great a need of it as are youngsters in our own society, who proverbially snack to their heart's content. No wonder the Arapesh are anxiously, proudly fascinated with food, pushing their interest to fetishistic extremes in feasting behavior, the exorbitances of the yam complex, and the gargantuan appetites of the Tambaran. In behaving as though they are on the brink of starvation, the adults are still reeling from a time in their lives when that's just what they were.

Limitations imposed by food technology rebound on the maternal relationship. With cruel irony, Arapesh culture gives prominence to the nurturant role of the mother.[19] Feeding her children is supposed to be, and in fact is, one of the most gratifying things a woman can do. And yet much of the time, circumstances prevent women from performing this role. From the child's point of view, much of the time the mother does not give food, she withholds it. Until recently a source of comfort,[20] satiation, and deep pleasure, the weanling's mother suddenly takes all of that away, betraying the trust that has accumulated to that point. To that extent she, like Nambweapa'w, "goes away," taking the magic of herself and her bounty with her.

The experience of weaning is probably traumatic for young ones in all societies, and therefore it hardly qualifies as a sufficient explanation for the dark side of Arapesh male attitudes toward women, beginning with their mothers and wives. Instead, the practice must be considered in conjunction with the limitations of local types of food, food technologies, the nutritional and psychological aftermath of weaning, as just described, the storminess of later mother-son relations, as observed by Rosa and myself, and the massive propaganda of the Tambaran, which begins aggressively to indoctrinate boys in early childhood. Thus situated, it can be seen that the weaning experience and its aftermath do contribute to the body of perceptions and predispositions that constitute manhood in the Ilahita mode.

By contrast, a girl at about the age of five proceeds into a childhood spent helping her mother in the gardens and groves, carrying little loads alongside her mother's big loads, learning women's crafts, looking after younger children of the group, sitting with the women, and in general building a positive relationship with her mother. Quickly enough, she learns that when the Tambaran sounds its approach from down the path, she must take flight with her mother and the other women. Distressing though it is, her terror at those times binds her to the women, teaches her what it is to a woman in Ilahita, and confirms her in that identity. Her brothers too flee in fear from the sound, but in their own direction, with no sense of solidarity with the women. From their first initiation at about the age of five, they know their day will come; that someday, if they survive at all, they will not run, but will stand with the Tambaran, where the men are. And when that time comes, they naively expect, they will never have to be afraid again.

* * *

For generations, the Tambaran had lived in fear of discovery by the women. Ideologically, the fear was that invasion by women would cause the Tambaran spirits to quit their patronage of prosperity and the social order. After a lifetime's experience with the Tambaran, senior cult elders came to understand this ritual reality in a combination of metaphorical and literal terms: the spirits were real, all right, but they were also manifestations of what men do, *as men;* when men stop doing what they do, desertion by the spirits and self-desertion by the men will be aspects of the same calamity. Insofar as men's works, by definition, depend upon the absence of women, the secrecy of the Tambaran was none other than the secrecy of the men—doing as they do. Likewise, the older men understood, and the younger men did not, that the details of the paraphernalia mattered less than the fact that they were male secrets. Here was the rub: like secrets between close family members, where what is hidden may be laughably unimportant or a thing of the past, once the moment for candor is lost, the secret acquires a seriousness all its own, eventually eclipsing its original purpose. Disburdening oneself becomes ever more painful, as the risk of humiliation mounts up, along with the evidence of weak moral character and betrayed trust. All the more so when the fear of discovery is institutionalized and transmitted down through the generations, each male playing the role of pious, reluctant deceiver to his wife and children.

The men knew that to reveal the Tambaran to the women meant conquering their fear that its secrets would be discovered. That is why, as later described to me, the occasion was triumphant, festive. The act was a catharsis, a brave, spiritual cleansing. Like the old man in "Nambweapa'w," the Tambaran could not simply be allowed to die; it had to be executed—with its last dying breath, if necessary. By returning the cassowary's skin to the women, so to speak, the men resolved a moral dissonance that had haunted male society from its mythic beginnings. The Revival had decreed that this contradiction bore Satan's imprint. Then came the letter announcing my return in a year. The news had prophetic overtones: Was this to be the fulfillment of "Nambweapa'w"? had I been fetched by dead Gidion from wherever it was he went? did my return mean that the Revivalist millennium was at hand? Once the connection was divined between these coincidental events and ideas, the course of action was clear: do away with the Tambaran, immediately, as the precondition of the great millenarian event. It all made perfect sense: since the Tambaran is the god of fear, destroy it, and you destroy the fear, making way for the god of love. What the men did not realize was that while the Tambaran may have engendered fears at one level, it dissipated fears on another. Those fears, older and more primitive than the Tambaran, were not really fears about women at all, but about Mother—though, of course, it was and is women who suffer because of them.

And so, having forsworn their fantasy of a gigantic, phallic, woman-hating monster, the men are now free to act it out. With no deceptions and secrets to hide, there is no need for masculine, conscience-soothing considerateness. Domestic relationships are increasingly raw and unbuffered. From both observed cases and the general impression gotten from living in Ilahita, it is clear that acts of violence by men against women—mostly against wives, but also against mothers—have greatly increased in frequency with the decline and death of the Tambaran. The reason is nearly always the same: with the Tambaran gone, wives no longer bend to their husband's will; indeed some wives, believing men are now powerless, attempt to dominate their husbands. What they find is that, with the Tambaran gone, husbands resort to their fists, which in the short term hurt far more than rhetoric does.

What all this means is that the central contradiction underlying traditional gender relations has survived, albeit inverted, into the present period. Formerly, the contradiction was that men feared women even as they dominated them; one might even say that the fear necessitated the domination, just as the domination produced the fear. But because the dominion of men was embedded in the images and procedures of the Tambaran, an institutional channel existed for the sublimation of mundane aggressive impulses, resulting in a relatively low incidence of actual violent acts by men against women. Today, the situation is reversed: men no longer dominate women and therefore they no longer fear them. The loss of the Tambaran has removed the sublimation channel, exposing women to a level of domestic brutality much higher than was previously observed. Ritual menace and rhetorical violence have gone, replaced with the real thing. Ironically, it would appear that the Cassowary-Mother's final revenge, the ultimate force of the Deluge, is not the liberated savagery of women, but the unsublimated savagery of men. Perhaps this should not surprise us, for it usually happens that the things that excite our most troubling fears come not from without, but from within.

Chapter Eight

SANCTUARY

At its violent end the Tambaran was old, decrepit, and anachronistic. It is the image of Baingap at his demise, halfway through his wife's story: enfeebled, unable to control their little boy except by sneakily using power he had long since stolen and hidden from Nambweapa'w, impotent when she recovers her skin and takes murderous revenge upon him.[1] The last major cult ceremony had occurred in 1972, a dozen years before the secrets were revealed. In those earlier days, the villagers had minimal cash, almost no education, limited mobility, little to occupy them beyond what life with the Tambaran contained. Within a few years circumstances changed, causing the Tambaran to age very rapidly.

Following national independence in 1975, the newly proclaimed village court responded to and by its presence stimulated new areas of litigation, delegitimizing old sentiments and jural reasonings and, in effect, helping to undermine the corporate bases of traditional social life. Relations within the village were further strained by runaway population growth, caused in large part by improved health services and (because the lactation interval was reduced at the urging of health authorities) a shortened period of postpartum sexual taboo. Productive resources were fought over as never before; desperate women began to rebel over having to bear, suckle, and mother long lines of children. One can imagine Nambweapa'w the Cassowary-Mother having the same complaint, only raised to a primal power.

Expanded coffee revenues and local wage-earning opportunities, as well as remittances from kinsmen holding good jobs in the towns, substantially increased the amount of money in the village. The new wealth altered the political economy to the detriment of traditional authority but unhappily did not produce sustainable community development. In the absence of reliable investment vehicles, not to mention business know-how in this sphere so alien to the Tambaran, most of the cash was simply consumed—in the form of beer, rice, tinned fish, assorted junk foods, cigarettes, fancy clothing, boom boxes, gambling debts, court fines, and marriage payments. And because consumer appetites only expand, the influx of cash and goods increased the desire for more, ironically turning the people's self-image of autonomy and spiritual strength into one of deprivation, dependency, and ineffectualness.

People were confused and demoralized. They felt cheated, but were not sure by whom; aggrieved by the loss of common cause and a mounting divisiveness between neighbors and kin; frustrated that Ilahita was going nowhere, while all the rest of the world seemed to be flourishing. One thing was certain: the Tambaran was not only unhelpful, it seemed to be obstructing the path to spiritual and material prosperity. As the icon of tradition, the Tambaran was easy to blame, predisposing many villagers to believe and to embrace the Revival when it condemned the Tambaran as the enemy, the great obstructor.

If increasing cash and a rising population did not cure Ilahita's ills, neither did education. National independence brought the establishment of a large state-run primary school at the northern outskirts of the village. Ultimately, this may prove to have been the most momentous change of all.[2] Within a short time, amid great hope and expectation by the parents, school attendance became virtually universal among Ilahita youngsters. Each year the cream of the sixth standard went off to board and study at the high school in Maprik or at one of the prestigious national high schools in Wewak or in other provinces. By the mid-eighties many young adults spoke passable English and knew or had experienced much about the world outside of Ilahita. In the current cant, young people were "empowered." Every few months, hundreds from a wide area would flock to attend rock-music *disko* held in a well-trampled meadow near the Ilahita school—admission, twenty toea. Their high-performance amplifiers, observed the old men, had a voice even mightier than the Tambaran's had when it sang in days gone by.

Some children of the village are now nurses, teachers, tradesmen, and public servants. The successful ones do not stay in Ilahita, though; they go away and stay away, returning rarely, if at all. For those left behind, pride and vicarious pleasure taken in the others' accomplishments are mixed with envy, diminution of self, and embarrassment at their own rusticity. Such ambivalence is probably inevitable, given a rate of change that is too fast for attitudes to adjust to it; for, indeed, some of the individual success stories (in 1985) would have been unimaginable as recently as 1972.

Supalo's son, for example, is a high-ranking national police official in Port Moresby. He and his Papuan wife sent their bright, beautiful, high-spirited teenager to live with her lion-faced old grandfather in Ilahita, there to be instilled with the disciplines of her father's remembered youth. Another young man, the manager of the Travelodge Hotel in Port Moresby, at last report was collaborating with an Australian to coproduce a documentary film about Ilahita. Yet another young man, a steward on Air Niugini's international service, on visits home would chat with me about the nightlife in Rome and about my ethnographies of Ilahita, both of which he had read with positive interest, cover to cover.

Under these radically new conditions, the Tambaran could no longer feel at home in Ilahita. Many young adults were too worldly to be impressed with the cult's pretensions. If, on visits home, these sophisticates refrained from challenging the remnants of Tambaran authority, it was not out of fear or credulity, but out of respect for their fathers and, especially, their grandfathers, for whom this tradition was life itself. Indeed, the most urbane young people, such as the airline steward, aware that the world's educated élite admired exotic customs and bemoaned their extinction, were already beginning to sentimentalize the Tambaran, the actual character of which was somewhat vague to them.

Those were the unusual cases. The majority of young people stayed at home, save for short stints of employment outside the village; they were not worldly, though many thought they were, and did not have the distance from custom that nostalgia requires. Bored and restless, these stay-at-homes tended to be stridently defiant of traditional authority, both ritual and secular, because, like young people everywhere, they felt stifled by it. Their defiance often took the form of more or less serious delinquency or was expressed by degrees of involvement with Christianity. If my impression is correct that these resistance behaviors were comparatively extreme, the reason may be that they were a measure of the comparably extreme controls exercised by the Tambaran's ritual authority system.

In the old days, defiance of any sort was severely punished by the Tambaran. From the middle 1970s, however, the Tambaran increasingly did not bestir itself because the men increasingly lacked the will and solidarity to mount the appropriate measures. A sense of malaise emerged, a flagging of masculine confidence, which, in the nature of the case, was perceived to be a loss of patronage by spirit guardians. For whatever reason, the Tambaran no longer essayed to champion its cult of masculine privilege. And when people are deserted by their old gods, they look for new gods, which again helps to explain why, despite having scornfully rejected the cargoistic Mount Hurun movement not so many years previously, many in Ilahita readily embraced the millenarian, cargoistic follies of the "Revival" movement.

These developments account for the Tambaran's final decrepitude, but not its assassination. Since it was virtually dead anyway, why did it have to be killed? This is the question I have repeatedly asked, the question that has driven this entire study.

There were, as we have seen, practical considerations. In the Christian idiom of the Revival, the Tambaran was Satan—reason enough to destroy it. Letting it wither away, unhurried, would not do, since the Revivalists held that only the Tambaran's lingering presence prevented a glorious millenarian event from visiting Ilahita. Exposing its secrets both killed the Tambaran and precluded any chance of backsliding into the old ways. But like the killing of Tsar Nicholas II and his family, the men's deed bore a symbolic significance far weightier than its instrumental aspects. The death of the Tambaran signaled, intentionally, an irrevocable rejection of the past and of the cultural self—a repudiation of tradition. What the reformers did not foresee, though the old men of the cult did, was that the death of the Tambaran was also the death of masculinity in the Ilahita mode.

What does it mean for masculinity to die? The story of Ilahita answers this question by highlighting the sometimes uneasy fit between culture and behavior. Men do as they do. In part, their behavior responds to creatural needs and desires little changed since the species began. In another part, men's behavior reflects understandings that to the actors may seem natural and imperative but to the outside observer are plainly precipitates of culture. Masculinity, in contrast, is a thing of ideology and ontology. It is the valorization of what men do, the symbolic resource members of a culture use to contemplate, understand, idealize, demonize, stereotype, place expectations upon, and otherwise identify men. Strictly speaking, masculinity is the distinctly human aspect of what men do.

Probably in most societies, most of the time, masculinity is relatively transparent and diffuse across the institutional order. Most of the time, men do not think of themselves as acting in a masculine fashion even when it is arguable that they are doing just that. Compared to gender constructions described for other societies, the Tambaran to an unusual degree personified and thus hypercognized masculinity, just as it did tradition.[3] The obsessive, misogynistic secrecy of Tambaran activities served constantly to remind men of the *masculine* significance of what they were doing. When cult elders privately confided that the Tambaran is "what men do," they meant—somewhat irreverently and somewhat erroneously—not only that the Tambaran is the remainderless product of male behavior, but also that masculinity consists of men doing Tambaran things.

By committing masculinity to a particular, albeit large and well-furnished, institutional sanctuary, the Ilahita forefathers achieved remarkable clarity and coherence in their collective identity. Toned by childhood memory and mythic imagery of women as an abiding threat to what they do and what they are, the men maintained themselves in a state of masculine readiness. The corresponding masculine solidarity, aided by a battery of organizational conventions, reduced the chances of serious division within this large village. In addition, concentrated masculinity was successfully projected into manly enterprise, as evidenced by the village's past greatness in war, diplomacy, ceremonialism, architectural and artistic works, social engineering, and other collective endeavors.

In the end, the Tambaran's intimate identification with masculinity had fatal consequences for the latter. By its inflexible, totalistic character, the institutional arrangement placed masculinity, and therefore the society in general, at risk. Institutions by their nature are buffeted and altered by history; sometimes they are abolished. Take away the Tambaran, as history has now done, and you take away masculinity—a dangerous subtraction for all concerned, since in the ensuing depression, anger, and disorientation, male behavior loses its meaning, its moral compass, its charity toward women—in a word, its humanity.

In individuals, so-called identity crises operate upon the "mythology" one has about oneself. Analogously, in a gender-inflected society such as Ilahita, where masculine (and feminine) identity is ritually constituted and mythically chartered, any modification inevitably reverberates through a wide web of ritual and mythic associations. By the same token, that web is a conservative structure, one that holds meanings together in proper symbolic arrangements, while absorbing shocks from outside the system. The Tambaran would have withered away in time all by itself; its web was fast deteriorating. But only a competing ritual system could have *killed* it. Such a system was the Revival—intense, charismatic, dazzling in its promises, and in significant respects the flip side of the Tambaran. With scarcely any hesitation, the reformers accepted the risk of obliterating their Tambaran identity, confident that the new identity awaiting them was robust and valid, and that in it man and woman, in all ritual respects, would be equal. A great Turning Point was at hand. However one may evaluate the costs exacted by the changeover, one cannot doubt the courage displayed in the men's act of self-determination.

By disrupting ordinary ontological understandings, this revolution naturally took on mythic characteristics and associations. Ecstasy, rapture, redemption, the sense of the miraculous—all were hotly evident in Ilahita at the time, making villagers ready to believe that all the usual metaphysical barriers were lifted. Past and present, living and dead, mythic and mundane, black skin and white, sequence and simultaneity—such dualities dissolved into a moment of absolute possibility. It was "Nambweapa'w" that told the truth about how these contrarieties began: of the Cassowary-Maiden deceived and avenged; of primal bliss achieved only to be lost by selfish disregard; of the Mother's curse, condemning posterity to an existence cut off from *her* and all that is in her power to bestow; and finally, of the promise of redemption through the little brother, whose return from America would liberate the people from this accursed era, which began with Nambweapa'w's punishing death. No wonder the people of Ilahita called upon the epic of Creation to be their interpreter and guide in this time of apocalyptic Re-creation: so much of what was happening seemed to be a fulfillment of possibilities enshrined in that special tale. As my new friends informed me on that first day so many years ago, "Nambweapa'w" was the story of who they were; to know the story was to know Ilahita.

Let me be clear as to the place of "Nambweapa'w" in my story, lest readers mistake me as being more metaphorical or less literal than I intend. My argument is that the story, despite its primordial setting, is not ancient to Ilahita's tradition, but, rather, entered it sometime after the middle of the last century—possibly as late as the 1880s. An earlier date is highly unlikely, in that the story's first half is plainly an adaptation of the "swan maiden," a motif traceable to Malay influences, which by my reconstruction did not reach this part of New Guinea until well after the founding of Hollandia in 1852. The Malay "swan maiden" blended with preexisting, imaginative notions the Ilahita had about cassowaries, and the result was a strange, riveting tale that quickly became supreme in the people's mythological canon.

The timing of Nambweapa'w's entry is crucial to understanding her involvement with the men's cult and its ultimate demise; the reason is that the Tambaran arrived independently in Ilahita at about the same time she did. Despite *its* primordial pretensions, the cult—at least, the upper grades of it—was adopted from the neighboring Abelam, who moved into the area from the south and began to pressure the Ilahita Arapesh during the period in question (Forge 1966; Tuzin 1976). Ilahita oral history confirms that diplomatic contacts and alliances occurred with some Abelam groups. In addition, several present-day Ilahita clans trace their ancestry to Abelam war refugees who joined the village, bringing their customs with them.

The Tambaran gave Ilahita a masculine ideology and organizational apparatus that were wonderfully suited to those perilous conditions. Ilahita village not only survived under the aegis of the Tambaran, it achieved a combination of population size, societal scale, military strength, and regional hegemony that was probably unsurpassed in traditional New Guinea. In part, Ilahita was favored by circumstance; in another part, its success had to do with the extraordinary literalistic zeal with which they deployed the foreign cult. Anthony Forge (pers. comm.) observed that the Abelam of the border region were amused at the extremes to which Ilahita and other Arapesh villages went in implementing the rhetoric of secrecy, ritual violence, and female antagonism. This was not true of the Mountain Arapesh, who, when pressured by the Abelam, retreated deeper and higher into the mountains. They too adopted the Tambaran, but only after tempering its secrecy, sexual hostility, and hazing procedures. For, as quoted in chapter 3, among the Mountain Arapesh "a cult that stresses hate and punishment is out of place" (Mead 1935, 67–68).

Hence the moral predicament the Ilahita forefathers embraced when they committed their masculine selves to the woman-hating, child-hating, punishing Tambaran. No less than among the Mountain Arapesh, the Tambaran, as glorious as it was, and despite its many triumphs as an institution, was culturally out of place in Ilahita (Tuzin 1982, 1995b, 1996). Men continued to be nurturant, protective, and valorous, but masculinity—the mystique surrounding what men do—became defined in terms of secrecy, deceit, and compulsory violence toward cult outsiders; furthermore, this baleful mystique determined men's deeds insofar as they were ritual actors—which they were a good deal of the time. The contradiction was recognized by the men themselves, who found it troubling because it stood as a source of moral unease and vulnerability, a secret indictment of ritual privilege; and, perhaps more seriously, it belied masculine identity. I suggest that "Nambweapa'w" became so quickly and deeply meaningful to Ilahita because, as modified from the "swan maiden" prototype, the story narratively encoded the moral dilemma brought on at that time by the adoption of the Tambaran.

To appreciate the story's symbolic functioning, it is helpful to know that Tambaran secrets were most often concealed by hiding them in plain sight. Typically, a secret would be represented to the women in a form bearing iconic resemblance to the idea or thing being hidden. For example, when boys were taken to the forest to be purged of maternal essences by having their genitals slashed and stung, the story given to the women was that they were forced to slide down the trunk of a thorny sago palm, ripping their soft parts against an object that, for the Ilahita, is a quintessentially maternal symbol (Tuzin 1992). Men took pleasure in the thought that women were actually being told the truth, if only they knew how to decipher it. Many times repeated, the maneuver enabled the men to profit from ritual secrecy[4] and yet disown moral responsibility for it.

"Nambweapa'w" is iconic in this way. With its sister "myths of matriarchy," the secrets it codifies are the insecurity of men and the illegitimacy of masculine authority. Indeed, the validity of masculinity itself is indicted, insofar as that principle originated in the duplicitous vulva-cutting, wife-taking creation of femininity, masculinity's defining Other. In aligning itself with the Tambaran, masculinity tricked, betrayed, and enslaved femininity—just as did Baingap, the personification of masculinity, when he stole Nambweapa'w's skin and took her home with him. In the story, Nambweapa'w recovers her skin and with it the power and autonomy that are hers by nature, with happy consequences for her primordial children. The prophetic implication is that in life too, women will one day be undeceived, with happy consequences for their children. In the story, Baingap died for his deceit; in life, so must the Tambaran. The killing of Baingap was redemptive; the killing of the Tambaran was intended to have the same effect. The actual result was dismally otherwise. Instead of inspiriting the village and triggering the Millennium, the effect of removing the Tambaran was to turn loose the rage and insecurity men had unknowingly felt toward their mothers and wives. The Tambaran was no longer there to ventilate the men's savage impulses, so the men had to do it themselves.

In a literal sense, then, the early wedding of ritual and myth ordained the death of the Tambaran almost from the moment of its adoption by Ilahita culture. The story of Nambweapa'w correctly intuited the moral contradiction that was the essence of Tambaran masculine identity. The millenarian detail of the youngest brother's departure "for America," with the promise he that would return to restore Nambweapa'w's magic to the people, was added following World War II under circumstances described in chapter 6. From there, an unlikely but not impossible series of events and coincidences—my arrival and departure, the withering of the Tambaran, the impatience with Mission Christianity and the lure of the Revival, my announced return coinciding with the death of Gidion—led to the moment when Nambweapa'w once again recovered her skin and destroyed her oppressor. This time, however, the death of masculinity did not preface the paradisiacal existence promised in the story, but rather a somewhat hellish condition in which men, shorn of their masculinity, male secrets, and male company and reduced to themselves alone, could no longer be what men are at their human best.

Although in Ilahita ritual and myth frame the issues with unusual vividness, it cannot be said that this is the only place experiencing gender turbulence. For some years, the American public has been treated to a rush of books and commentaries about the plight of men; this in the wake of feminism's comprehensive, effective, and prolix attack on masculine privilege, on masculinity itself, and, most hurtfully, on men. Authors speak of "the masculine dilemma" (Rochlin 1980), "the male ordeal" (Skjei and Rabkin 1981), and "masculinity in crisis" (Horrocks 1994). With an ironic nod to Freud, they wonder "what men want" (Ross 1994). They prescribe an unapologetic return to manly virtues, guided by the primal Wild Man within men (Bly 1990).

Unless these authors are overstating the demoralized state of the American male—and I believe they are not—the evolution of this condition bears some similarity to what happened in Ilahita, albeit much larger in scope and duration. I refer to the two-phase aspect of the process:

in Ilahita, the withering away of Tambaran authority over a period of a dozen years, culminating in the revelation of the cult secrets; in the United States, the protracted withering away of male-exclusive occupational sectors during this century, culminating in a traumatic, ideological assault on masculinity during the latest generation.

Due to major economic and demographic changes, there has been a wholesale loss of traditional male occupations in agriculture and other primary industries, certain transportation modalities, trades, and heavy manufacturing. If country-and-western music lyrics are any indication, the romance of masculinity is now personified in that latter-day cowboy who rides his chrome-plated eighteen-wheeler across long, lonely stretches of highway. Yesterday's manly pursuits, to a great extent, have been replaced by less gendered occupations in ultramechanized manufacturing and light industry, government bureaucracies, the professions, and the so-called service sector (Murphy and Murphy 1985, 239).[5] The large patriotic wars of this century valorized what men do—until the Vietnam War, when moral condemnation of America's involvement turned many young men against pursuing manhood on the battlefield, splashed Vietnam veterans with the stain of immorality, and discredited masculinity because of its close identification with that discredited militarism. As Kimmel (1996, 267) puts it, the antiwar movement of the late 1960s and early 1970s was "a central expression of the growing crisis of masculinity."

Such was the weakened state of masculinity when, starting in the early 1970s, militant feminism seized the advantage, as it were, claimed back its cassowary skin, and proceeded to define, demonize, and then destroy masculinity.

This rhetorical abuse did not go unanswered indefinitely. The responses have tended to be weak and ineffectual, however, suggesting that masculinity, unlike femininity, is not skilled at arguing on its own behalf. In the presidential election of 1980, Ronald Reagan's defeat of Jimmy Carter was hailed in some quarters as a sign that American manliness was back in the saddle again (Kimmel 1996, 291). The euphoria waned along with Reagan's popularity during his second term in office. Nowadays, the so-called men's movement strives for effect by linking itself to better-defined causes and constituencies: thus, the Million Man March on Washington in 1995 drew upon images of the 1960s civil-rights movement in an attempt to rescue black males from their appalling decline into crime, drug abuse, and domestic delinquency; the organization known as Promise Keepers fills football stadiums with "men only" bonding in the belief that Christian evangelism can reverse society's slide by putting masculinity back in charge, where it belongs; male advocacy groups work to combat antimasculine biases in legal areas such as child custody, spousal abuse, and sexual harassment; at this writing, the assault on affirmative action is being defined largely as an assertion by straight white males of Republican persuasion against the rest of the color-gender-party spectrum. If American society was not self-consciously "gender-inflected" to begin with, it is certainly becoming so as the problematic of gender works its way through one institutional setting after another.

As often happens when grown-ups behave with self-conscious idealism, many of these attempts to rescue masculinity have an artificial, pathetic, unmanly quality about them. The picture of Robert Bly's followers out in the woods beating tom-toms and staging initiation ceremonies does raise a smile. It all seems terribly juvenile; gender in the adult should be effortless, unaffected, transparent to behavior. Such condescension, while tempting, risks ignoring the symptomatic nature of these antics and the serious social consequences that come from depriving men of their masculinity. The story of Ilahita has something to say about this difficult and controversial issue, and I cannot end my account without addressing the matter, however brief and provisional my remarks must be.

Among anthropologists, Lionel Tiger was one of the first to spot danger on the horizon, though his warning was neither welcomed nor heeded by gender reformers of the time, who regarded it as an apologetic for old-fashioned structures of male dominance. In his book *Men in Groups* (1969), Tiger argues that the importance of male bonding and the high incidence of male organizations around the world are part of our phylogenetic heritage, a legacy of hunting and warfare adaptations that exerted selective pressures on humans and prehumans for hundreds of thousands of years. By their very nature, then, suggests Tiger, "men 'need' some haunts and/or occasions which exclude females" (p. 208).

The life and death of the Tambaran offers no brief for arguing the genetic case either way, but the story of what happened in Ilahita does lend support to Tiger's idea that men—probably more than women—have a need for sanctuary and secrecy or, if you will, privacy. It matters little what men *do* in private; rather, as Tambaran elders correctly perceived, it is the crucial element of exclusiveness that makes the activity "masculine." The circular link with behavior is that it is men doing things known to be masculine that refreshes their sense of intrinsic worth and validity as (male) persons; that is why men come away from such occasions pumped up and feeling good about themselves—*as men.*

Without such opportunities, there is no sanctuary. Without sanctuary, people eventually forget what it means, and what it is worth, to be masculine, leaving men the beastly choice of running to hide or standing to fight. Militant feminists from Germaine Greer to Andrea Dworkin have argued that masculinity is the enemy; from the standpoint of society's long-term interests, they could not be further from the truth.[6] Robert Bly and his happy campers at least know this much: that any genuine improvement in gender relations, upon which much of society depends, must include revalorizing masculinity, not destroying it utterly. This would require restoring a modicum of gender separation by providing masculinity with privileges and privacies of its own.

During the last quarter century, a major feminist goal has been to breach male secrecy by obtaining access for women to traditionally male-dominated institutions. Their success has been such that today many people—women and men alike, and their elected representatives—accept the principle that institutions which exclude women, especially those using public funds, are automatically anachronistic and prejudicial to women's interests. The results have been epoch making. The armed services, military academies, men's colleges and clubs, the learned professions, police and fire departments, high-profile athletics, the America's Cup sailing competition—these are just a few of the domains where males no longer enjoy sanctuary as they once did.[7] Even the Boy Scouts of America has been challenged, as yet unsuccessfully, for its supposed sexism in admitting only males. Each such barrier falls noisily, as those protecting cultural monuments usually do, with fanfare provided by news media, commentators, politicians, lawyers, judges, and advocates. Each successful siege announces to men the loss of one more sanctuary, one less way for all men to think of masculinity, and themselves, as unique and indispensable.

The process has gone ahead in less formal arenas as well. Little of men's clothing, for example, is strictly gendered any longer; that trousers are as much feminine as they are masculine is a fact that would have seemed extremely curious not so long ago. Nor is the trend confined to the United States. In rural and working-class districts of England and other former Commonwealth countries, one can still find drinking establishments that are divided between a saloon bar and a public bar, the latter being the side where women of good reputation do not go. That separation too is on its way out, and among the urban middle and upper classes it is already a thing of the past.

My point is that within the social, demographic, and occupational trends that have weakened masculinity during the twentieth century, there has been a striking, wholesale invasion of male sanctuaries by women with very little movement in the opposite direction.[8] Some of the former exclusions seem silly and unnecessary in retrospect: as a possible instance, when merry-go-rounds started to appear in the late nineteenth century, they were thought to be too thrilling and dangerous for women and children to ride safely.[9] Other exclusions, such as from the right to vote and from other basic liberties, were not silly at all, but were foundational elements in a structure of male privilege that probably few men or women today would wish to see restored.

In achieving many of these reforms, society's gaze has been directed at the privilege-bearing, advantage-gaining, old-boy-networking aspects of these traditionally male-dominated institutions. Some years ago, when a female sports reporter was censured for following her story into a (male) football team's locker room, where she received certain lewd gestures, her defense was that the freedom of access her male colleagues enjoyed put her at an unfair disadvantage. Likewise, men's clubs proverbially are places where business deals and relationships are struck, which is why businesswomen demand equal access to them. That many of these traditional institutions are, or were, like the Tambaran, bastions of male privilege is true beyond question. That their abolition is a necessary step in the progress toward gender equality is perhaps also undeniable, though reasonable people might debate the point. But the matter of gender-based privileges and their place in the pursuit of social justice should not obscure a fact of theoretical and practical importance: namely, that such institutions, like the Tambaran, are at the same time masculine sanctuaries and that their abolition may be having unanticipated, unwelcome social and behavioral effects.[10]

The issue here is not whether male exclusiveness confers male privilege (it does by definition) or whether the privilege being denied nonmales is serious or trivial (that is a matter of opinion in each case). My argument, rather, is that the destruction of masculine sanctuaries sets loose male defensive aggressiveness, in both active and passive forms, which society might pause to consider in its campaign to obliterate structures that, from time to time, set men apart (cf. Skjei and Rabkin 1981, 36). The problem lies with the fragility of the American male's ego—a condition that Gregory Rochlin (1980) attributes to the impossibility of the performance demands placed upon him. Just how far this attribution can be generalized to other cultures I cannot say; but, putting aside the etiological question, the following passage in my view does pinpoint the relationship of male ego fragility to the need for masculine sanctuary on the part of Ilahita men. "Whether in its development or in its maturity," writes Rochlin (p. xi),

> masculine narcissism . . . is especially vulnerable. It is, for instance, Joseph Conrad more than psychoanalysts who commented that a man's self-esteem remains precarious and demands that he put out of sight all reminders of his folly, of weakness, of morality . . . the memory of failures. I must add that in these characteristics the boy was never more father to the man.
>
> Precariously footed self-esteem being the condition, masculinity is besieged—prone to injury, sensitive to and fearful of limitations. Aggressiveness and at times a ready hostility, typical of ever-vigilant masculinity, issue easily to its defense.

Sanctuaries exist to separate and to protect. The Ilahita case suggests that masculine sanctuaries exist both to protect men from threats to their ontological validity and sense of phallic adequacy and to protect them and others from the grim consequences of having those pretensions exposed as self-serving illusions. The implications of this view are several. To begin with, the element of male ego fragility explains why gender-exclusive institutions are so predominantly masculine in societies around the world. As observed in an earlier chapter, secret male cults are about *male secrets;* in this respect, all institutions exclusive to males have a male-cultish character. One of those secrets is the vulnerability of the male's sense of self-worth.

The same line of argument enables one to see why gender-exclusive institutions tend not to be feminine. While there are many reasons in all societies why adult women might feel vulnerable, doubts concerning sexual adequacy and intrinsic self-worth are rarely among them. If for no other reason than their biological prepotencies for coitus, conception, pregnancy, childbirth, suckling, and, to press the point, maternal sentiment, women fundamentally do not doubt themselves the way males do.[11] As if to obscure their implied inadequacy in this psychobiological realm, men have learned to do the next best thing: by fair means or foul, they appropriate and claim ownership of women's sexual, reproductive, and maternal potencies.[12] But as wretched Baingap discovered, such hegemony is precarious in the extreme, and in the end only adds to the male's insecurity and self-doubt. In our society, significantly, the feminine version of this kind of doubt—often centered on the maternal role—arises among women who pursue careers outside the home as a matter of choice rather than by dint of economic necessity. Ironically, then, self-doubts stereotypic of career women, such as fear that one may be deficient in maternal feeling, are not inherently feminine but are perverse refractions or emulations of the male predicament. They do not threaten the feminine persona—unless of course the ego-ideal in question is itself patterned on conventional masculinity, in which case the woman is feminine no more.

Finally, the protective requirements of sanctuary account for why power, privilege, and misogynistic rhetoric are so often associated with male-exclusive settings. These elements may assume an arrogant, aggressive, even violent form; but it is important to understand that such expressions are primarily defensive or preemptive in character.[13] As the Tambaran and other men's cults exemplify with particular clarity, this kind of male behavior is the stylized, often ritualized, masculine apotheosis of phenomenal aggression. Orderly and conventionalized, this type of aggression—if "aggression" is quite the right name for it—normally affirms social arrangements and cultural understandings. Indeed, paradoxically, through acts of self-mitigation such as were performed by men under the rule of the Tambaran, aggression at the rhetorical level may systematically stimulate its opposite at the behavioral level. In this manner, the benefits of masculine sanctuary may bestow themselves on all of society.

A very different kind of aggression erupts when the sanctuary is violated. At these junctures men are, so to speak, fighting for their lives. There is nothing orderly or edifying about these outbursts: no mercy, no mitigation, nothing to benefit the wider society. Though men are usually the perpetrators, it is a dangerous mistake to believe that it is masculinity that makes them so; rather, it is the very *loss* of masculinity. Much of the violence in contemporary American society has this character, and it is perhaps no accident that the explosive increase in crime and related social pathologies has occurred during the period when formal and informal measures were destroying masculine sanctuary.

Let the experts debate the causes of runaway violence and social decay: racism, joblessness, gangs, incivility, spousal abuse, divorce, the aptly named "drug culture." Each of these factors contributes to the problem, but underlying or running through them all is the specter of lost, damaged, or eroded masculinity. The idea of violence on television and in films as the cause of violent behavior is something of a red herring in that it begs the question of why such depicted, increasingly lurid violence is as popular as it is. Why else does the public have this appetite for hypermasculine violence on the screen if not to compensate for a lost masculinity?

The consequence of father absence in many inner-city black families expresses this problem with particular literalness and severity: the absence of worthy masculine sanctuaries for the father—hence the man's own "absence"—and the absence of a worthy masculine model for the son create a vicious cycle of manly deprivation that is as dangerous to society as it is intractable to workable solutions. Not just in the black family, but in the wider society as well, the behavior patterns that produce epidemic rates of teen pregnancy, divorce, and spousal abuse are often traceable to active or passive aggression on the part of men for whom masculinity no longer affords adequate shelter.

Another set of social problems rooted in abolished, flawed, or devalued masculinity concerns the recent growth in the numbers and stridency of armed militia groups.[14] I write this on the first anniversary (April 19, 1996) of the bombing of the federal building in Oklahoma City. The attack killed 168 men, women, and children. Investigators have evidence that the terrorist incident was staged partly to avenge the bloody climax of the siege, by federal agents, of the Branch Davidian headquarters near Waco, Texas, one year earlier. The shoot-out at Ruby Ridge, Idaho, and the prolonged standoff at the Freemen headquarters in Jordan, Montana, are other publicized instances of militia confrontations with government agencies. The American public is coming awake to a developing threat that law-enforcement officials have known about for some time: across this country there are a large number of potentially dangerous men, armed to the teeth and decked out in military camouflage fatigues, who are hoping for—in some cases, plotting—the violent overthrow of the government.

These campers are not happy at all, nor do their antics raise a smile, at least not any longer. More than any of the other examples given, theirs is a blatant, defiant, last-stand assertion of stereotypic masculinity under siege: the weapons, the military styling of discipline, clothing, vehicles, and other gear, the command of a fortresslike center and a defended perimeter, the patriarchlike polygyny of some of the leaders. All of this indicates that the rage driving these men is a response to ego vulnerabilities being aroused by the loss—actual or potential, real or imaginary—of masculine sanctuary. Indeed, the Hollywood image of the siege comes closest to being a master metaphor for these kinds of groups: circled wagons or a walled fort on the prairie or a log cabin in the woods; gun barrels bristling from every aperture; inside, desperate heroes willing to die rather than surrender themselves or their right to bear arms. Again, it all seems terribly juvenile and atavistic; so did Hitler and his Brownshirts in the early days of the Nazi rise to power.

Their enemy is the governmental Establishment. For men whose acts, I am arguing, are an attempt to compensate for, restore, or deny a depleted sense of masculine self-esteem, the government may seem an oddly irrelevant target. More logical—primitive and horrifying, but logical—might seem the 1989 case of the antifeminist man who selectively slaughtered fourteen women at a university in Montreal simply because they were women. There is a logic in the militia case, however, and it follows from the collective, institutionalized character of their masculine insecurity and defensive strategy. To prove one's manliness to oneself and others, one selects the biggest, strongest target in sight. For individuals like Lee Harvey Oswald and Sirhan Sirhan, killing a Kennedy made sense to their hollow egos and limited capacities. For organizations such as these militias, however, nothing short of the violent overthrow of the government, and seizure by themselves of power, would suffice to repair their collective masculine insecurity. If the ambition is irrational, so are the needs generating it.

Furthermore, it is entirely possible that many of these militiamen maintain gratifying relationships with women and have wives who agree with their politics. They may not be feminists, and they may decry the government as "effete" and "impotent"; but my argument does not require that each member, individually, be hostile to women or blatantly insecure about his masculinity. Along with institutional development and a widening of appeal to prospective members, secondary formations occur in these, as in all, movements. The focus of attention epigenetically evolves from sexual (in)adequacy to masculine (in)security, to gender politics, and finally to politics concerning the government's supposed betrayal of freedom, autonomy, individualism, and other values stereotypic of American masculinity. Men may join at any stage, think of themselves as motivated by any of these issues; but whether or not all members are aware of it or are personally describable according to it, the pervasive, motivating theme of the institution remains the prospective loss of masculine sanctuary and the frightful exposure of male inadequacy.

The events surrounding the loss of masculine sanctuary in Ilahita parallel, in a compressed form, the prolonged, more diffuse process that has been going on in American society. In giving up their Tambaran secrets, exposing their manly substance to the glare of feminine skepticism, the men tore down the last and greatest bulwark of Ilahita masculinity. That they did so voluntarily gave the Revival men some slight protection from the ensuing feminine onslaught; it even enabled them to preserve a particle of ritual authority into the post-Tambaran era. What those men did could be viewed from outside as noble or treacherous, visionary or benighted, reckless or sly; in fact, it was all of these at once. For traditionalists, though, the revelation was an unmitigated, apocalyptic reliving of the primal event of Nambweapa'w seizing back her cassowary skin, with its awful entailments of abandonment, impotence, and oblivion. That is why the old men grieved so when the Revivalists revealed the ritual secrets; why they were grimly certain that without the Tambaran great hardships would befall Ilahita and people would behave badly. Their gloomy predictions were dismissed, but, as often happens where the Tambaran or Nambweapa'w is concerned, they were prophetically accurate.

As we have seen, many of the adversities were entirely predictable, if, like the cult elders, one could but intuit the secret wisdoms of Ilahita myth and ritual. In the weeks and days leading up to our final departure, several additional calamities befell the village. Whether predictable or not, their timing darkened our parting impressions of Ilahita.

To begin with, there had been no rain for about a month. Prolonged dry spells are not unusual in this part of the Sepik region, which is subject to wet-and-dry seasonality; nor would the dryness normally have posed a problem, since yams prefer such conditions at the time of harvest. This crop year, however, Revivalist distractions had greatly delayed yam plantings, causing the tubers to be correspondingly immature when, on time, the rains ended. Not even magical intervention, said the garden magicians, could prevent the harvest from being poor.

To make matters worse, yam vines lucky enough to be rooted near groundwater were saved only to be host to a scourge of black caterpillars. The insects started with the coffee leaves, decimating next season's crop (and cash revenue) before moving on to devour the people's subsistence base. Government extension officers had a poison adequate to the caterpillars, but the chemical was so toxic as to require special training for those who administered it. The remedy would not arrive soon enough to save Ilahita's coffee and yams.

That was not nearly the end of it, so far as Ilahita's travail in our last few weeks was concerned. After years in the courts, a land dispute involving the village was finally resolved. According to a senior officer of the Lands Titles Commission in Port Moresby, with whom I later spoke, the case of "Komanata'wa" had lasted longer than any other in the history of the country; an act of parliament had been directed solely at the case. With the Tambaran no longer there to enforce solidarity, some men of the village supported the enemy side. The judgment went against Ilahita—unjustly and unfairly, based on what I know of the case—disastrously stripping Ililip ward of a vast area of productive resources and exacerbating population-driven shortages that were already serious. The old men had said it: without the Tambaran, Ilahita would be unprotected, weak, and divided before its enemies.

Meanwhile, as if intending to drive the misery deeper, an epidemic pounded the village. Its flulike symptoms included prolonged diarrhea, leading to severe dehydration, which can make a minor ailment lethal under these conditions. We emptied our medical kit of antidiarrhetics, dispensed the remaining Tang in an effort to rehydrate sufferers—to little avail. People were dying. The Revival halted in mid-prayer, while parishioners and traditionalists alike held their breaths to await the revealed significance of these catastrophes.

The many deaths enabled the villagers, led by the Revivalists, to practice a new procedure proclaimed on May 24, 1986, two weeks before our departure. Like the prohibition on slitgong knelling that had so distressed

Supalo (chapter 3), this innovation tore at the social fabric in ways the Tambaran never would have allowed. The moral confusion surrounding the death of the Tambaran, the death of masculinity, may be temporary; the future may see orderly, satisfying meanings and behaviors of its own. One would not know this from the closing events of fieldwork, however, which were faithful in tone to all that preceded them.

The occasion was a memorial feast for Safa'akw, Kunai's older sister, who had died two months earlier. "Jesus has brought us a New Law," said one of the speakers, "and we must now put behind us the evil, destructive ways of the Tambaran." Accordingly, it was announced that this would be the last memorial feast and that future bereaved families would no longer have to make food payments to the matrikin of the deceased. Missionaries had long objected to these practices, damning them as wasteful and heathenish and thus displaying complete ignorance of the important functionality and considerable beauty of these exchange traditions. On the contrary, said the speaker, again echoing opinions native to Smallville, USA, but not Ilahita, it is the immediate family of the deceased who stand in greatest need of material assistance at a time like this.

Then and there a collection was raised and handed over to Safa'akw's somewhat bewildered widower, Baiwam. People stood around, awkward but curious, as the money was publicly counted. The total was announced to be K65.94. Then a strange thing happened: a silence fell over the crowd, as people looked at each other blankly. Finally, someone asked out loud what everyone seemed to be wondering: under the circumstances, was K65.94 a lot or a little? No one knew.

On a morning two weeks later, packed and loaded, we were ready to depart for home. For me, as I suppose for many ethnographers, leave-taking is emotionally the most trying moment of fieldwork: the prospect of never returning, never again seeing these faces and mannerisms, releases a storm of pent-up love, gratitude, relief, and, most of all, guilt. This time, amid death and despair, washed by the accumulated sadness about what was happening to Ilahita and its people, the distress was such that even today, ten years later, I still experience it.

Among those who came to wave us good-bye was a woman whom I shall call by a pseudonym—Kwaninga. One of our closest friends in the village, at middle age Kwaninga still had the bones, eyes, smile, and poise that had made her one of the legendary beauties of her day. Not on this day, however. Having not seen Kwaninga during the previous, hectic few days, I was stunned at the look of death she had suddenly acquired: wasted flesh, waxy skin, rheumy, unfocused eyes—she was obviously ill with the epidemic disease and very weak. Coming the distance to say farewell must have cost Kwaninga considerable effort; but when I gently upbraided her for exerting herself, she forced a smile and said, unconvincingly, that she had been sick but was getting well.

Three weeks later we arrived home in California to find a note from an Ilahita neighbor, bearing the unhappy news that Kwaninga had died a few days after our departure. Some time later another letter arrived, this one from Kwaninga's widower. There can be no doubt that Silembin (a pseudonym) had always esteemed Kwaninga very highly: during our first fieldwork, their passion for each other was something people talked about; fifteen years later, the mutual devotion was still plain to see. I could well imagine that her death was a terrible loss for him.

Silembin's communication did not comment, however, on the tragedy of Kwaninga's death or his reaction to it. Instead, the letter was an unsettling tirade over the paltry amount of money he had received as donations at her funeral. Only K80 had come in, Silembin complained bitterly. He had expected more, had deserved more. People are mean and stingy. "They do not care that I have expenses," he railed. "Kwaninga was worth more than K80!"

I do not know Kwaninga's monetary worth. I do not know if K80 is a lot or a little. But as I reached for my checkbook, I felt a great sadness—about Kwaninga, about Silembin, about myself, and about the new valuations of life and death that were taking shape in Ilahita.

Notes

Chapter One

1. M. J. Meggitt (1979, 112–13) discusses the implications of his having returned to the Mae Enga several times in relatively quick succession. Among the advantages he names are greater ethnographic efficiency owing to the researcher's familiarity with the people and the sociocultural setting, increasing acceptance as a "repository" of cultural knowledge resulting from his or her having passed from fresh-faced youth to gray-haired elder over the course of many visits, and the researcher's evolving intellectual maturity as regards the varying problems examined from one visit to another. As will be seen, although these features applied to my return visit to Ilahita, the length of my absence and the peculiar circumstances of my return created enormous practical difficulties as well.

At the other extreme, Kenneth E. Read (1986) describes returning to the Gahuku-Gama after an absence of thirty-one years. Although Read's return was traumatic to him in certain lyrically told ways, the great length of his absence and the circumstances of the community during the period of his return meant that the sorts of problems I experienced in Ilahita did not arise.

2. Shirley Lindenbaum excellently observes that Papua New Guineans live in a "gender-inflected universe" (1987, 222). In Ilahita, with its profound investment in male identity, the Tambaran was the grammatical vehicle, so to speak, of that inflection.

3. Six of the thirty tok profet were men. In every case they had been either early converts to mission Christianity or marginal members of the Tambaran cult—who presumably had not been transformed by the rigors of the initiation process. With the exception of Samuel (Tuzin 1989), these male tok profet were not effectual, and I am not aware of any actions taken on account of their inspired pronouncements.

It is not easy to know which of these Revivalist beliefs and practices originated in Ilahita and which were introduced or adapted from similar movements going on in many parts of the country at this time (e.g., Barr 1983). Despite its relative recency in the village, local accounts are somewhat vague as to how it arose. One notion is that the "Revival" was introduced by a visiting mission worker from the Solomon island of Malaita (Tuzin 1989). Another story is that

Banabas Kain, an Ilahita man who was prominent in the regional South Sea Evangelical Church (formerly Mission), experienced visions while hospitalized in the provincial capital of Wewak. The visions directed him to institute the Revival in Ilahita and from there spread the News throughout the region. Banabas's efforts at leading a mass movement were quite successful during the early 1980s, and they helped to make Ilahita the center of the Revival over an area covering perhaps two dozen villages. The militant, millenarian, rather anti-Establishment character of Banabas's movement did, however, alienate him from the hierarchy of the European-dominated, religiously more conservative South Sea Evangelical Church and its dwindling circle of adherents in the village.

For present purposes, it suffices to say that Ilahita's Revival had multiple sources, both inside and outside the village, but that, once formed, the Ilahita Revival became intensely the village's own, reflective of highly localized issues of culture, history, and society.

4. Under Papua New Guinea law, people are free to believe and preach what they like. Cargo cultists generally run afoul of legal authorities, however, by soliciting money from their followers, with the understanding that fabulous benefits will be returned to the donor. Regardless of whether or not the leader is acting in good faith, the courts construe such unkeepable promises as fraudulent and hence punishable.

5. The other wards are Balanga, Nangup, Hengwanif, Bwi'ingili, and Ilifalemb. See Tuzin 1976 for the sociological features of these wards and their interactions.

6. These letters were written in Melanesian Pidgin, the lingua franca of New Guinea. By the 1970s, literacy in this language was no longer rare among the younger Ilahita men, thus enabling me to communicate with anyone in the village, directly or through a literate intermediary.

7. If Naipe'w was correct in calling it "liver cancer," Gidion's fatal condition would probably have been the effects of hepatitis B, which is endemic in the Sepik area, and which in advanced stages can produce cirrhosis of the liver and malignant hepatoma. In the village, when I discussed the case with a medical missionary, a New Zealander with formal nursing training, she recalled thinking that Gidion's death had been caused by malaria that had invaded the liver. This diagnosis seems unlikely, however, in view of the usual rapidity with which death from *Plasmodium falciparum* normally occurs, if it occurs, after the presentation of symptoms. Gidion's had been a steady terminal decline lasting about three months. I am grateful to Clifford C. Dacso, formerly associate adjunct professor of medicine at the University of California, San Diego, for explaining to me the association between the malaria parasite and various liver disorders.

8. The passage is from Act I, Scene I of William Shakespeare's *Second Part of King Henry IV.*

> Rumour is a pipe
> Blown by surmises, jealousies, and conjectures;
> And of so easy and so plain a stop
> That the blunt monster with uncounted heads,
> The still-discordant wavering multitude,
> Can play upon it.

9. According to the late Donald C. Laycock (pers. comm.), foremost authority on Sepik area languages, *dowank* almost certainly belongs to a family of terms found among the mountain peoples of northern New Guinea, which is etymologically derived from the Malay *tuan,* meaning "lord." Although Malay plume hunters are known by scholars to have operated in the mountains west-northwest of Arapesh country, there is no indication that they ever reached the vicinity of Ilahita.

Chapter Two

1. By the 1960s the policy of the local Catholic Mission (Society of the Divine Word), encouraged by the actions of Vatican Council II, had changed completely in its attitude toward these spirit houses, so much so that village churches were sometimes modeled after them; see Tuzin 1980, 186, for a photograph of the one at Ariseli, in the mountains north of Ilahita. These magnificent "tambaran churches" were troubling to evangelical Protestant missionaries, many of whom regarded the mixing of Christian and heathen styles as a blasphemy that would only befuddle the parishioners. By the 1960s, the Catholics were also doing a thriving business in the sale of artifacts, which were supplied by outstations to the Mission's large warehouse store in the port town of Wewak.

2. Margaret Mead (1978, 74) reports such an event among the Iatmul. The effect did not last long, according to Mead (pers. comm.): soon the cultists and their audience were back at it, pretending successfully that the revelation had never occurred.

3. Prior to World War II, the only mission in the East Sepik region was the Roman Catholic Society of the Divine Word (SVD), which since German times had been established on the coast and along the lower and middle reaches of the Sepik River (Townsend 1968, 225). With the opening of the Sepik hinterland after the war, Protestantism entered the area through various mutually cooperative evangelical organizations, principally the South Sea Evangelical Mission, the Assemblies of God Mission, and, more recently, the Christian Mission of Many Lands and the New Tribes Mission. Although the Catholic Mission also expanded after the war, the greater part of the new field appears to have been occupied by these Protestant groups, which generally maintain a cool but respectful distance from their Catholic counterparts.

4. The American Liebenzell Mission is an independent organization, which,

however, worked with German Liebenzell Mission in Manus between 1951 (the time of its arrival there) and 1988. At present no members of American Liebenzell remain in Manus, and in the Pacific region this Mission is principally active in Micronesia. In this study, "Liebenzell" refers only to the *German* Liebenzell Mission, since no member of American Liebenzell has ever worked with the SSEM in the East Sepik.

5. Founded in Upper Silesia around 1890 by Eva von Thiele-Winkler (b. October 31, 1866), this humanitarian sisterhood specialized in establishing and supervising orphanages. With the post–World War II takeover of this part of Germany by Poland, Friedenshort shifted its headquarters to Bavaria, where Miss Schrader lived in retirement until her death in 1993.

6. Someone had told me that ethnographers newly arrived in the field should be guarded and noncommittal about their initial associations, lest they become innocently, but prejudicially, aligned with one or another interest group in the community. This good advice is difficult to apply, however, in the context of the novice's greater dread that *nobody* will want to associate with him. In most situations, I suspect, the risk of irremediable political entanglement is minor compared with the emotional and practical advantages of responding warmly to any and all friendly gestures.

7. I also owe Miss Shrader a personal debt. In March 1970, I left Ilahita for two weeks in order to be married in Sydney, Australia, where Miss Schrader was sojourning for a time before retiring to Germany. When the complicated, long-distance arrangements for our civil ceremony collapsed in a heap, Miss Schrader—who did not hold with registry-office weddings anyway—leapt into action. Within hours she produced a church, a preacher, flowers (borrowed), a small band of well-wishers, and a reception, complete with cake and unfortified punch, at the Mission headquarters. This was an instance of Miss Schrader's generous spirit, an act of kindness for which Beverly and I remain grateful.

8. This problem was alleviated when the British and Foreign Bible Society in Australia (1969) published a Melanesian Pidgin translation of the New Testament. Miss Schrader herself never acquired a knowledge of the Ilahita Arapesh language, but another SSEM worker during the 1950s, Shirley Matthews, made headway on a related dialect and had compiled a useful word list. The complex noun-class structure characteristic of Arapesh languages was brilliantly described by Reo Fortune (1942), based on a six-month visit to the Mountain Arapesh in the early 1930's. By the mid-1980s Robert Conrad, a member of the Bible-translating Summer Institute of Linguistics, had produced Arapesh versions of a few books of the New Testament. Village Christians literate in Pidgin had great difficulty in reading their own language and seemed to regard these translations as little more than a novelty.

9. There were a few villagers, nearly all of them men, about whom Miss

Schrader was ready to believe the worst. From stories and rumors that had reached her, confirmed by calculatedly scary manners and appearances, she had decided that these individuals were more than mere dupes of Satan, they were his dedicated henchmen in the village. Salvation might still be possible for such sinners—salvation is always a possibility for *anyone*—but Miss Schrader was pessimistic, and she would not hesitate to show them the road whenever she caught one of them sneaking around the Mission compound.

10. What Miss Schrader did not know was that Kwamwi continued a secret interest in the clinic. Over the years he operated behind the scenes to ensure that one of his young protégés was always chosen to be the next clinic assistant. With a man on the "inside," Kwamwi was able to maintain a small stock of raw penicillin, which had become the principal secret ingredient of his curing magic. In conjunction with a muttered spell, raw penicillin applied directly to a festering wound or dermal ulcer is spectacularly effective. This procedure was the chief source of Kwamwi's considerable reputation and income all the rest of his days.

Chapter Three

1. This aesthetic, which operates throughout Arapesh dual organization and dual cosmology (Tuzin 1976), was understood by the artist Edouard Manet. In 1880, referring to the depiction of single figures, he wrote to his friend Antonin Proust, "combien il est malaisé de camper une figure seule sur une toile et de concentrer sur cette seule et unique figure tout l'intérêt, sans qu'elle cesse d'être vivante et pleine. Fair deux figures qui puisent leur attraction dans la dualité des personnages est à côté de cela un jeu d'enfant" (how difficult it is to place a figure alone on a canvas, and to focus all interest on this single and only figure, without which it ceases to be living and real. To paint two figures that get their interest from the duality of the two personalities is child's play in comparison) (Manet 1945, 59–60).

2. For example, family members lived with the corpse of a loved one, which was allowed to rot in a shallow open grave in the groundhouse floor. This procedure both protected the remains from necrophagous *sangguma* sorcerers and enabled the living reverently to imbibe—as a kind of cannibalism of its own—the fumes of the deceased. See Tuzin 1975, 1976, 1977 for a discussion of Arapesh beliefs and practices associated with death.

3. By contrast, birth, marriage, and male puberty are subject to relatively few cultural understandings. Female puberty rites, while they do not compare in complexity or social scale to those of death, do involve a period of ritual seclusion for the newly menstruating woman, followed by a feast in which, arrayed in paint, feathers, and shell jewelry, she is formally presented to neighbors, kin, and other well-wishers. See Tuzin 1980, 17–23, for a description of this practice, and also of certain customs invoked at the time of marriage.

4. These are hardwood logs of various sizes that are hollowed out with a slit running longitudinally along one side and are beaten with long hardwood clubs. Slitgongs are used for long-distance signaling—the sound of a large one carries for miles—and as accompaniments to some dances. Even with the benefit of steel tools, it requires enormous effort to make a slitgong, which is why they were formerly protected from the elements and were, accordingly, made to last for generations. Nowadays, with the eradication of many of their ceremonial applications, slitgongs that would have been treated as heirlooms are neglected and are fast deteriorating.

5. Portions of the following discussion appeared in the journal *Oceania* (Tuzin 1988). I am grateful to the editors for permission to use passages from that article in the present context.

6. Initially, the Australian administration sought to establish its control and influence by encouraging villagers to bring their disputes to Maprik. The news that this armed, manipulable, third-party power was offering to settle their disputes for them was received with great enthusiasm; the Maprik magistrate found his docket crammed with lawsuits and complaints of dubious legal merit. Within a very short time, many of the more trivial complaints were being turned away, their petitioners enjoined by the weary judge to settle these matters at home, according to customary procedures.

7. Traditionally, men tended to marry for the first time in their late teens or early twenties. By the mid-1980s, the premarital sex taboo had lost its force, and, in addition, men appeared to be marrying at a slightly younger age.

8. Councilor Kunai avoids potential strife by allowing his six wives to keep all the money they earn from their coffee activities. He does this in recognition that he contributes little or nothing to the household's productive activities. Increasingly, and for many years, his involvement in council and village court affairs has absorbed much of his time. He is paid for this employment. With their separate incomes, he and his wives are mutually self-sufficient, and loans of money pass both ways between the two sides of the household.

This discussion omits the large proportion of polygynous unions in which a man, usually in his prime, assumes care of a woman who has been widowed or divorced. Oftentimes, especially in cases of leviratic succession, the additional wife is older than the man, and, depending on their actual ages, there may or may not be cohabitation. It is a marriage of convenience: Eros sits lightly on the parties, and everyone gets along fairly well.

9. The Papua New Guinea currency system is based on the kina. There are one hundred toea to the kina. At the time of fieldwork, the value of the kina was about equal to that of the United States dollar.

10. These figures understate the magnitude of natural increase by excluding a number of nuclear families—perhaps totaling as many as two hundred per-

sons—which, during the 1969–85 period, permanently emigrated to one of the resettlement centers in West New Britain Province. No such instances had occurred as of the time of my 1969 census. In both censuses, however, I include individuals who were temporarily absent at work or school, were expected to return, and were considered members of the community.

11. Those seeking to stem population growth face a number of obstacles. Some local leaders, picking up on rhetoric from some national parliamentarians, hold that national strength lies in numbers and that the country is underpopulated—by Indonesian standards, for example. In Ilahita, local German missionaries are averse to population-control measures, in part because they fear that artificial contraception will foster promiscuity. As regards direct birth-control measures, local medical authorities are reluctant to prescribe contraceptive pills to village women for fear that they will not be able to maintain the dosage routine. Tubal ligation is available at the Wewak Hospital, but families are deterred by the trouble and expense of journeying to the coast and are justifiably fearful of the risks of major surgery. Intrauterine devices are available in Maprik, but not without a gynecological examination by a (usually Papua New Guinean, usually male) physician, a procedure Ilahita husbands will not allow.

Vasectomy is not available, nor was it known about in Ilahita, until Dr. Philip E. Young, a gynecologist friend, visited us in the village. Sitting with a small group of married men, the subject of birth-control options came up. Dr. Young inquired whether vasectomies were available to male villagers. I translated his question, wincingly fearful that the subject would pain and embarrass our companions. On the contrary! The men were quite taken with the effectiveness and medical simplicity of the idea; one of them, already known to me as a "quick study," observed that his having a vasectomy would enforce chastity on his wife.

12. As seen earlier in the case of Ta'af, one sign of a husband's loss of affection is that he stops giving his wife daily work assignments. Assigning work is seen as a husband's duty, and the lack of caring implied by the husband's neglecting to do so is considered to be grounds for divorce. Asao was never guilty of this.

13. Unlike Gidion, whose memory was a constant presence in this return fieldwork, Asao was hardly talked about. His name appears in my notes only in the death registry and in connection with Akwaliwa's visit.

14. In my experience, the Ilahita are quick to personify entire traditions, such as the Tambaran. In dirges and eulogies performed at important funerals, the idea that the death represents the passing of an era is invariably evoked. On philosophic grounds, I would agree with them.

Chapter Four

1. In Tuzin 1980, 5, 7, the original Arapesh, *meho'w,* is inexplicably but erroneously translated as "tree kangaroo."

2. The English love affair with swans—no castle moat is complete without a nuptial pair of them—showed itself in Portsmouth on August 11, 1415, as Henry V's armada was setting sail to invade France. As the great convoy took position, an accident occurred in which three ships were destroyed by fire. This was interpreted as a bad omen for the military expedition; but the king felt that God was on his side and so refused counsel that he not leave the country. As the fleet sailed south, writes Hibbert (1964, 46), "The wind was strong out at sea and the painted sail-cloth bulged tightly over the decks. In the clear sky above the *Trinité Royale* a flock of swans gathered. The burning of the boats was forgotten. The omens were good now." Henry went on to meet the French at Agincourt, there to achieve one of the greatest victories in military history.

Likewise, in his history of the Plantagenet dynasty, Costain (1964, 123) recounts that King Edward I, in the presence of two swans, swore "'by the gracious God of all and the two swans'" that he would not rest until he had killed the Scottish rebel, Robert the Bruce. The use of swans in oath taking is related to their supposed prophetic qualities, a subject reserved for the end of this chapter.

3. Robert Barakat (1965) attempts to argue that "la Llorona" is as much Aztec in origin as she is European. Aztec mythology, he notes, usually depicts goddesses in or near *water,* just as la Llorona is imaged to haunt pools, fountains, wells, and rivers. This detail proves nothing, in that the water association is equally ubiquitous in European swan-maiden stories. On the other hand, it must be said that neither Leavy's recent study (1994) nor Taggart's study of Spanish folktales (1990), promisingly entitled *Enchanted Maidens,* mentions swan maidens in Spain or Portugal (but see Thompson 1956, 34). La Llorona's derivation aside, Barakat's material does raise the possibility, albeit remote, of an Aztec "swan maiden" tradition.

4. For excellent discussions of the motif, see Thompson 1946, MacCulloch 1964, Lessa 1961, and Leavy 1994.

5. Early in his stay with the Black Sea Turks, my colleague Michael E. Meeker (n.d.) was told how to acquire a peri as a guardian (*sahipli olmak*):

> If you go down to the river, you might discover the peri girls (peri kzlar) bathing there. When you know the place where they bathe, you go there at night, take off all your clothes, and hide in the bushes. When the peri girls come, they take off their clothes and leave them on the bank. As they bathe, you pick out the one you like (seviyorsun) and you steal her underwear (külot). When the peri girls have finished bathing, they come out of the river and don their clothes, except for the one you have picked out. She cannot find her underwear. She will then discover you hiding with her clothes, and she will try to frighten you to compel you to return them. She will take the form of all sorts of ani-

mals and things: a dragon, an elephant, a pig, a wolf, a lion, and so on. She will even cause storms and shake the earth in her efforts to terrify you. But you must not give the underwear to her (the story teller here mimes a terrified person clutching the underwear to his breast). This goes on until morning at the time of the first call to prayer. But this is not the end. You must return the next night and endure the same ordeal all over again. If you prevail, the peri girl becomes your friend and will tell you all manner of secrets, the location of hidden money and treasure, the means to find it, and so on.

6. Although Cross, writing in 1915, realizes that these forms could change over time and space, his prejudice gets in the way of a genuine understanding of how mythic images (including swan maidens) evolve and adapt within cultural circumstances. Referring to two Old French poems, he observes (1915, 619–20),

> It is obvious that in both *Graelent* and *Guingamor* the garments by which the fountain ladies set such store are rationalized feather-skins, and are derived ultimately from stories of animal marriages. To peoples in the animistic or totemistic stages of culture unions between men and animals are perfectly natural and acceptable, but to later and more enlightened peoples the moral and intellectual shock is too great. The bride, at first an animal *sans phrase,* becomes a supernatural woman in animal form, and finally a fairy maiden whose power resides in her clothing. The predominance among civilized peoples of the swan over the many other forms of animal bride known to savages is probably due to a recognition of its peculiar appropriateness as a disguise for a beautiful fée. The natural association of swans with water furnishes an easy explanation of the confusion between swan-women and water-fées, as in so many versions of the Offended Fée, including our two Old French poems.

Such a progression of forms may have occurred in many places, but the interpretation would require more than Cross's teleological assumption of an evolving repugnance toward the implied bestiality of the swan maiden story. In addition, Cross seems to regard the water element as an incidental feature of the story—present only because swans happen to be water birds. The worldwide inclusion of water formations, notably in versions where the maiden is not a swan or other water animal, suggests that this element may have dictated the mythmaker's choice of a swan, rather than the reverse. See Tuzin 1977 for an analysis of the feminine significance of water symbolism among the Ilahita Arapesh.

7. Even as I write (May 1995), at least two current films draw upon her story. John Sayles's *The Secret of Roan Inish* is about an Irish family with a history of

romantic interaction with local Selkies, who are the seal-people of Irish legend. Maria Luisa Bemberg's *I Don't Want to Talk About It* is about an Argentine dwarf whose doting mother hides from her the knowledge of her dwarfness and who happily marries a handsome man of normal height—just before the circus comes to town.

8. Hence the apparent nonexistence of *indigenous* swan maidens in New World cultures. Throughout native North America, were-animals, demon lovers, and Orpheus-type stories are surely common enough that the hunting would seem to be excellent for genuine swan maidens (Leavy 1994; cf. Lessa 1961, 160). And yet the evidence for their indigenous occurrence is far from definitive (see note 3, above). Wendy Doniger O'Flaherty (1980, 204) mentions in passing that the motif appears in "numerous forms among North American Indians"; Stith Thompson (1946, 88) likewise avers that the swan maiden is found "in practically every cultural area of the North American Indians." Nevertheless, elsewhere Thompson (1919, 366–78) takes pains to show that swan maiden elements occurring in the tales of, for example, the Menominee, Shuswap, Chilcotin, and Natchez were the result of French or French Canadian influence; and that, indeed, *all* North American versions were probably transatlantic imports.

As regards mutually close swan maiden variants among Arctic peoples, those of the Central Eskimo (Boas 1888, 615–18), Baffin Island and Hudson Bay Eskimo (Boas 1901, 179–82), Smith Sound Eskimo (Kroeber 1899, 170–72), and Kodiak Islanders (Golder 1903, 87–90) are almost certainly derived from the Chuckchee and other northeastern Siberian tribes known also to possess them (see Thompson 1946, 92).

In summary, although the swan maiden motif is extremely widespread in world cultures (Thompson 1956, 34), there is little evidence of recurrent independent invention. This accords with the idea, to be argued on various grounds (see below), that Ilahita's version is a local variant of this widely diffused story and that the modifications wrought upon it there are precisely indicative of psychocultural problems peculiar to that village.

9. See, for example, Perry 1924 and Smith 1933.

10. Stephen C. Leavitt reports (pers. comm.) trying to elicit a version of the story from the Bumbita Arapesh, immediately to Ilahita's west. "Without fail," he recalls, "the response was that this was an Ilahita story, and that they could not tell it adequately. They were quite adamant about it."

11. The Ilahita counting system has three primary numbers (1, 2, 3), enabling one to specify, using compounds, numbers 1 through 9—beyond which the counter must resort to fingers, toes, body joints, knots on a string, sticks, and the like to make the count. Quantities greater than nine are verbally described as *hiamwi* ("many"), with a normal accent on the middle syllable. Greater degrees

of "many" can be signaled by intensifying the syllabic stress. By this measure, storytellers indicate that Nambweapa'w had a *great* many children.

12. The notion is that a line of siblings is divided into three segments: oldest, youngest, and those in between. The triad is usually expressed dualistically by contraposing either oldest or youngest (depending on context) against the other two segments combined. See Tuzin 1991 for an examination of this sibling pattern and its behavioral implications.

13. Cf. the ritual image of the cassowary "Great Mother" among the Yafar of the Border Mountains of the West Sepik Province (Juillerat 1992, 58f.). This figure's single pendulant breast—a powerfully phallic image—is modeled on the cassowary's wattle. Among the many exotic ideas attached to the cassowary by New Guinea peoples, that of chicks nursing from the mother's wattle appears to be one of the more common.

14. In a story from Maeva (Vanuatu), Qat's sky-maiden wife, after quarreling with Qat's mother, recovered her wings and flew back to the sky.

> Qat made an arrow ladder to the heavens. Having found her he began
> to take her back to earth. As they were descending on a banyan root,
> *someone* chopped off the root before they had time to reach the ground.
> Qat fell down and was killed, but the woman flew back to heaven.
> (Lessa 1961, 129; emphasis added)

In a closely cognate story from Lepers Island (Vanuatu), the banyan root is cut by the swan maiden herself, who insists that her husband, Tagaro, climb down ahead of her. In that version, Tagaro is not said to die, in so many words; but the story does end there, implying that he does not survive the fall (Dixon [1916] 1964, 139). Comparing the two versions, one detects a seeming unwillingness to admit (a) that the husband dies for his follies and (b) that he dies by the swan maiden's hand. The Ilahita display no such reluctance.

15. The local species is the large, single-wattled, lowland cassowary, *Casuarius unappendiculatus*. The bird grows to a height of 160 centimeters (Perrins and Middleton 1985, 20), which happens to be exactly the average height of Ilahita adult males. The average height of Ilahita adult females is 149 centimeters (Tuzin 1976, 6).

16. During the 1930s, on the coast near Aitape, A. J. Marshall (1938, 241) also encountered ideas about cassowary femininity and supposed suckling behavior.

17. One story is told that there was once a man who had an enormously long penis, which, from time to time, he would uncoil and send off underground to prowl for a woman. One woman, annoyed at having this persistent thing enter her whenever she bent over, chopped the penis to bits with her ax, causing the

man at the other end of it to die. Ever since then, men have had short penises. There will be cause to refer back to this story in chapter 7.

In another story with castration overtones, the protagonist was captured by a village of evil men, each with two tails. When seated, the men would insert their tails into holes in the ground, which were there for that purpose. The hero escaped and undid his captors by putting biting and stinging insects in the holes. When next the men went to sit down, the insects *chewed their tails off,* causing them to die in agony. (See text, below, for the coital significance of "biting and stinging insects," and the feminine significance of "holes in the ground.") In both cases listeners react to the moment of severance with hilarity.

18. From the Mianmin, a group of the northern fringes of the highlands near the Indonesian border, comes a myth fragment about an old woman "who bore many children." When her husband died, she lovingly cut off his penis and kept it permanently in her vagina. It rotted and stank; her sons discovered what she had done and banished her. She went off and eventually turned into a cassowary (Gardner 1984, 141). "This myth," writes Gardner,

> suggests an equation between a-woman-with-a-penis-in-her-vagina
> and the cassowary . . . [I]t indicates the possibility that the significance
> of the cassowary derives from its being more than a straightforward em
> bodiment of potent female powers. Rather, this remarkable animal,
> which is endowed with certain essential characteristics of both men and
> women, displays the same capacity for self-sufficient and self-closing pro
> ductive cycles [that] is emphasized and exalted in sacred rituals.

A similar constellation of cassowary-as-maiden-with-penis images occurs among the Gimi of the Eastern Highlands (Gillison 1993, 328f.).

19. See Tuzin 1980, 242f.; 1989, 291, for the use of coital imagery in Tambaran ceremonies.

20. E. g., Feld 1982, Gardner 1984, Gell 1975, Herdt 1981, and Juillerat 1992. For a criticism of the familiar nature/culture opposition as applied to cassowary classifications, see Pouwer 1991. For interesting parallels concerning emu "femininity" in Australian Aboriginal mythology, see Maddock 1975 and Hamilton 1988.

21. Burton and Burton (1969) dispute the oft-repeated claim that cassowaries—supposedly "the only birds that can kill a man at one blow" (p. 385)— regularly kill people. The authors find only one documented case of this ever having occurred; the victim was not disemboweled—the usually imagined method—but bled to death after the bird slashed his jugular vein. Be this as it may, no one disputes that cassowaries are highly dangerous when aggressively aroused.

22. "For the largest land animals in New Guinea [cassowaries] have kept

their secrets well; we still have only the barest outline of their life history" (Perrins and Middleton 1985, 25).

23. The Portuguese discovered the Moluccas in 1512. Of the five vessels that set forth from Spain in 1519 under the command of Ferdinand Magellan, only *Victoria* ever returned, laden with cloves of Tidore. And in 1580, Sir Francis Drake's *Golden Hind* returned to Plymouth carrying a large cargo of cloves from Ternate.

24. Other scholars confirm the strict geographical limits of Moluccan activity prior to 1852. When William Cornelison Schouten reached Biak and Numfoor from the east, in July 1616, he encountered "Indians" who offered for trade

> some Chinay porceline, for we bartred for two dishes whereby we
> were perswaded that many Christian shippes had bin there, for they
> wondered not, as others did, at our ship. They were another kind of
> people than the former, of a yealower colour, and greater of body, some
> of them hadde long haire, some short, and also used bowes and arrowes,
> where of wee had some in barter. They were desirous of beades, and
> iron worke, and had greene blew, and white glas rings, sticking in their
> eares: which we gest they had from the *Spaniardes.* (Schouten 1619, 70)

Nearly three and a half centuries later, G. J. Held (1957) observed that the metal tools and ornaments of Indonesian origin that he found among the Waropen of the east coast of Geelvink Bay arrived there from Numfoor and Biak, the offshore islands whose inhabitants traded directly with the Birdshead and the Moluccas (see also Elmberg 1968, 128). "Occasionally," writes Held,

> there was also direct contact between the Waropen and the world of
> the Moluccan islands. So for instance there are flags of which it is said
> that they are from Tidore, at least as far as their model is concerned . . .
> but all in all this traffic cannot have been very intensive. (1957, 15)

See Andaya 1993 for a comprehensive history of Ternate and Tidore during their heyday.

25. Without mentioning how she came by the information, Cheesman (1938) indicates that Malay plume hunting in the Hollandia area flourished for "at least two hundred years before white men took part" (p. 36).

26. This estimate accords with Gell's data from the Border Mountains area (Gell 1975, 2) and also with Allen's excellent historical review of Malay and Chinese penetrations of the Torricelli Mountains northwest of Ilahita, beginning within the living memory of men still alive in the early 1970s (Allen 1976, 56–63).

27. In 1849, the Dutch man-of-war *Circe* was unable to land at Humboldt Bay, where Hollandia was later sited, "because of strong southeast winds and a

lee current" (Swadling 1996, 211). Sailing along the north shore in July 1616, Schouten speaks of progressing "stil west northwest, along by the coast with faire wether . . . with help of the streame, that set us about the west, as it did all along the coast of *Nova Guinea*" (Schouten 1619, 67). It should be mentioned that if Schouten had been making this passage in January rather than July, the northwest monsoon of that season would have inflicted less favorable wind conditions. Admitting some seasonality to these patterns—a weak countercurrent flows during the northwest monsoon season—there is nonetheless a distinct bias favoring movement from east to west along this coast, especially in the vicinity of Cape d'Urville. For similar reasons, modern yachtsmen regard Point Conception as something of a barrier to sailboats beating north along the California coast.

28. Named for the Italian physicist, Giovanni Battista Venturi (1746–1822), who studied the effects of compressing fluid flows from a conically reducing space.

29. Whereas the German colonial authorities required only a license to hunt birds of paradise, one of the first acts of the ensuing Australian Civil Administration was to outlaw the shooting and sale of these creatures. Nevertheless, during the 1920s, Malay hunters continued to slip across the border to poach on the Australian-controlled side (Townsend 1968, 65–66).

30. In his survey of Afek mythology among Mountain-Ok peoples, Brumbaugh (1990, 85) suggests that this tradition is not very old; if true, this could allow for a Malay source. Brumbaugh favorably mentions (pp. 69–70) the possibility that Afek originated on the south coast (i.e., Marind-anim), but the bulk of his evidence hints at influences from westerly and/or northeasterly directions. A Malay swan maiden in Afek's ancestry is not impossible, though the figure would have been much changed in the retellings.

31. Trade links to the north coast—one likely conduit of Malay influences—were traditionally very active, as evidenced by the large quantities and cultural importance of seashells in the Sepik hinterland. Ripples of a Malay presence are indicated by the use of cognates of *tuan* (Malay: "lord") throughout the coastal mountain societies as the term for "white man" (or "ghost"), the Ilahita word being *dowank*. And, working among the Urat, a group at only one remove to the west of Ilahita, B. J. Allen (1976, 57) interprets certain oral histories as describing an outbreak of smallpox, presumably traceable to Malay contacts.

32. In his published play, *The Death of a Muruk,* Bernard Narokobi, a prominent Papua New Guinea lawyer and politician who is from a coastal Arapesh village, introduces the cassowary maiden not as lacking a vagina, but as one "still untouched by the moon," meaning she has not yet begun to menstruate (Narokobi 1982, 74). In either case, the creature is not sexually whole until she is made so by her human male captor.

33. The Boiken, southeasterly neighbors of the Mountain Arapesh, have a cassowary maiden story that lacks the genital wounding detail in which the casso-

wary maiden knows all along that the man has her "clothes." In one version she voluntarily stays with the man (Paul Roscoe, pers. comm.); in another version, she recovers her clothes by bribing her son and runs off, never to be seen again (Freudenburg and Hwasimani 1976, 107–8).

34. In the Shetland Islands, the swan maiden is a "Finn"—a kind of local sea monster able "to take any shape of any marine animal, and also that of human beings" (MacRitchie 1890, 3). A human male gets possession of a Finn maiden by seizing her skin when she is not wearing it.

> Had the foolish man who was her husband burnt or destroyed the skin, the Finn woman could never have escaped. But the man had the skin hidden, and it was found by one of the bairns, who gave it to his mother. Thereupon she fled; and it is said that she cried at parting with her family very bitterly. The little ones were the only human beings she cared for. (Ibid.)

35. For example, in a Swedish tale the couple are married, "lovingly and contentedly," for seven years, when the young man makes the mistake of telling his swan wife how he had sought and won her. "He brought forth and showed her, also, the white swan feathers of her former days. No sooner were they placed in her hands that she was transformed once more into a swan, and instantly took flight through the open window. In breathless astonishment, the man started wildly after his rapidly vanishing wife, and before a year and a day had passed, he was laid, with his longings and sorrows, in his allotted place in the village churchyard" (Booss 1989, 250).

36. The Ilahita Arapesh word for "cassowary" is *unalo'w,* which is also the word for "praying mantis." Interestingly, the same terminological coincidence occurs among the Umeda, a society located far to the west of Ilahita, near the Indonesian border (Gell 1975, 225). If this polysemy is based on any resemblance between the bird and the insect, it probably has to do with the similarities in the shape and carriage of the head and neck.

37. Richard Scaglion (pers. comm.), who has worked for many years in Neligum, an Abelam village a short distance east of Aupik, has never heard any Abelam version of the swan maiden story. The Aupik story is almost certainly a recent import from the Ilahita Arapesh.

38. Other Sepik subregional Cassowary-Mother traditions, for example among the Manambu (Simon Harrison, pers. comm.) and Kwoma (Bowden 1983, 109–10; cf. Newton 1973), may be traceable to other coastal sources. A movement of this sort may have reached the region of the Keram River—the second-lowest tributary of the Sepik, after the Porapora. A cassowary maiden story occurs among the Keram River Banaro but not, according to Philippe Peltier, among the Adjorab of the Porapora area (Bernard Juillerat, pers. comm.) or

the Mundugumor or Bun of the Yuat River, the next tributary upstream from the Keram (Nancy McDowell, pers. comm.) This patchy distribution suggests the Rai coast and littoral as the possible source of this tradition (Höltker 1965). See Thurnwald 1916 and Juillerat 1993 for discussions of trade and cultural diffusion between the Banaro and these coastal and hinterland regions.

39. This is not to disparage general interpretations of the swan maiden motif, which may be useful for purposes other than my own. Franz (1993, 137–39), for instance, takes a Jungian view, suggesting that the swan maiden represents the male's ever-elusive anima. Leavy's comparative study (1994) takes a feminist view, arguing that swan maiden stories are gender allegories that envision freedom from the arduous captivity of domestic life. Stories about cassowary maidens and cassowary wives would have nicely supported Leavy's argument, but are not mentioned in her book.

40. Similarly, a story heard in *Inakor,* a Kwanga village southwest of Ilahita, states only that a man captures a cassowary woman by stealing her animal skin; she recovers her skin from hiding and runs away, never to be seen again. The brother of the woman telling the story explained that it is really an Ilahita story and that the Kwanga do not know it well (Karen Brison, pers. comm.). See note 10 above for the same deference expressed in Bumbita.

41. See, for example, MacCulloch 1964, 262 and note 2 above.

Chapter Five

1. Bihinguf is referring to the Great Seal of Australia, which features the emu and the kangaroo and is embossed on the badge worn by administrative officers.

2. See, for example, Kroeber 1915, 1917, and Sahlins 1976.

3. For example, with regard to mathematics, Lévi-Strauss (1962, 248) observes that,

> mathematical thought . . . reflects the free functioning of the mind, that is, the activity of the cells of the cerebral cortex, relatively emancipated from any external constraint and obeying only its own laws. As the mind too is a thing, the functioning of this thing teaches us something about the nature of things: even pure reflection is in the last analysis an internalization of the cosmos. It illustrates the structure of what lies outside in a symbolic form.

4. Kenelm Burridge (1970, 33) terms this criterion of mythic placement "consent." In his treatment of the ideology and history of cargo movements in the Madang area, Burridge conceives of the "myth-dream" in terms consistent with the method of cultural annotation I apply in pursuit of the swan maiden. For Burridge (p. 27), the "myth-dream is a body of notions derived from a variety of sources such as rumours, personal experiences, desires, conflict, and ideas about

the total environment which find expression in myths, dreams, popular stories, and anecdotes. If those involved in a myth-dream were capable of fully comprehending and intellectualizing its content and means then 'aspiration' might have been a better word." As the Ilahita case unfolds, it will make plain that there are "historical" moments when a people's myth-dream becomes sufficiently cognized, that it may constitute an aspiration, motive, or directive force.

5. The last paragraph of Sigmund Freud's *The Interpretation of Dreams* ([1900] 1965, 659–60) asks,

> And the value of dreams for giving us knowledge of the future? There is of course no question of that. It would be truer to say instead that they give us knowledge of the past. For dreams are derived from the past in every sense. Nevertheless the ancient belief that dreams foretell the future is not wholly devoid of truth. By picturing our wishes as fulfilled, dreams are after all leading us into the future. But this future, which the dreamer pictures as the present, has been moulded by his indestructible wish into a perfect likeness of the past.

The formal similarity to the prophetic truth content of "Nambweapa'w" is quite striking, assuming a liberal definition of "wish" that could include the men's troubled fascination with an existential dilemma—or, if you will, a cognitive dissonance—in perennial need of resolution.

6. This interpretation was the centerpiece of Saint Augustine's Christian theory of time, according to which all time was but the instant "present" in God's mind.

7. Once the shaft descended more than arm's length in depth, the man would continue to use a long stick to loosen the soil at the bottom of the hole, but would employ a bamboo device to excavate the backfill (Tuzin 1980, 131–32). He would first splinter the end of the culm and then reinforce the splintered part with a rope cuff tied around it about one foot back from the end. With tension thus placed on the split ends, the bamboo culm would be plunged into the loosened, gluey soil at the bottom of the hole, seizing the equivalent of a large handful of the soil that was easily lifted to the surface. Using this secret technique, which was also used to dig deep holes in preparation for the planting of long yams, a man could excavate a ten-foot shaft in a surprisingly short period of time.

8. The method is somewhat reminiscent of Marcel Proust's *A la recherche du temps perdu,* except that it depends less on subjective evocation than on an objective marshaling of ethnographic annotata. In other words, the method looks mainly to culturally constituted ideas, not personal fantasies, for its data. Of course, "public" and "private" symbols are interrelated in important, complex ways; but that is not my topic here. See Obeysekere 1981 for an interesting treatment of this issue in a Sri Lankan context.

9. Sacred landscapes and spatialized memories occur throughout Melanesia and Australia (Biernoff 1978; Spencer and Gillen [1899] 1968, 123–24, 391 et passim; Stanner 1963, 254), and an important new literature has grown up around the subject (e.g., Poole 1986; Battaglia 1990; Weiner 1991; Hirsch and O'Hanlon 1995; Shama 1995). Embuing natural features with legendary significance may, in fact, be a universal tendency. American folk culture is certainly filled with such lore. I recall that the ten thousand lakes of my Minnesota childhood were fabled to be the soggy footprints left by Paul Bunyan and Babe the Blue Ox as they lumberjacked through the north woods. Nathaniel Hawthorne evokes the romance of landmark features in his twice-told tale, "The Great Stone Face." Referring to the facelike rock formation brooding high over the village in this story, the author writes, "Creation was not finished till the poet came to interpret, and so complete it" (Hawthorne 1907, 292).

Such culturally elaborated, spatial representations of memory are perhaps traceable to a basic cognitive proclivity in humans, one that memory wizards have exploited for centuries. See Spence 1984 for an account of Matteo Ricci, the sixteenth-century Jesuit missionary to China, whose astonishing feats of memory utilized mental palaces built and furnished with mnemonic images.

10. The Arapesh word, *maolinimuna* (sing.), is derived from *maolas,* the name given to powerfully malevolent spirits that inhabit pythons and large eels. That is why only ritually accomplished elders, whose own power is of the same order, may eat them without harm to themselves. Giant yams also contain *maolas* spirits, put there by means of python ashes, which are an ingredient of yam-growing magic. Because of the *maolas* element, caution requires that giant yams be eaten only by men of senior ritual standing—one step below those who are able to eat python flesh. From a gustatory point of view, this is a dubious privilege, since giant yams tend to be woody and flavorless, far less appetizing than the everyday kitchen yams.

11. Any animal that looks or acts abnormally may be suspected, but exceptionally large or menacing pigs, pythons, and eels are routinely assumed to be masalai.

12. The contrast between masalai and ancestral spirits parallels that between short and long yams. See Tuzin 1972 for a description of spiritual and other attributes of yams.

13. See Tuzin 1975 for a study of Arapesh ghosts and nightmares.

14. Opinions differ as to whether the spirit of a married woman goes to her own or her husband's patriclan waters. Although women's spirits are particularly active and dreaded as *ghosts,* they seem simply to drop out of sight in subsequent phases of death. The spirits of dead children are even less signified, and I never heard anyone refer to a child ghost.

15. This notion comes from observing that the products of putrefaction are

liquid. The flesh appears to melt from the bones, as it reverts to its basically liquid nature. See Tuzin 1975, 1977.

16. Note that at any given time a water shrine is inhabited by permanently resident, patrilineal spirits, as well as a number of residents from other patriclans, who are there temporarily by virtue of their *mothers* having been natal members of that patriclan. The assemblage projects an ideal of consanguineal togetherness, which, apart from certain ceremonial moments (see, e.g., Tuzin 1992), is not attainable in everyday social existence.

17. Also recall that, at the time, Nambweapa'w was preparing vegetal salt, potassium chloride. The process entails burning sago spathes and leaching the salt from the ashes. Although sodium chloride (from nearby salt springs or purchased at trade stores) is preferred as a flavoring, vegetal salt is still required for ritual feasts. Beyond the fact of this prescription, I could not obtain exegetical information on this substance, nor does it appear in any other stories I collected. Without such associations, I cannot offer an interpretation as to why Nambweapa'w was engaged in this activity at the moment her son's grass spear reached her.

18. There are clues that these positive attributions belie feelings of guilt and hostility toward parents, which may be projected after the parent dies, even beyond the ghostly phase. See Tuzin 1975 for a discussion of these projective fantasies and their behavioral correlates.

19. On one occasion that I observed, however, a season inversion and its correspondingly poor yam harvest were divined as having been the work of Tambaran spirits, angry over a recent wave of Christian conversions.

20. The word *nggwal* is of Middle Sepik origin. Among the neighboring Abelam, *nggwalndu* are "clan spirits" of ancestral significance, which are responsible for the renewal of pigs and long yams (Forge 1966, 28–29). Among the Iatmul, *nggwail* refers to "father's father, father's father's sister, son's son, son's daughter," and to the "totemic ancestors of a clan" (Bateson 1936, 310).

21. In the Mountain Arapesh version (Mead 1940, 376), when the man of the story first addresses the cassowary-woman, he asks, "Are you a ghost or a woman?" She replies, "I am a woman." Her name is Shaliom.

22. This concept is intended to evoke Sigmund Freud's "dream-work," the title subject of chapter 6, the longest, most important chapter of his *The Interpretation of Dreams* (Freud [1900] 1953). The dream-work consists of mental operations the dreamer uses to formulate, represent, disguise, and express thoughts that are unacceptable to consciousness. These operations include displacement, condensation, secondary revision, forgetting, and other symbolic maneuvers that also occur, mutatis mutandis, in the formation of myths, in respect of deeply embedded existential and psychocultural themes.

23. One prominent storyteller claimed that Imoina is none other than Baingap himself by another name.

24. In kinship terminology, the spouse of a man's same-sex cross-cousin is called "wife," and she reciprocates with "husband." In a system of bilateral cross-cousin marriage, such a usage would, in effect, register the equivalence of "sister" and "wife," in that Ego and Alter would be uterine siblings. The Ilahita do not, in fact, practice such a prescriptive marriage system, but there is circumstantial evidence that they once did (Tuzin 1976, 146–48) and that their sister-exchange marriage preference is a vestige of that former system.

25. See Tuzin 1972 for a discussion of Arapesh yam spirits and the sacramentalism entailed in eating yams that are themselves the lineal descendants of the yams of one's ancestors. These and other features contribute to the symbolic significance of yam exchange. See also Tuzin 1976, 245–49.

26. The same association between marriage exchange and incest appears, less elaborated, in "Kataomo" (Tuzin 1980, 332–34), a story that refers to the time before people knew about pigs. In that mythic time hereditary partners did not exchange pigs to eat, as they do today, but exchanged son-and-daughter pairs to be eaten. This notion is suggestive in Ilahita symbology of sexual *cum* marital exchange, possibly bilateral cross-cousin marriage (Tuzin 1976, 1978; note 24 above). One brother-sister pair are warned by their mother that they are about to be sent to the father's partner. They escape and grow to adulthood in a hidden cave. One day, a python and a pig come into the cave and copulate to produce piglets. Brother and sister marry. Eventually, the brother, who has become a Tambaran spirit by virtue of eating pork, visits their home village. He gives pigs to the villagers and instructs them to desist from using children and to use pigs instead in their exchange practices.

27. When, rarely, such behavior occurs in the village, public opinion is severe against the man, who is despised as weak and irresponsible. Except in the myths we are talking about, incest among primary kin is considered to be repulsive and can lead (in the male) to short-windedness, carbuncles, and various ugly lumps and sores on the face and head.

28. See Tuzin 1976, 189–93, for the full text of the story.

29. In other stories, and in ribald usage, the action of stinging insects is suggestive of the penis's experience of coitus. The same association applies to the effect of stinging nettles. Likewise, referring to the neighboring Abelam, Forge (1962, 10) notes the coital imagery of long-yam growth, responding to magical paint. As described to him,

> the paint is so "hot" that it irritates the sides of the yam (my informant compared this to the rubbing of the ribs of men with stinging nettles during initiation ceremonies), and the yam squirming and stretching to relieve the irritation drives itself further into the ground thus getting longer and longer.

The Ilahita visualize yam growth in very similar terms, without, however, quite so explicit a sexual imitation.

30. This contrast accords with a thoroughgoing distinction in Ilahita social and cultural ideology between "elder brothers" and "younger brothers." See Tuzin 1991 for an examination of this topic.

31. This theory does not account for menarche, since this bleeding is normally not preceded by sexual penetration. It should be noted, however, that, under traditional conditions of child betrothal and prenuptial coresidence, marriage and sexual cohabitation do occur soon after the woman experiences menarche. According to research conducted by Beverly Tuzin, menarche occurs as late as age seventeen or eighteen, presumably because of nutritional factors, by which time the woman is otherwise well ready for marriage.

32. Among the Mountain Arapesh:

> The special symbolism attached to trees as the natural embodiment of a long line of human links with the natural world, now supernaturally tinged by the presence of the ghosts . . . binds all of the individuals of a locality closer together regardless of gens affiliation, for a child is reared "beneath his father's trees" and his father's trees are scattered far and wide. (Mead 1940, 342)

33. Melanie Klein (1882–1960) was a child psychoanalyst trained by Sándor Ferenczi, who was an early associate of Sigmund Freud. Klein's clinical observations led her to conclude that the Oedipus complex developed far earlier in psychic ontogeny than Freud supposed and that children fantasize quite horrific impulses of cruelty, aggression, and cannibalism against the mother. Since these fantasies are unacceptable to later consciousness, they are projected onto the maternal image itself, producing the witch, the ogress, the Kali-like figure of many cultural traditions. See Hays 1964 and Lederer 1968 for compendious treatments of such images from around the world and throughout history.

Chapter Six

1. As examples of the skeptical view of such phenomena in other contexts, Thomas cites Machiavelli's *Discorsi* and Montaigne's *Essais* (1993, 42). As applied to the Aztec conquest, he cites recent works by Todorov (1982) and Fernández-Armesto (1992). See Davies 1982 and Gillespie 1989 for additional comments in the skeptical tradition surrounding Aztec auguries.

2. Hugh Thomas (1993, 187) quotes an Aztec proverb:

> Another time it will be like this, another time things will be the same, some time, some place. What happened a long time ago, and which no longer happens, will be again, it will be done again as it was in far-off times: those who now live, will live again, they will live again.

3. For a time during the 1960s, a movement on the island of New Hanover pinned its millenarian hopes on the idea that U.S. President Lyndon B. Johnson could be induced to come and be its leader.

4. From the Murik Lakes area, near the mouth of the Sepik River and a short distance up the coast from the Madang homeland of Ambwerk and Tuman, the "Two Brothers" myth features yet another pair of fraternal rivals. The trickster younger brother seduces the elder brother's wife and is punished by the elder brother, but finally has his revenge. The story ends with the younger brother going away and eventually finding his way, it seems, to the United States, where he marries many women and has many intelligent white descendants (Meeker et al. 1986, 47–48).

5. See Tuzin 1983 for the use of "the Unthinkable"—another kind of Otherness—in assimilating, cognitively and emotionally, the experience of Japanese cannibalism during World War II. See Sahlins 1983 for a similar argument, which concludes that "the historical practice of cannibalism [in Fiji] can alternatively serve as the concrete referent of a mythical theory or its behavioral metaphor" (p. 91).

6. One was Moses, my neighbor with the pet cassowary, who was mentioned in chapter 4.

7. Further on this issue, see Sahlins 1989, Parker 1995, and Obeyesekere 1995.

8. Marilyn Strathern (1990, 25) writes,

> It has been something of a surprise for Europeans to realise that
> their advent in the Pacific was something less than a surprise. A number
> of accounts give the sense that their coming had been expected; that
> they were previously known beings "returned" or manifest in new
> form. Such ideas certainly fuelled the millenarism of cargo cults in Papua New Guinea. A further return was indicated in the future.

9. On this last point, anomalies, such as oddly shaped trees or kiaps camping in graveyards, are anxiety arousing. Explanations or meanings are sought; current events are reflected upon; stories are invoked or invented. The behavior has a narcissistic, even paranoid, quality, in that it refers an independent, indifferent object to oneself. But because this mode of thought is culturally standardized and socially reinforced, the thinking derived from it is not pathological, unless, as sometimes happens, the individual is delusional. On the other hand, it is not impossible—it may even be likely—that these cultural modes of thought originated in delusional states, including dreams. See Devereux ([1956] 1980) for a classic treatment of this issue.

10. The date was September 13, 1969. A few weeks earlier, on July 20, Neil Armstrong, an American, had been the first person to set foot on the moon. The

people of Ilahita had heard of this event from administrative officials. Although unable to conceive the distance involved or the technical enormity of the accomplishment—some wondered why, if the reports were true, the astronauts could not be seen walking around up there—the people easily accepted world opinion, as described to them, that the moon landing was proof of America's special knowledge, amounting to a kind of wizardry.

11. With my height of 193 centimeters, the choice of names was not difficult.

12. Such constructiveness is not uncommon in Ilahita mythology. Many stories are formed, modular fashion, by mixing and matching from a limited set of images and scenarios.

13. If there is an air of uncertainty in this part of my presentation, the reason is partly that names are not straightforward topics of inquiry in Ilahita. People are acutely embarrassed at being asked their name and will employ sometimes extravagant ruses to pretend they did not hear the question. If a third party is present, that person typically provides the answer, often in response to a pleading look or a stony staring at the ground from the person being questioned. In a one-on-one situation, after the shock of the interviewer's gaucherie is past, the name produced may be an official "book" (i.e., government census) name, which the individual has not used for decades. Alternatively, it may be one of a number of obsolete past names, a trivial "plantation" name, a Christian name, the name of a father; it may be a lie. All according to the person's perception of the interview situation.

These complexities stem from the extreme importance of personal names in the practical, ever-changing constitution of Ilahita persons. For me, they imposed unspeakable hardships on the obtaining of accurate, consistent census and genealogical information in this village of fifteen hundred name-crazed souls. The whole village seemed to breathe a huge sigh of relief when, after six months of effort and concentration, I had mastered the names of every adult (and many of the children) and did not have to ask that question anymore. The struggle was worth every calorie, because in Ilahita—as in our own society, only far more so— it is a great compliment to remember a person's name and to use it in address. In fact, learning their personal names was possibly the single most important component of developing rapport with the people of the village.

14. As a grisly parallel, the Nazis planned to erect a museum of Jewish culture and history after they had destroyed the living tradition and the people who carried it.

15. This transformation was manifested when Mr. Don Niles, an ethnomusicologist from the Institute of Papua New Guinea Studies, visited me in Ilahita to record the flutes, trumpets, drums, whistles, and singing that make the music of the Tambaran. The Revivalists voiced only fleeting concern over the propriety

of staging performances now seen as religiously offensive; by far the greater objection was heard from anti-Revival traditionalists, who took umbrage at what they saw as the trivialization and cynical abuse of these customs by hypocrites who would loudly denounce them at other times. The performances went ahead over their objections, and before long everyone—women and children, too, and even some of the naysayers—was caught up in the festive, nostalgic atmosphere. When Niles left, the instruments were discarded and life returned to its tuneless rhythm. What the experience demonstrated, however—rather subversively, from the standpoint of the traditionalists—was that Tambaran art can be secularized, and that doing so might be preferable to totally abandoning it. Was it *really* the Tambaran that had been singing? Nobody thought so. Nevertheless, it was generally agreed that there were moments when the feeling was right, and all the good memories came flooding back.

16. There were, in addition, six male tok profet, whose pattern of revelations was indistinguishable in content from that of their female colleagues and who were graced by virtue of having been early Christians or of little account as Tambaran men (Tuzin 1989).

17. In this transformation Salalaman strikingly resembled his sister Ribeka's husband, Samuel, except that Samuel's original indolence was dreamier, less discontented, and appeared to lack Salalaman's idle ambitiousness. In part, the likeness may have been due to similar processes underlying their respective rises to prominence. It is also likely that Salalaman sought to emulate his distinguished brother-in-law. See Tuzin 1989 for a description of Samuel's remarkable career—his rise from political and ritual obscurity to a position of supreme ritual authority across a wide geographical area, his visions and their derivation from emotional crises in his life—and for further details concerning the Revival movement in Ilahita.

18. Wa'akea used the Melanesian Pidgin term *samsam,* which refers to a stylized battle prance in which the warrior brandishes his spear while executing lunging motions. Empty-handed, the gesture is sometimes used during oratory to emphasize a point, or as part of an agonistic display between men who are in a heated argument.

19. This semiosis subversively implies that objects and events in the other reality exist because folks in *this* reality believe in them. See Tuzin 1980, 263, 203–4, 212–14, for a discussion of religious illusion as a precipitator of religious truth.

20. The stamina of these parishioners was both phenomenal and tyrannous, as was that of the Tambaran ritualists of old. Nowhere in the entire ward could one go to escape the tiny repertoire of maddeningly repetitive, largely tuneless hymns. Our house being less than three hundred meters downwind and slightly uphill from the church, we could hear every cough, every sour note, with an illusion of nearness that was sometimes eerie. The blaring incessancy of the

illusion of nearness that was sometimes eerie. The blaring incessancy of the hymns quickly became for us a kind of torture, like some inane jingle that keeps grinding through one's mind—only worse, for these could not be turned off or overridden from inside. Continuing long into the night and resuming at first light, these hymns were sounding when we went to bed, sounding when we woke up, churning whatever sleep was achieved during the long hours of the service. Hardest hit was our musically inclined six-year-old, Alex, who once awoke as if from night terrors, and frantically begged me, in vain, to go down there and tell the people to stop singing.

21. I once administered a Rorschach psychodiagnostic test to Kumbwiata, a middle-aged man of some fame as a storyteller. After identifying Plate I as a scene, a landscape, he went on to improvise a story that, step by step, narratively *connected* the first four plates of the series. So comfortable was he in the story's unfolding, that he seemed to know what Plate IV would "be," before I turned the card. Guided dreaming proceeds in a similar fashion; so does mythogenesis.

Chapter Seven

1. In his analysis of an instance of mythopoetic creation among the Huli of the Southern Highlands of New Guinea, Clark (1993, 754) concludes that "myth is not necessarily constructed over centuries, and people transform it in the telling to meet and interpret novel social situations. It has, in this instance at least, a relevance for people's everyday lives and constitutes a kind of 'auto-anthropology.'"

2. In his great work, *La nueva scienza,* published in 1725, Giambattista Vico propounded a very similar dialectic in explaining the movement of culture history and the corresponding evolution of human spirituality. The human spirit is knowable only by its external products, he reasoned, which are the things of culture and history. But the beholding of those products itself modifies the spirit, renewing its need for outward expression. Human works, therefore, are the manifestations of human spirit, always and ever in quest of itself (Berlin 1976). For a wonderfully insightful and elegant examination of the interaction of myth and biography in a Melanesian society, see Young 1983.

3. Some of these stories appear as chapter prologues in Tuzin 1980.

4. It is fairly certain that they were not imported from the Abelam, in the same way the Tambaran itself was. Ethnographers (e.g., Kaberry 1941, 359–60; Forge 1966, 24; 1970, 288) report that the Abelam have virtually no mythology at all, and the few stories they tell are borrowed from neighboring peoples, including the Arapesh (Tuzin 1995b). As in the case of "Nambweapa'w," the moral implications of these "incriminating" stories appear to be Arapesh in origin.

5. The Ilahita have no memory of ever having lived near large, potentially dangerous bodies of water. It is therefore provocative that their mythic calamities

nearly always entail a devastating *flood*. Long ago, long before the death of the Tambaran, I analyzed this mytheme as a male castration fantasy, an image of feminine (because watery) essences erupting out of control, rising up, and violently swamping male power and dominion (Tuzin 1977; cf. Horney [1932] 1966, 84). The social and cultural ruination following the revelation of the Tambaran did indeed bear an uncanny spiritual likeness to the aftermath of a flood—a flood, moreover, feminine in nature.

6. Based on material from Tierra del Fuego and the Amazon Basin, Bamberger treats the "myth of the Rule of Women" as a social charter. Thus, in recounting how women misused their primal authority, the story reaffirms "dogmatically the inferiority of their present position" (1974, 279; cf. Chapman 1982, 66–70). Bamberger implies, somewhat contradictorily, that the South American stories are not secret to women (p. 280), which, if so, would enable them to exercise their "charter" function. In Ilahita, the stories are not only secret, they do not recount that women formerly abused their ritual privileges, other than by frightening the men with them. Furthermore, as noted in the text, some stories feature not women but little boys or dogs as original owners of the sacred objects. In short, the Ilahita stories are not "social charters" in any straightforward sense.

7. The case of the Amazonian Mundurucú bears startling similarities to what I am describing for Ilahita. According to the Murphys, the Mundurucú "myth of matriarchy" is a "parable of phallic dominance, of male superiority symbolized in, and based upon, the possession of the penis. But it is an uneasy overlordship, obtained only by expropriation from the original custody of the women" (Murphy and Murphy 1985, 121). Further, the "dogma of male dominance is . . . pervaded with doubt and contradiction. It must be regarded less as a statement of what things are really like than as the posing of a riddle, the expression of a dilemma, and an ideological device for its resolution" (p. 137).

8. This attitude is reported in other societies possessing secret men's cults. Writing of the Mundurucú, Murphy and Murphy (1985, 126–27) "never found any great curiosity among the women" as regards the men's ritual secrets. Though "none would admit peeking," the women knew all about the secret paraphernalia, and "they were neither mystified nor cowed. It is as if they had investigated the secret sources of the men's power—and had found absolutely nothing" (p. 167).

Compare, also, the Ilahita women's blasé response to the revelation of the Tambaran secrets with a comment by L. R. Hiatt (1971) concerning similar gender separations in Aboriginal Australia. Acknowledging that Aboriginal women are evidently "not always impressed" by the men's intimidating gestures, Hiatt (p. 88n) writes that "one of Annette Hamilton's female informants at Maningrida told her that the *Kunapipi* ceremony was 'man's rubbish,' adding that 'men make secret ceremonies, women make babies.'" Most Ilahita women would agree, I think.

9. The passage appears in Jean-Baptiste Molière's preface to the 1669 version of his satiric play *Tartuffe*.

10. The phallic character of male spiritual strength is revealed with great clarity in the prestige complex centered on the growth and competitive exchange of giant long yams; see Tuzin 1972.

11. Such views are very commonly reported from societies with systems of gender-inflected ritual secrecy. For example, among the Kuranko of northern Sierra Leone, who possess both men's cults and women's cults, Michael Jackson (1977, 220–21) was told that

> the "work" of the cult associations was "to keep men and women separate, to make them respect each other; the women cannot understand the men's cults and the men cannot understand the women's cults, therefore a darkness exists between them which maintains the mutual respect between womanhood and manhood." Some informants confessed that within the cult "there isn't really very much, though for the women it is awesome." The secret objects themselves are far less significant than the principle of secrecy and the mystical powers which they symbolise. The betrayal of cult secrets leads not only to the punishment of the offender (by the cult adepts), it also threatens the social order. For, "if women have no respect for men then the principles of manhood will be as nothing."

12. Rosa would not be pleased at the unflattering depiction of Hageners by the Telefolmin of the Mountain Ok region. According to Jorgensen (1991, 262), young men returning from work on tea plantations around Mount Hagen portray the Hageners as "shameless." "The men are lazy and leave all the work to the women; old men have many wives, while many young men are shiftless bachelors who cause trouble. What is worse, Hageners are greedy and try to make a *bisnis* out of their sisters or daughters; they eagerly marry them off to outsiders, providing the latter can come up with large amounts of money to pay for the bride." While none of this discredits Rosa's criticisms of Ilahita family life, it does indicate an element of personal and ethnic bias operating in her invidious comparisons.

13. By 1985, the year in which this conversation took place, bride-price had indeed replaced sister exchange as the mode of marriage transaction. The new form having not yet assimilated to Ilahita social organization, the burden of raising expensive bride payments rested with the groom or, at most, his nuclear family, not with a wider kinship or clan grouping, such as occurs in societies where bride-price is an established tradition. Conversely, payment received for an

out-marrying daughter was enjoyed by her immediate family, rather than being distributed to a larger social group. One consequence of this narrow compass was the tragic asymmetry in the valuation of sons and daughters, as described by Rosa.

14. Gilbert Herdt (1987) reports that among the Sambia of the Eastern Highlands, who have a men's cult, parents are loath to punish boys; mothers are even inclined to pamper them. When necessary, however, "Mothers more than fathers are involved in controlling children" (pp. 251–52). There, as among the Ilahita, it would appear that fathers depend upon their wives and the cult organization to control their sons.

15. With reference to the Balif Arapesh, Macdonald (1995, 315) observes that "where men had customarily taken much of the responsibility for the socialization of young males, colonial practices ensured that women, of necessity, were responsible for the socialization of all children, but without the authority over their sons that a more equitable apportionment of power and influence between men and women would have enabled." In Ilahita, where the Tambaran remained a force in male socialization for almost the entire colonial period, the change Macdonald reports may have been less dramatic. Perhaps of greater significance in male socialization was the colonial-era cessation of endemic warfare, which reduced the urgency of the male authority system and increased the role of mothers in the raising of sons, with resulting problems of the kind Macdonald describes.

16. The survey was based on a stratified random sample of twenty children in each society. Each evening for a week, recall of the day's crying events was elicited from each subject's caregiver(s), who, in nearly all cases, was the uterine mother.

17. The survey turned up interesting divergences between boys and girls. For Ilahita boys, 43 percent ($n = 44$) of crying incidents were food related; the next most frequent cause, fighting with siblings or playmates, amounted to 18 percent of the total. Of crying incidents by Ilahita girls ($n = 33$), 36 percent were food related, and 27 percent were the result of fighting with siblings or playmates. In addition, 11 percent of boys' tears were the result of wanting to be carried, usually by the mother, whereas no such incidents occurred involving girls. Though too modest in scale to permit firm conclusions, the survey does support my general impression that little boys experience more craving and frustration than little girls do, when it comes to nurturant attention from their mothers.

18. Nutritional information is provided by Beverly Tuzin, a professional dietitian, who conducted systematic dietary-intake studies in Ilahita during 1970–71.

19. Similarly, the Mountain Arapesh assign criterial importance to the nurturant role of mothers—and, according to Mead (1935), fathers as well. Among

the Ilahita, the same emphasis exists, but with the idea that fathers provide the food, while mothers *feed* the children.

20. Ilahita women sometimes must utilize a wet nurse for their suckling infants. The woman, usually a relative, lives and sleeps with mother and infant, ready to feed on demand. But only to feed. There is a strong injunction against wet nurses cuddling infants, which is something only the mother should do.

Chapter Eight

1. Age and decrepitude also compose the image projected upon initiates of the last grade of the cult, the grade of the "old men" (Tuzin 1980, chap. 8). Recall (chapter 5) that the large taro leaf under which old Baingap crouched before being killed is represented as the inner-sanctum structure in the house belonging to this grade. In addition, a story told in association with this grade is that of Imoina, Baingap's little brother grown old, who by some accounts is Baingap himself in old age. (See chapter 5; also Tuzin 1980, 250–53.) In associating the elderly initiates with Imoina, who has the power to doff his wrinkled skin and emerge as a strong, handsome young man, the Tambaran seeks to deny their apparent decrepitude and powerlessness.

2. The school draws its pupils from Ilahita and two other villages toward the south: Ingamblis and Kamanakor, the latter of which is Kwanga-speaking. In 1985, all the teachers were from far out of the area, and they lived with their families in a housing compound on the school property. Note that the Mission school mentioned in chapter 2 was a small facility—only one or two classes— attended mostly by boarding students from other, nearby villages. If a few Ilahita men currently in their fifties can read and write Melanesian Pidgin, it is because they were among the small number from the village who briefly attended the school during the late 1950s. As best as I can tell, the Mission school had little or no impact on the culture of the village.

3. I have elsewhere argued (Tuzin 1980, 322) that the Tambaran's self-conscious identification with Ilahita tradition emerged during the two decades following 1935, as part of a redefinition of cultural identity that was prompted by exposure to a radically alien (European) Other.

4. Moreover, the trick of *simultaneously* revealing the secret to and concealing it from the women was essential to the magical efficacy of the ritual. See Tuzin 1995b for a discussion of this subject.

5. See Kimmel 1996 for a comprehensive history of manhood in America, one that includes the cultural and institutional backdrop to the trends being discussed here. In a chapter entitled "A Room of His Own," Kimmel describes the reactive, hypermasculine ideology that prevailed at the turn of this century and its decay in succeeding decades, largely in response to changes in the nation's

occupational profile. Aside from his tendency to make light of the contemporary "men's movement" (e.g., p. 318f.), Kimmel's historical account is in agreement with my treatment of "masculine sanctuaries."

6. Earlier works by feminist writers such as Simone de Beauvoir (1952) and Betty Friedan (1963) sought, constructively and with considerable analytic acumen, to improve women's lot, not to blame and defame men. Indeed, were it not for the relatively moderate, affirmative tone of their critiques, modern feminism would not have attracted the sizable following among women (and men) that it did. The strains of phallophobic feminism arising in the 1970s and onward were something else entirely.

7. On the day of this writing (May 1, 1996), the House National Security Committee voted to ban the sale of girlie magazines on U.S. military bases. Whatever satisfaction such a restriction might bring to its sponsors and advocates—to whom the ban would not apply—the initiative is a clear indication that the military is no longer the masculine sanctuary it once was.

8. In the last thirty years, as unprecedented numbers of married women have taken jobs outside the home, the expectation has been that husbands would assume their fair share of child care and routine housekeeping chores. While some movement along these lines has undoubtedly occurred, in both ideology and behavior, "time-budget studies suggest that most husbands of working wives have assumed only a minor part of the housework" (Putnam 1995, 74; also Hochschild 1989, 277–79). Clearly, men have not been clamoring to enter this traditional area of feminine sanctuary. For a sensitive, practical discussion of "peer marriage" in the new world of gender relations, see Schwartz 1994.

9. Some of today's counterexclusionary notions are equally silly. In the *New York Times* of April 28, 1996, it is reported that the prison commissioner of Alabama resigned after the governor "squashed" his serious suggestion that female chain gangs be instituted—the idea being that chains on males were "discriminatory because women did not have to wear them."

10. For example, the systematic destruction of male sanctuary may be seen as an aspect of, but also a contributor to, the sharp decline of civic engagement in American society during recent years (Putnam 1994, 1995).

11. See Chodorow 1978 for excellent psychodynamic insights into gender differences in the character and formation of ego boundaries. Simply put, for boys, according to Chodorow, separation from the mother and identification with the father result in strong but easily threatened ego boundaries; whereas for girls the same process results in weak but resilient and adaptable ego boundaries. Chodorow's etiology is quite consistent with the notion of "masculine sanctuary" being developed here.

12. In 1971, when Beverly asked a middle-aged woman if women too had

secrets, she was told, in a matter-of-fact tone: "Oh, yes—but the men know them all."

13. These coping behaviors begin at an early age. In his rousing critique of the stereotyping tactics of today's gender warriors, Cose (1995) decries the extent to which young boys are imprisoned in illusions. "We tell them," Cose writes (pp. 256–57),

> though not necessarily directly, that they are smarter and more emo-
> tionally stable than girls, that they can handle power and pain so much
> better. And because these things are not true, boys learn early to pre-
> tend, to hide their inadequacies behind a mask. Or, worse, they take the
> premise of superiority as a fact and endeavor to personify it—even if it
> kills them, as it sometimes does.

14. As reported on the PBS television broadcast of *The NewsHour with Jim Lehrer,* April 24, 1996, the Southern Poverty Law Center counts 441 armed mili-tia groups active in all fifty states—approximately twice the number of a year earlier. It is not known precisely how many of these groups, or how many mem-bers, represent a danger to civil society.

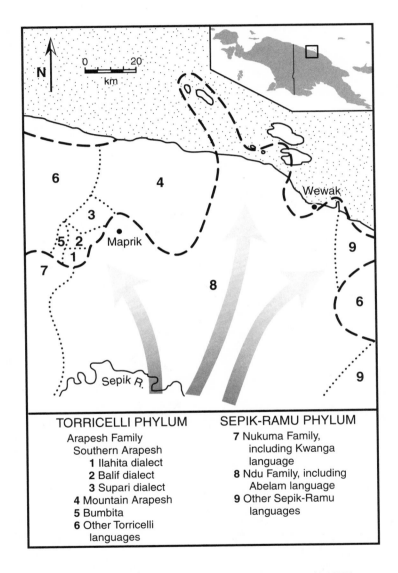

N

0   20
         km

6

4

Wewak

3

5 2   Maprik

1

7

9

8

6

9

Sepik R.

TORRICELLI PHYLUM	SEPIK-RAMU PHYLUM
Arapesh Family	**7** Nukuma Family,
Southern Arapesh	including Kwanga
1 Ilahita dialect	language
2 Balif dialect	**8** Ndu Family, including
3 Supari dialect	Abelam language
4 Mountain Arapesh	**9** Other Sepik-Ramu
5 Bumbita	languages
6 Other Torricelli	
languages	

1. Languages of the Maprik–Wewak area (after Laycock 1973)

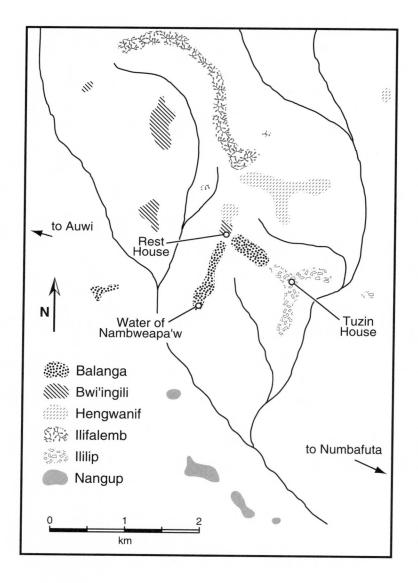

to Auwi

Rest
House

N

Water of
Nambweapa'w

Tuzin
House

- Balanga
- Bwi'ingili
- Hengwanif
- Ilifalemb
- Ililip
- Nangup

to Numbafuta

0   1   2
        km

2. Ilahita village

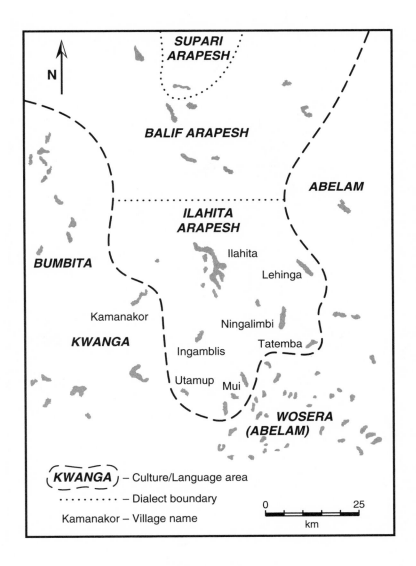

N

SUPARI
ARAPESH

BALIF ARAPESH

ABELAM

ILAHITA
ARAPESH

Ilahita

Lehinga

BUMBITA

Kamanakor

Ningalimbi

KWANGA

Tatemba

Ingamblis

Utamup   Mui

WOSERA
(ABELAM)

KWANGA – Culture/Language area
. . . . – Dialect boundary
Kamanakor – Village name

0   25
km

3. Language-culture areas of Ilahita and its environs

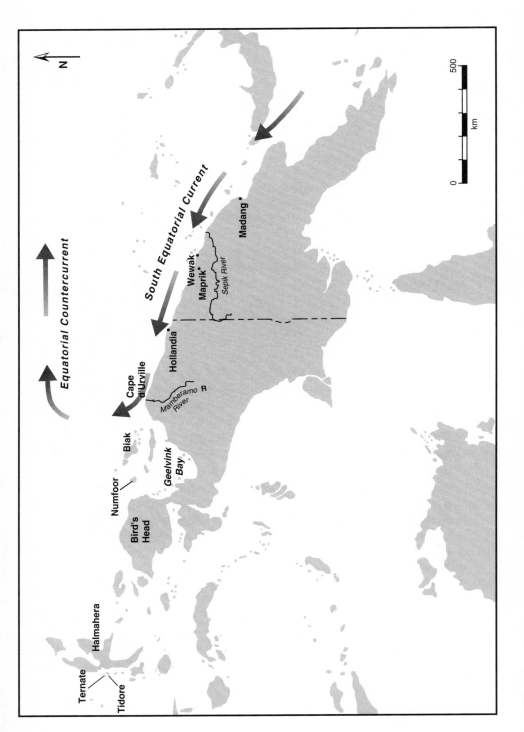

4. The New Guinea north coast, showing features referred to in the text

References

Akimoula, Menis. 1980. The Origin Story Told at Aupik Village, Maprik Dialect Area of Abelam Speakers. *Oral History* 9(8):6–7.

Allen, B. J. 1976. Information Flow and Innovation Diffusion in the East Sepik District, Papua New Guinea. Ph.D. thesis, Australian National University, Canberra.

Allen, M. R. 1967. *Male Cults and Secret Initiations in Melanesia.* Melbourne: Melbourne University Press.

Amadon, Dean, and E. Thomas Gilliard. 1954. Birds of the World. In *The Animal Kingdom.* Vol. 2, edited by Frederick Drimmer. New York: Greystone Press, pp. 875–1188.

Andaya, Leonard Y. 1993. *The World of Maluku: Eastern Indonesia in the Early Modern Period.* Honolulu: University of Hawaii Press.

Aufenanger, Henry. 1972. *The Passing Scene in North-east New-Guinea (A Documentation).* St. Augustin, Germany: Anthropos-Institut.

———. 1975. *The Great Inheritance in Northeast New Guinea.* St. Augustin, Germany: Anthropos-Institut.

Bamberger, Joan. 1974. The Myth of Matriarchy: Why Men Rule in Primitive Society. In *Women, Culture, and Society,* edited by Michelle Rosaldo and Louise Lamphere. Stanford: Stanford University Press, pp. 263–80.

Barakat, Robert A. 1965. Aztec Motifs in "La Llorona." *Southern Folklore Quarterly* 29(4):288–96.

Barr, John. 1983. A Survey of Ecstatic Phenomena and "Holy Spirit Movements" in Melanesia. *Oceania* 54(2):109–32.

Barth, Fredrik. 1987. *Cosmologies in the Making: A Generative Approach to Cultural Variation in Inner New Guinea.* Cambridge: Cambridge University Press.

Bateson, Gregory. [1936] 1958. *Naven: A Survey of the Problems Suggested by a Composite Picture of the Culture of a New Guinea Tribe Drawn from Three Points of View.* Stanford: Stanford University Press.

Battaglia, Debbora. 1990. *On the Bones of the Serpent: Person, Memory, and Mortality in Sabarl Island Society.* Chicago: University of Chicago Press.

Beauvoir, Simone de. 1952. *The Second Sex.* New York: Alfred Knopf.

Berlin, Isaiah. 1976. *Vico and Herder: Two Studies in the History of Ideas.* New York: Viking Press.

Bettelheim, Bruno. 1954. *Symbolic Wounds: Puberty Rites and the Envious Male.* Glencoe, Ill.: Free Press.

Biernoff, David. 1978. Safe and Dangerous Places. In *Australian Aboriginal Concepts,* edited by L. R. Hiatt. Canberra: Australian Institute of Aboriginal Studies, pp. 93–105.

Bly, Robert. 1990. *Iron John: A Book about Men.* Reading, Mass.: Addison-Wesley.

Boas, Franz. 1888. The Central Eskimo. *Annual Report of the Bureau of American Ethnology* 6:409–669.

———. 1901. I. The Eskimo of Baffin Land and Hudson Bay. *Bulletin of the American Museum of Natural History* 15:1–370.

Booss, Claire. 1989. *Scandanavian Folk and Fairy Tales.* New York: Avenel Books.

Bowden, Ross. 1983. *Yena: Art and Ceremony in a Sepik Society.* Oxford: Pitt Rivers Museum.

Brumbaugh, Robert. 1990. "Afek Sang": The Old Woman's Legacy to the Mountain-Ok. In *Children of Afek: Tradition and Change Among the Mountain-Ok of Central New Guinea,* edited by Barry Craig and David Hyndman. Oceania Monograph no. 40. Sydney: University of Sydney, pp. 54–87.

Bulmer, Ralph. 1967. Why Is the Cassowary Not a Bird? A Problem of Zoological Taxonomy among the Karam of the New Guinea Highlands. *Man,* n. s., 2(1):5–25.

Burridge, Kenelm. 1969. *New Heaven New Earth: A Study of Millenarian Activities.* New York: Schocken.

———. [1960] 1970. *Mambu: A Study of Melanesian Cargo Movements and Their Social and Ideological Background.* New York: Harper and Row.

Burton, Maurice, and Robert Burton. 1969. Cassowary. In *The International Wildlife Encyclopedia.* Vol. 3. New York: Marshall Cavendish.

Cantor, Norman F. 1994. *The Sacred Chain: A History of the Jews.* New York: HarperCollins.

Chapman, Anne. 1982. *Drama and Power in a Hunting Society: The Selk'nam of Tierra del Fuego.* Cambridge: Cambridge University Press.

Cheesman, Evelyn. 1938. *The Land of the Red Bird.* London: Herbert Joseph.

Chodorow, Nancy L. 1978. *The Reproduction of Mothering: Psychoanalysis and the Sociology of Gender.* Berkeley: University of California Press.

Clark, Jeffrey. 1993. Gold, Sex, and Pollution: Male Illness and Myth at Mt. Kare, Papua New Guinea. *American Ethnologist* 20(4):742–57.

———. 1995. Highlands of History: Images of Deviance and Desire. In *Papuan Borderlands: Huli, Duna, and Ipili Perspectives on the Papua New Guinea Highlands,* edited by Aletta Biersack. Ann Arbor: University of Michigan Press, pp. 379–400.

Coates, Brian J. 1982. *Papua New Guinea Birds in Colour.* Bathurst, N.S.W.: Robert Brown.

Cose, Ellis. 1995. *A Man's World: How Real Is Male Privilege—And How High Is Its Price?* New York: HarperCollins.

Costain, Thomas B. 1964. *A History of the Plantagenets: The Three Edwards.* New York: Popular Library.

Cross, Tom Peete. 1915. The Celtic Elements in the Lays of Lanval and Graelent. *Modern Philology* 12(10):585–644.

Davies, Nigel. 1982. *The Aztecs: A History.* Norman: University of Oklahoma Press.

Devereux, George. [1956] 1980. Normal and Abnormal. In *Basic Problems in Ethnopsychiatry.* Chicago: University of Chicago Press, pp. 3–71.

Dixon, Roland B. [1916] 1964. *Oceanic.* Vol. 9 of *The Mythology of All Races,* edited by Louis Herbert Gray. New York: Cooper Square.

du Toit, Brian M. 1969. Misconstruction and Problems in Communication. *American Anthropologist* 71(1):46–53.

Elmberg, John-Erik. 1968. *Balance and Circulation: Aspects of Tradition and Change among the Mejprat of Irian Barat.* Stockholm: Etnografiska Museet.

Feld, Steven. 1982. *Sound and Sentiment: Birds, Weeping, Poetics, and Song in Kaluli Expression.* Philadelphia: University of Pennsylvania Press.

Fernández-Armesto, Felipe. 1992. "Aztec" Auguries and Memories of the Conquest of Mexico. *Renaissance Studies* 6:287–305.

Fleetwood, Lorna. 1984. *A Short History of Wewak.* Wewak: East Sepik Provincial Government.

Forge, Anthony. 1962. Paint—a Magical Substance. *Palette* 9:9–16

———. 1966. Art and Environment in the Sepik. *Proceedings of the Royal Anthropological Institute 1965,* pp. 23–31.

———. 1970. Learning to See in New Guinea. In *Socialization: The Approach from Social Anthropology,* edited by Philip Mayer. London: Tavistock, pp. 269–91.

Fortune, Reo. 1942. *Arapesh.* New York: J. J. Augustin.

Franz, Marie-Louise von. 1993. *The Feminine in Fairy Tales.* Rev. ed. Boston: Shambhala Publications.

Freud, Sigmund. [1900] 1953. The Interpretation of Dreams. In *Standard Edition of the Complete Psychological Works of Sigmund Freud.* Vols. 4–5, edited by James Strachey. London: Hogarth Press.

Freudenburg, Allen and Demon Hwasimani, compilers. 1976. *Kueliwalanka Tiere Huafu.* Ukarumpa: Summer Institute of Linguistics.

Friedan, Betty. 1963. *The Feminine Mystique.* New York: Dell.

Gardner, D. S. 1984. A Note on the Androgynous Qualities of the Cassowary: Or Why the Mianmin Say It Is Not a Bird. *Oceania* 55(2):137–45.

Gelber, Marilyn G. 1986. *Gender and Society in the New Guinea Highlands: An Anthropological Perspective on Antagonism Toward Women.* Boulder, Colo.: Westview Press.

Gell, Alfred. 1975. *The Metamorphosis of the Cassowaries.* London: Athlone Press.

———. 1992. Under the Sign of the Cassowary. In *Shooting the Sun: Ritual and Meaning in West Sepik,* edited by Bernard Juillerat. Washington, D.C.: Smithsonian Institution Press, pp. 125–43.

Gesch, Patrick F. 1985. *Initiative and Initiation: A Cargo Cult-Type Movement in the Sepik against Its Background in Traditional Village Religion.* St. Augustin: Anthropos-Institut.

Gewertz, Deborah, ed. 1988. *Myths of Matriarchy Reconsidered.* Oceania Monograph no. 33. Sydney: University of Sydney.

Gillespie, Susan. 1989. *The Aztec Kings.* Tucson: University of Arizona Press.

Gillison, Gillian. 1993. *Between Culture and Fantasy: A New Guinea Highlands Mythology.* Chicago: University of Chicago Press.

Glasse, Robert M. 1995. Time Belong Mbingi: Syncretism and the Pacification of the Huli. In *Papuan Borderlands: Huli, Duna, and Ipili Perspectives on the Papua New Guinea Highlands,* edited by Aletta Biersack. Ann Arbor: University of Michigan Press, pp. 57–86.

Golder, F. A. 1903. Tales from Kodiak Island. II. *Journal of American Folk-lore* 16:85–103.

Gregor, Thomas. 1985. *Anxious Pleasures: The Sexual Lives of an Amazonian People.* Chicago: University of Chicago Press.

Hall, D. G. E. 1981. *A History of South-east Asia.* 4th ed. New York: St. Martin's Press.

Hamilton, Annette. 1988. Knowledge and Misrecognition: Mythology and Gender in Aboriginal Australia. In *Myths of Matriarchy Reconsidered,* edited by Deborah Gewertz. Oceania Monograph no. 40. Sydney: University of Sydney, pp. 57–73.

Harrison, Simon. 1990. *Stealing People's Names: History and Politics in a Sepik River Cosmology.* Cambridge: Cambridge University Press.

Hawthorne, Nathaniel. 1907. The Great Stone Face. In *Modern Stories,* selected by Eva March Tappan. Boston: Houghton Mifflin, pp. 271–98.

Hays, H. R. 1964. *The Dangerous Sex: The Myth of Feminine Evil.* New York: Putnam.

Hays, Terence E. 1988. "Myths of Matriarchy" and the Sacred Flute Complex of the Papua New Guinea Highlands. In *Myths of Matriarchy Reconsidered,* edited by Deborah Gewertz. Oceania Monograph no. 40. Sydney: University of Sydney, pp. 98–120.

Held, G. J. 1957. *The Papuas of Waropen.* The Hague: Martinus Nijhoff.

Herdt, Gilbert H. 1981. *Guardians of the Flutes: Idioms of Masculinity.* New York: McGraw-Hill.

———. 1987. The Accountability of Sambia Initiates. In *Anthropology in the High Valleys: Essays on the New Guinea Highlands in Honor of Kenneth E. Read,* edited by L. L. Langness and Terence E. Hays. Novato, Calif.: Chandler and Sharp, pp. 237–81.

Hiatt, L. R. 1971. Secret Pseudo-procreation Rites among the Australian Aborigines. In *Anthropology in Oceania,* edited by L. R. Hiatt and C. Jayawardene. Sydney: Angus and Robertson, pp. 77–88.

Hibbert, Christopher. 1964. *Agincourt.* London: Pan Books.

Hirsch, Eric, and Michael O'Hanlon, eds. 1995. *The Anthropology of Landscape: Perspectives on Place and Space.* Oxford: Oxford University Press.

Hochschild, Arlie. 1989. *The Second Shift.* New York: Avon.

Höltker, Georg. 1965. Mythen und Erzählungen der Monumbo- und Ngaimbom-Papua in Nordost-Neuguinea. *Anthropos* 60:65–107.

Horney, Karen. [1932] 1966. The Dread of Woman. In *Psychoanalysis and Male Sexuality,* edited by Hendrik M. Ruitenbeek. New Haven, Conn.: College and University Press, pp. 83–96.

Horrocks, Roger. 1994. *Masculinity in Crisis: Myths, Fantasies and Realities.* New York: St. Martin's Press.

Hwekmarin, L., J. Jamenan, D. Lea, A Ningiga, and M. Wangu. 1971. Yangaru Cargo Cult 1971. *Journal of the Papua New Guinea Society* 5(2):3–27.

Jackson, Michael. 1977. *The Kuranko: Dimensions of Social Reality in a West African Society.* London: C. Hurst.

Jorgensen, Dan. 1991. Big Men, Great Men and Women: Alternative Logics of Gender Difference. In *Big Men and Great Men: Personifications of Power in Melanesia,* edited by Maurice Godelier and Marilyn Strathern. Cambridge: Cambridge University Press, pp. 256–71.

Juillerat, Bernard. 1993. *La révocation des Tambaran: Les Banaro et Richard Thurnwald revisités.* Paris: CNRS Editions.

———, ed. 1992. *Shooting the Sun: Ritual and Meaning in West Sepik.* Washington, D.C.: Smithsonian Institution Press.

Kaberry, Phyllis M. 1941. The Abelam Tribe, Sepik District, New Guinea: A Preliminary Report. *Oceania* 11(3):233–58, (4):345–67.

Kimmel, Michael. 1996. *Manhood in America: A Cultural History.* New York: Free Press.

Kroeber, Alfred L. 1899. Tales of the Smith Sound Eskimo. *Journal of American Folk-lore* 12:166–82.

———. 1915. Eighteen Professions. *American Anthropologist* 17(2):283–88.

———. 1917. The Superorganic. *American Anthropologist* 19(2):163–213.

Langer, Susanne K. 1953. *Feeling and Form.* New York: Charles Scribner's Sons.

Lawrence, Peter. 1964. *Road Belong Cargo: A Study of the Cargo Movement in the Southern Madang District New Guinea.* Manchester: Manchester University Press.

Laycock, Donald C. 1973. Sepik Languages: Checklist and Preliminary Classification. *Pacific Linguistics,* ser. B, no. 25.

Leavitt, Stephen C. 1989. Cargo, Christ, and Nostalgia for the Dead: Themes of Intimacy and Abandonment in Bumbita Arapesh Social Experience. Doctoral dissertation, University of California, San Diego.

————. 1995. Political Domination and the Absent Oppressor: Images of Europeans in Bumbita Arapesh Narratives. *Ethnology* 34(3):177–89.

Leavy, Barbara Fass. 1994. *In Search of the Swan Maiden: A Narrative on Folklore and Gender.* New York: New York University Press.

Lederer, Wolfgang. 1968. *The Fear of Women.* New York: Harcourt Brace Jovanovich.

Lessa, William A. 1961. *Tales from Ulithi Atoll: A Comparative Study in Oceanic Folklore.* Berkeley: University of California Press.

Lévi-Strauss, Claude. 1962. *The Savage Mind.* Chicago: University of Chicago Press.

Likita, Stephen. 1980. The Cassowary Woman and the Beginning of Awi (Auwi) Village. *Oral History* 8(9):82–85.

Lindenbaum, Shirley. 1987. The Mystification of Female Labors. In *Gender and Kinship: Essays Toward a Unified Analysis,* edited by Jane Collier and Sylvia Yanagisako. Stanford: Stanford University Press, pp. 221–43.

MacCulloch, J. A. [1930] 1964. *Eddic.* Vol. 2 of *The Mythology of All Races,* edited by Louis Herbert Gray. New York: Cooper Square.

Macdonald, Wendy Mortill. 1995. Social Transformations and Gender Distinctions: "Locating" Balif Arapesh Women in Contemporary Papua New Guinea Society. Ph.D. thesis, Northern Territory University, Darwin, Australia.

MacRitchie, David. 1890. *The Testimony of Tradition.* London: Kegan Paul, Trench, Trübner.

Maddock, Kenneth. 1975. The Emu Anomaly. In *Australian Aboriginal Mythology,* edited by L. R. Hiatt. Canberra: Australian Institute of Aboriginal Studies, pp. 102–22.

Malinowski, Bronislaw. [1926] 1948. Myth in Primitive Psychology. In *Magic, Science and Religion and Other Essays.* Garden City, N.Y.: Doubleday.

Manari, Mary. 1980. How Yams and Mamies Came to Akasamei Village in the Nuku District, West Sepik Province, as Told by Amos Melasa. *Oral History* 8(9):52–56.

Manet, Edouard. 1945. *Manet: Raconté par lui-même et par ses amis.* Paris: Pierre Cailler.

Marshall, A. J. 1938. *The Men and Birds of Paradise: Journeys through Equatorial New Guinea*. London: William Heinemann.

Mauss, Marcel. 1925. Essai sur le don: Forme et raison de l'échange dans les sociétés archaïques. *Année Sociologique* 1:30–186.

McCarthy, J. K. 1963. *Patrol into Yesterday: My New Guinea Years*. Melbourne: F. W. Cheshire.

Mead, Margaret. 1933. The Marsalai Cult among the Arapesh, with Special Reference to the Rainbow Serpent Beliefs of the Australian Aboriginals. *Oceania* 4(1):37–53.

———. 1935. *Sex and Temperament in Three Primitive Societies*. London: George Routledge and Sons.

———. 1938. The Mountain Arapesh: I. An Importing Culture. *American Museum of Natural History. Anthropological Papers* 36(pt. 3):139–349.

———. 1940. The Mountain Arapesh: II. Supernaturalism. *American Museum of Natural History. Anthropological Papers* 37(pt. 3):317–451.

———. 1978. The Sepik as a Culture Area: Comment. *Anthropological Quarterly* 51(1):69–75.

Meeker, Michael E. n. d. The Black Sea Turks: The Formation of a Modern Political Identity. Unpublished manuscript.

Meeker, Michael E., Kathleen Barlow, and David M. Lipset. 1986. Culture, Exchange, and Gender: Lessons from the Murik. *Cultural Anthropology* 1(1):6–73.

Meggitt, M. J. 1979. Reflections Occasioned by Continuing Anthropological Field Research among the Enga of Papua New Guinea. In *Long-Term Field Research in Social Anthropology*, edited by George M. Foster, Elizabeth Colson, Thayer Scudder, and Robert V. Kemper. New York: Academic Press, pp. 107–25.

Meigs, Anna S. 1984. *Food, Sex, and Pollution: A New Guinea Religion*. New Brunswick, N.J.: Rutgers University Press.

Murphy, Yolanda, and Robert F. Murphy. 1985. *Women of the Forest*. 2d ed. New York: Columbia University Press.

Narakobi, Bernard. 1982. The Death of a Muruk. *Bikmaus* 3(1):72–80.

Newton, Douglas. 1973. Why Is the Cassowary a Canoe Prow? *Art Journal* 33(1):41–45.

Nupela Testamen bilong Bikpela Jisas Kraist. 1969. Canberra: British and Foreign Bible Society in Australia.

Obeyesekere, Gananath. 1981. *Medusa's Hair: An Essay on Personal Symbols and Religious Experience*. Chicago: University of Chicago Press.

———. 1992. *The Apotheosis of Captain Cook: European Mythmaking in the Pacific*. Princeton: Princeton University Press.

———. 1995. Re-weaving the Argument: A Response to Parker. *Oceania* 65(3):268–73.

O'Flaherty, Wendy Doniger. 1980. *Women, Androgynes, and Other Mythical Beasts.* Chicago: University of Chicago Press.

Oliver, Douglas. 1975. *The Pacific Islands.* Rev. ed. Honolulu: University of Hawaii Press.

Parker, Samuel K. 1995. The Revenge of Practical Reason? A Review Essay on Gananath Obeyesekere's *The Apotheosis of Captain Cook. Oceania* 65(3):257–67.

Perrins, Christopher M., and Alex L. A. Middleton, eds. 1985. *The Encyclopedia of Birds.* New York: Facts on File.

Perry, W. J. 1924. The Dual Organization. Appendix 3 to *Social Organization,* by W .H. R. Rivers. London: Kegan Paul, Trench, Trubner, pp. 205–22.

Plato. 1961. *The Dialogues of Plato,* translated by Benjamin Jowett. New York: Washington Square Press.

Poole, Fitz John Porter. 1986. The Erosion of a Sacred Landscape: European Exploration and Cultural Ecology among the Bimin-Kuskusmin of Papua New Guinea. In *Mountain People,* edited by Michael Tobias. Norman: University of Oklahoma Press, pp. 169–82, 208–10.

Pouwer, Jan. 1991. The Willed and the Wild: The Kalam Cassowary Revisited. In *Man and a Half: Essays in Pacific Anthropology and Ethnobiology in Honour of Ralph Bulmer,* edited by Andrew Pawley. Auckland: The Polynesian Society, pp. 305–16.

Putnam, Robert D. 1994. Social Capital and Public Affairs. *Bulletin of the American Academy of Arts and Sciences* 47(8):5–19.

———. 1995. Bowling Alone: America's Declining Social Capital. *Journal of Democracy* 6(1):65–78

Read, Kenneth E. 1986. *Return to the High Valley: Coming Full Circle.* Berkeley: University of California Press.

Rochlin, Gregory. 1980. *The Masculine Dilemma: A Psychology of Masculinity.* Boston: Little, Brown.

Ross, John Munder. 1994. *What Men Want: Mothers, Fathers, and Manhood.* Cambridge: Harvard University Press.

Sahlins, Marshall. 1976. *Culture and Practical Reason.* Chicago: University of Chicago Press.

———. 1983. Raw Women, Cooked Men, and Other "Great Things" of the Fiji Islands. In *The Ethnography of Cannibalism,* edited by Paula Brown and Donald Tuzin. Washington, D.C.: Society for Psychological Anthropology, pp. 72–93.

———. 1985. *Islands of History.* Chicago: University of Chicago Press.

———. 1989. Captain Cook at Hawaii. *Journal of the Polynesian Society* 98:371–425.

———. 1995. *How "Natives" Think: About Captain Cook, For Example.* Chicago: University of Chicago Press.

Scaglion, Richard. 1990. Legal Adaptation in a Papua New Guinea Village Court. *Ethnology* 29(1):117–33.

Schieffelin, Edward L., and Robert Crittenden, eds. 1991. *Like People You See in a Dream: First Contact in Six Papuan Societies*. Stanford: Stanford University Press.

Schouten, William Cornelison. 1619. *The Relation of a Wonderfull Voiage made by William Cornelison Schouten of Horne. Shewing how South from the Straights of Magelan, in Terra Delfuogo: he found and discovered a newe passage through the great South Seaes, and that way sayled round about the world.* London: Nathanaell Newberry.

Schwartz, Pepper. 1994. *Peer Marriage: How Love Between Equals Really Works.* New York: Free Press.

Shama, Simon. 1995. *Landscape and Memory.* New York: Alfred A. Knopf.

Simmel, Georg. 1950. The Secret and the Secret Society. In *The Sociology of Georg Simmel,* translated and edited by Kurt H. Wolff. New York: Free Press.

Skjei, Eric, and Richard Rabkin. 1981. *The Male Ordeal: Role Crisis in a Changing World.* New York: G. P. Putnam.

Smith, G. Eliot. 1933. *The Diffusion of Cultures.* London: Watts and Co.

Spence, Jonathan D. 1984. *The Memory Palace of Matteo Ricci.* New York: Viking.

Spencer, Baldwin, and F. J. Gillen. [1899] 1968. *The Native Tribes of Central Australia.* New York: Dover.

Stanner, W. E. H. 1963. On Aboriginal Religion: VI. Cosmos and Society Made Correlative. *Oceania* 33(4):239–73.

Strathern, Andrew J. 1984. *The Line of Power.* London: Tavistock.

Strathern, Marilyn. 1988. *The Gender of the Gift: Problems with Women and Problems with Society in Melanesia.* Berkeley: University of California Press.

———. 1990. Artefacts of History: Events and the Interpretation of Images. In *Culture and History in the Pacific,* edited by Jukka Siikala. Helsinki: Finnish Anthropological Society, pp. 25–44.

Swadling, Pamela. 1990. Sepik Prehistory. In *Sepik Heritage: Tradition and Change in Papua New Guinea,* edited by Nancy Lutkehaus, Christian Kaufmann, William E. Mitchell, Douglas Newton, Lita Osmundsen, and Meinhard Schuster. Durham, N.C.: Carolina Academic Press, pp. 71–86.

———. 1996. *Plumes from Paradise: Trade Cycles in Outer Southeast Asia and Their Impact on New Guinea and Nearby Islands until 1920.* Boroko: Papua New Guinea National Museum.

Taggart, James M. 1990. *Enchanted Maidens: Gender Relations in Spanish Folktales of Courtship and Marriage.* Princeton: Princeton University Press.

Thomas, Hugh. 1993. *Conquest: Montezuma, Cortés, and the Fall of Old Mexico.* New York: Simon and Schuster.

Thompson, Stith. 1919. *European Tales among American Indians.* Colorado College Publication, vol. 2. Colorado Springs.

———. 1946. *The Folktale.* New York: Holt, Rinehart and Winston.

————. 1956. *Motif-Index of Folk-Literature: A Classification of Narrative Elements in Folktales, Ballads, Myths, Fables, Mediaeval Romances, Exempla, Fabliaux, Jest-Books, and Local Legends*. Vol. 2. Copenhagen: Rosenkilde and Bagger.

Thurnwald, Richard. 1916. Banaro Society: Social Organization and Kinship System of a Tribe in the Interior of New Guinea. *American Anthropological Association, Memoirs* 3:253–391.

Tiger, Lionel. 1969. *Men in Groups*. London: Thomas Nelson.

Todorov, Tzvetan. 1982. *La conquête de l'Amérique*. Paris: Seuil.

Townsend, G. W. L. 1968. *District Officer: From Untamed New Guinea to Lake Success, 1921–46*. Sydney: Pacific Publications.

Tuzin, Donald. 1972. Yam Symbolism in the Sepik: An Interpretative Account. *Southwestern Journal of Anthropology* 28(3):230–54.

————. 1975. The Breath of a Ghost: Dreams and the Fear of the Dead. *Ethos* 3(4):555–78.

————. 1976. *The Ilahita Arapesh: Dimensions of Unity*. Berkeley: University of California Press.

————. 1977. Reflections of Being in Arapesh Water Symbolism. *Ethos* 5(2):195–223.

————. 1978. Sex and Meat-Eating in Ilahita: A symbolic study. *Canberra Anthropology* 1(3):82–93.

————. 1980. *The Voice of the Tambaran: Truth and Illusion in Ilahita Arapesh Religion*. Berkeley: University of California Press.

————. 1982. Ritual Violence among the Ilahita Arapesh: The Dynamics of Moral and Religious Uncertainty. In *Rituals of Manhood: Male Initiation in Papua New Guinea*, edited by Gilbert H. Herdt. Berkeley: University of California Press, pp. 321–55.

————. 1983. Cannibalism and Arapesh Cosmology: A Wartime Incident with the Japanese. In *The Ethnography of Cannibalism*, edited by Paula Brown and Donald Tuzin. Washington, D.C.: Society for Psychological Anthropology, pp. 61–71.

————. 1989. Visions, Prophecies, and the Rise of Christian Consciousness. In *The Religious Imagination in New Guinea*, edited by Gilbert Herdt and Michele Stephen. New Brunswick, N.J.: Rutgers University Press, pp. 187–208.

————. 1991. The Cryptic Brotherhood of Big Men and Great Men in Ilahita. In *Big Men and Great Men: Personifications of Power in Melanesia*, edited by Maurice Godelier and Marilyn Strathern. Cambridge: Cambridge University Press, pp. 115–29.

————. 1992. Sago Subsistence and Symbolism among the Ilahita Arapesh. *Ethnology* 31(2):103–14.

————. 1995a. Discourse, Intercourse, and the Excluded Middle: Anthropology and the Problem of Sexual Experience. In *Sexual Nature Sexual Culture*, edited by Paul R. Abramson and Steven D. Pinkerton. Chicago: University of Chicago Press, pp. 257–75.

———. 1995b. Art and Procreative Illusion in the Sepik: Comparing the Abelam and the Arapesh. *Oceania* 65(4):289–303.

———. 1996. The Spectre of Peace in Unlikely Places: Concept and Paradox in the Anthropology of Peace. In *A Natural History of Peace,* edited by Thomas A. Gregor. Nashville: Vanderbilt University Press, pp. 3–33.

Wagner, Roy. 1996. Mysteries of Origin: Early Traders and Heroes in the Trans-Fly. In Pamela Swadling, *Plumes from Paradise: Trade Cycles in Outer Southeast Asia and Their Impact on New Guinea and Nearby Islands until 1920.* Boroko: Papua New Guinea National Museum, pp. 285–98.

Webster, E. M. 1984. *The Moon Man: A Biography of Nikolai Miklouho-Maclay.* Berkeley: University of California Press.

Weiner, Annette B. 1992. *Inalienable Possessions: The Paradox of Keeping-While-Giving.* Berkeley: University of California Press.

Weiner, James F. 1991. *The Empty Place: Poetry, Space, and Being among the Foi of Papua New Guinea.* Bloomington: Indiana University Press.

Williams, F. E. [1923] 1977. The Vailala Madness and the Destruction of Native Ceremonies in the Gulf Division. In *Francis Edgar Williams: "The Vailala Madness" and Other Essays,* edited by Erik Schwimmer. Honolulu: University of Hawaii Press, pp. 331–84.

Young, Michael W. 1983. *Magicians of Manumanua: Living Myth in Kalauna.* Berkeley: University of California Press.

Index